D0974411

THE FREE PRESS

THE ROAD TO HELL

The Ravaging Effects of Foreign Aid and International Charity

MICHAEL MAREN

THE FREE PRESS
A Division of Simon & Schuster, Inc.
1230 Avenue of the Americas
New York, NY 10020

THE FREE PRESS and colophon are trademarks
Of Simon & Schuster, Inc.

Designed by Carla Bolte
Manufactured in the United States of America

10 9 8 7 6 5 4 3 2 1

Library of Congress Cataloging-In-Publication Data

Maren, Michael.
The road to hell : the ravaging effects of foreign aid and
International charity / Michael Maren.
p.cm.
Includes bibliographical references and index.

ISBN 0-7432-2786-7
    1.   Economic assistance-Africa 2. Africa-Economic
    Conditions-1960- 3. Charities-Africa-Management. 4. Charities-
    Africa-Corrupt practices. I. Title
    HC800.M3527 1997
    338.9'1'096-dc20   96-41168
                                         CIP

For information regarding special discounts for bulk purchases, please contact Simon &
Schuster Special Sales at 1-800-456-6789 or business@simonandschuster.com

FOR MY PARENTS
BILL AND BUNNY MAREN

The evil that is in the world always comes out of ignorance, and good intentions may do as much harm as malevolence, if they lack understanding.

—Albert Camus, *The Plague*

Behold how the Infidel lays traps for you [Somalis] as you become less wary. The coins he dispenses so freely now will prove your undoing.

—Sayiid Mohamed Abdille Hassan (The Mad Mullah), 1920

CONTENTS

AUTHOR'S NOTE

This book would not have been possible without the assistance of many people in the U.S., Africa, and Europe. Because of the nature of this investigation and the unsettled state of Somali politics, some of them cannot be named, and others can only be partially identified. They know who they are.

Thanks are due to Scott Malcomson, Jonathan Larsen, and Amy Virshup, all formerly at the *Village Voice*, for backing me on several trips to Somalia and making much of this reporting possible.

In Somalia, Mohamed Jirdeh Hussein, proprietor of the Sahafi Hotel, offered advice, contacts, and credit when my funds began to dwindle. Thanks to my crew: Abass, who was with me day after day as a translator and became a friend; Osman, who drove like a maniac and kept us moving through the mean streets of Mogadishu; Hassan, Nur, and Abdi, who watched my back.

A number of my colleagues were also instrumental in the completion of this book. Special thanks to Joshua Hammer, Keith Richburg, and Mark Huband. Photographers Steve Lehman and Peter Jones worked with me on several projects. Thanks to Richard Ben Cramer for guidance and for suggesting I write this book in the first place. Ken Menkhaus, Bernhard Helander, and Michael Madany were generous with their extensive knowledge of Somalia. Matthew Bryden devoted months of his time to answering my endless questions.

Julie Lang, Jennifer Meagher, and Ted Hannon helped with research and transcriptions. Thanks also to Linda Rubes, Barry Shelby, Tami Hausman, Chris Lavin, Judy Hart, Patrick Dillon, Marc Aronson, Amina Abdi Issa, Daphne Pinkerson, Thomas Keenan, Don Wallace, and my friends at soc.culture.somalia. The Charlotte Geyer Foundation provided some funding.

Finally, I want to express my deep appreciation to Bruce Nichols at The Free Press for patience way beyond the call of duty, and to my agent, Flip Brophy, for hanging with the project for nearly a decade.

Some elements in this book are based on material previously published in *The Village Voice, Penthouse, Forbes Media Critic,* and *The New Republic.* A few names have been changed to protect sources.

ON THE SPELLING
OF SOMALI WORDS

While the Somali language has a rich oral tradition, it did not receive an orthography until 1972 when Mohamed Siyaad Barre, in what will likely be remembered as the only enduring accomplishment of his regime, assembled scholars and linguists to create a standardized system for writing Somali in the Latin alphabet. Still, English-language publications use a random array of spellings for Somali words and names. In part this is the result of Somalia's diverse colonial heritage. The Somali people were colonized by the Italians, British, and French, each of whom spelled the words as they sounded to them. Thus Somalia's capital is spelled Mogadiscio by the Italians, Mogadishu by the English, and Muqdisho in proper Somali. In addition, the wide use of maps from the French Michelin company has extended French style into areas beyond French influence so that the town of Beledweyne is often spelled as Belet Uen.

For this book I had originally intended to solve this problem by using proper Somali spellings in every instance. This quickly proved awkward. For example, the name of Somalia's most famous warlord would appear as Maxamed Farax Caydiid. And some readers found it confusing when I referred to Muqdisho instead of Mogadishu. The towns of Baidoa and Bardera are more properly written as Baydhabo and Baardheere, but using these spellings would have proved puzzling to anyone who routinely followed press reports from Somalia.

To solve the problem I have compromised, using the proper Somali spellings whenever possible, and approximating them when appropriate. Thus the man known as Aidid, or Aideed in the Western press and as Caydiid in Somalia appears in this text as Aydiid. I use the proper spelling for the port of Kismaayo, which is often rendered as Chismayo or Kismayo. For the town of Gaalkacyo I have used Galkayo instead of Galcaio or any of the other variations that have appeared in print. Most of the spellings chosen for the text should be self-evident. Some of these compromises are certain to irritate Somali scholars and Somali language purists, and for that I apologize. My goal has been to communicate ideas to an audience beyond those with a specific interest in Somalia. The spellings I have chosen serve that purpose.

INTRODUCTION: DARKNESS AND LIGHT

The conquest of the earth, which mostly means the taking it away
from those who have a different complexion or slightly flatter noses
than ourselves, is not a pretty thing when you look into it too
much. What redeems it is the idea only. An idea at the back of it;
not a sentimental pretense but an idea; and an unselfish belief in
the idea—something you can set up, and bow down before, and
offer a sacrifice to. . . .

—Joseph Conrad, *Heart of Darkness*

I n October of 1977, I traveled from my home near Boston to Kenya,
East Africa, via Nashville, Tennessee. Nashville was the site of a Peace
Corps staging, a preliminary training program to prepare a group of us for
two years of teaching in Kenya. About thirty volunteers showed up, mostly
young, recent college graduates, predominantly middle class, all of us
white. I was twenty-one years old, the youngest of the group.

We gathered for the first time in a campus lounge on a cool and colorful
fall day, not sure what to expect from each other, completely clueless
about what the next few years would bring but sure that we were about to
share an amazing adventure. On that first day, we were asked to introduce
ourselves to the rest of the group. Beyond the standard biographical

1

data, each of us was to answer the question: Why are you joining the Peace Corps?

None of us had taken the decision to join lightly. The application process that dragged on for months, and in some cases years, weeded out those without a burning desire to join up. But the question of why elicited only vague and ambiguous answers about adventure, exploration, and personal growth. But then in a final flourish of certitude, nearly everyone capped his or her list of reasons with a statement about wanting to help people. The idea was to help Africans. Whatever else this adventure would be, it was built on a solid mission of charity and good will.

I don't recall what exactly I said that day; I hadn't really thought much about why I was going to Africa. It probably had something to do with wanting to spend a few years in a tropical climate. I would have been just as happy to be sent to Malaysia or Bolivia. I'd earlier spent a semester studying in India and had enjoyed the sights, sounds, and even the smells of the Third World environment. And graduating from college with a degree in English I had no idea what I wanted to do with my life. The Peace Corps seemed like a low-key graduate program with a full scholarship and a healthy stipend. Whatever reasons I did have, I must admit that helping people was not high among them. It's not that I didn't care; I just wasn't entirely certain that people in Kenya needed help. And if in fact the Kenyans did need help, it wasn't at all apparent that any of us young and eager American kids was really in a position to offer any. None of us had ever been to Africa before, nor did we have any background in development studies. We all just knew, somehow, that our breeding, education, and nationality had imbued us with something valuable from which these less fortunate people could benefit.

It was easy to presume that people needed our help. For us, Africa was more than a place on the map, it was a location in our collective psyche. Our idea of Africa had been shaped by years of advertisements and news coverage that portrayed the continent as poor and helpless. Growing up in an affluent Western society we were invested with a stake in the image of helpless Africa, starving Africa. In public affairs discussions the term "starving Africans" (or "starving Ethiopians" or "starving Somalis") rolls from the tongue as easily as "blue sky." "Americans leave enough food on their plates to feed a million starving Africans." Charities raise money for starving Africans. What do Africans do? They starve. But mostly they starve in our imaginations. The starving African is a Western cultural archetype like the greedy Jew or the unctuous Arab. The difference is that we've learned that trafficking in these last two archetypes is wrong or, at least, reflects badly upon us. But the image of the bloated helpless child adorns advertisements for Save the Children and World Vision. The image of the starving African is said to edify us, sensitize us, mobilize our good will and awaken us from our apathy.

The starving African exists as a point in space from which we measure our own wealth, success, and prosperity, a darkness against which we can view our own cultural triumphs. And he serves as a handy object of our charity. He is evidence that we have been blessed, and we have an obligation to spread that blessing. The belief that we can help is an affirmation of our own worth in the grand scheme of things. The starving African transcends the dull reality of whether or not anyone is actually starving in Africa. Starvation clearly delineates *us* from *them*.

Sometimes it appears that the only time Africans are portrayed with dignity is when they're helpless and brave at the same time. A person about to starve to death develops a stoic strength. Journalists write about the quiet dignity of the hopelessly dying. If the Africans were merely hungry and poor, begging or conning coins on the streets of Nairobi or Addis Ababa, we might become annoyed and brush them aside—and most aid workers have done that at one time. When they steal tape decks from our Land Cruisers we feel anger and disgust. It is only in their weakness, when their death is inevitable, that we are touched. And it is in their helplessness that they become a marketable commodity.

As I got to know the people in my Peace Corps group, I learned more about why people had joined. We were refugees from failed marriages, broken engagements, and other traumas. We all needed time to figure out what we wanted to do with our lives. The Peace Corps was a temporary escape, like joining the French Foreign Legion but with a much shorter commitment. Most of us associated the Peace Corps with JFK and carried with us a nostalgia for the dream that died in Dallas in 1963. Those of us in our early twenties at that time were the first post-Vietnam generation, slightly too young to have been drafted, but just old enough to have been politicized by the war.

In the post-Vietnam world, the Peace Corps offered us an opportunity to forge a different kind of relationship with the Third World, one based on respect. Vietnam had sowed within us enough suspicion of our own culture to have us looking for answers to the world's problems in other cultures. As Americans, we claimed a certain distance from Kenya's colonial past. We were self-consciously anticolonial. Most of us would have early experiences with colonials and other expatriates who spoke in flippant and demeaning generalizations about "the Africans." We were even shocked by experienced volunteers who talked about how the kids didn't learn or how you have to be firm with your hired help lest they steal everything you own. We bristled when Kenyans called us "Europeans," by which in fact they just meant "white people." Our country, after all, had not been a colonial power in Africa.

On several occasions Kenyans came and shook my hand while declaring that we, Kenyans and Americans, shared a historic bond, both of us colonized people who had thrown out the British. It was a profound misunderstanding, one which I never bothered to contradict. It was, I wanted to think, at least true in spirit.

But the reality was that the colonial experience of the European powers had taught us how to view Africa. Many of us discovered just how deep our Western prejudices ran, built as they were on the literature of colonialism. Certainly there had been an early 1960s, romanticized view of African independence movements that deified the likes of Ghana's Nkrumah, Guinea's Sékou Touré, Kenya's Kenyatta. But it was difficult to hold those notions when the icons of independence showed themselves to be incompetent, corrupt, and worse. This "new" Africa of bold revolutionary heroes was, in retrospect, just another chapter in the same Western mythology that gave us Tarzan and further evidence of the patronizing relationship between the powerful and the powerless.

By the time I arrived in Africa, a second generation of African leaders was taking command. Hypocrites were replaced by tyrants and madmen such as Uganda's Idi Amin, and Jean Bedel Bokassa and his Central African Empire, men who killed their enemies and kept them in refrigerators for snacks. The very week we arrived in Nairobi, Bokassa threw himself a multimillion-dollar coronation in Bangui, the capital of his impoverished country. A wave of nostalgia for colonialism was beginning to surface among expatriates and even among some Africans.

This nostalgia played perfectly into my "experience" with Africa, shaped by films like *Khartoum*, *Beau Geste*, *The African Queen*, *Casablanca*, and a selection of Tarzan movies. These images endured despite my having read Frantz Fanon, Chinua Achebe, Ngugi wa Thiong'o, and other African thinkers. We arrived in Nairobi to find that our white skin was an immediate passport to the best clubs and restaurants in town. We soon learned the joys of drinking on the verandah of the Norfolk Hotel, or of visiting game lodges in Kenya's national parks. The lure of the hedonistic colonial lifestyle became even more seductive when we were sent out beyond the metropolis to the towns in the hinterland. There we found refuge in the colonial sports clubs with their billiards tables, dart boards, and squash courts that the servants of the Crown had carved out of the wilderness. There, in the remote colonial refuges, we could gather with a few other expatriates—and even some Kenyans—to talk about, complain about, and even ridicule the Africans for their inability to grasp what it was we were trying to teach them. We had effortlessly become what we had so recently despised. The fit was easy, all of it redeemed by the big idea of aid. They needed our help. We were there to serve.

My first two years were spent as a secondary school teacher in an isolated village in the district of Meru on the eastern slope of Mount Kenya. I was dropped off by a Peace Corps staffer who left me standing outside of a little wooden shack with my duffel bag in hand. I gazed across an idyllic scene of thatched roofs, lush greenery and majestic hills. Then as I watched the old Land Rover rattle away down a rutted dirt road, my mind focused on a single thought: My god, I'm going to be here for two years. What have I gotten myself into?

The experience was overwhelming, so much in fact that I never really had the time to worry about the economic development of my hosts. They seemed to be getting along fine without me. It was I who needed help. I was the one who had to adapt to life without running water or electricity. I had to get used to living in a place where the nearest telephone was ten miles away.

The people in the village were endlessly amused by my ignorance about agriculture. I couldn't plant maize or raise chickens. They snickered when my uncalloused hands couldn't hold a scalding hot glass of tea.

It brought to mind an H. G. Wells short story I'd read in high school, "Country of the Blind." In that story a mountaineer, "a reader of many books," falls into a deep precipice and finds himself trapped in a lost valley among a race of people who centuries before had lost the use of their eyes. From his perspective, the people of the valley lead a simple and laborious life and he immediately sets out to "bring them to reason"—to enlighten them about the wonders of sight. But inseparable from the notion that he can enlighten them is the notion that he can rule them. Is that not the role, even the responsibility, of the enlightened person who lives among the blind? He recalls the adage, "in the country of the blind, the one-eyed man is king."

He learns, however, that the populace has adapted itself to sightlessness. When he speaks of "seeing," they think he is mad. They have no windows in their houses and prefer to work at night, when it is cooler. Quickly the mountaineer learns that the king of the blind is "a clumsy and useless stranger among his subjects." In the kingdom of the blind, the one-eyed man can't see.

For the following twelve months I struggled to survive. I was the one who learned to raise and slaughter chickens, grow vegetables, plant cassava. I learned how to live on a diet consisting primarily of maize and beans in various forms. I learned how to shower with a bucket of cold water and cut the chiggers out of my feet with a Swiss Army knife. I learned to speak Swahili and spent my mornings with the old men at a local tea shop listening to stories about the past. These old men viewed me as a curiosity. It never occurred to them that I could bring anything of value to the village.

There were a few people who thought I could, however. A few men in the village had Land Rovers and lived in large stone houses: the local administrative chief, the preacher, the school headmaster. These men had brought me to the village. Later I learned that they had paid someone in the ministry of education some large bribes to get me there. (I was told this when I hiked to a neighboring village that had lost the bribe war.) It was their idea that a white teacher would help attract more students, school fees, and donations to the school. Which I did. (The local pastor was devastated to learn that I was a Jew. He had planned on my active participation in church services and fund-raisers. The headmaster looked at the bright side and confided to me that his biggest fear had been that the Peace Corps would send them a black teacher.) They raised money to build more classrooms. But when the shipments of cement and stone blocks arrived, the headmaster and his buddies carted them away at night and built additions to their own houses and expanded their shops in the market.

These were the people who benefited most from my presence in the village; they were educated, Westernized, and living lives far removed from most of the people in the village. They knew how to manipulate the system that ran on foreign aid. They knew how to get a piece of every contract or public project in the area. It was disheartening, and I complained about it loudly when I traveled to the town of Meru on the weekends and joined with other expatriates at the Pig and Whistle Hotel or at the Meru Sports Club. Unlike the mountaineer in Wells's story, I had a support group to remind me where I came from.

Back in the village, I learned to go with the flow and enjoy myself. I dropped any pretenses that I had anything to offer. I stopped trying to help and began to observe. And I learned some important lessons about economic development. I learned to respect people for what they did. People usually do things for good reasons, even though it might not be immediately apparent to outsiders.

The relevance of Wells's story continued to resonate with me. The more time I spent in the village the more aware I became of the connection between the desire to enlighten, to do development work, and the desire to rule. It was difficult to sit back and watch the village leaders taking money from the farmers who worked so hard to pay their children's school fees. Yet the only thing I could have done would have been to get involved politically, to take power, to lead, ultimately to rule. (Indeed, several teachers at the school wanted me to become headmaster.) Earlier missionaries had delivered enlightenment as the word of God and had paved the way for political and economic domination from Europe. We were delivering enlightenment in the form of Western culture dressed up as education and development. Like the missionaries, we could not know what would follow.

When my Peace Corps term was up I wanted to stay in Kenya, so I went to Nairobi looking for work. I'd heard that Catholic Relief Services was looking for a Peace Corps volunteer to roam the country starting food-for-work projects. I went to the CRS office and met a smiling man named Jack Matthews. Matthews told me long stories about his work in Korea and India. He then told me that CRS had received a $900,000 grant from the United States Agency for International Development (USAID) to start food-for-work projects around the country. Whoever got the job would be given an apartment in Nairobi, a Land Cruiser, and instructions to drive around the country starting projects. Of course I was interested. Kenya is one of the world's uniquely beautiful places. Few people had the money to spend a year in a four-wheel-drive truck exploring its most remote regions. I asked Matthews what I had to do to get the job.

He told me that he wanted the Peace Corps director to make the choice. The new director had only been in the country a short while and knew very few of the volunteers. When I walked into her office that afternoon, it was the first time I had ever seen her. She immediately told me that she didn't feel right choosing from a group of volunteers she didn't know. So I told her that Matthews wanted to hire me; all she had to do was phone him and say it was okay with her. I had the job that afternoon.

I moved into a beautiful garden apartment in a nice neighborhood in Nairobi. My first day on the job I drove home in a brand-new Land Cruiser. In the morning I drove to my office to figure out ways to give away bags of rice that were already enroute to Kenya from a port in Texas. Meanwhile, CRS notified the country's parish priests and government officials that this rice was available. All they had to do to receive it was fill out a one-page application describing their proposed project and specifying the number of "recipients"—the number of the project's workers who would receive sacks of rice in exchange for their labor. Hundreds of applications were submitted.

I took some of the USAID money and customized the Land Cruiser, adding extra-large fuel tanks and a really nice stereo system, and then I set off across Kenya to inspect the proposed projects. It was a dream come true. I was getting paid to cross one of the world's most beautiful land-scapes. I was so awestruck by my own good luck that sometimes I'd stop in the middle of a huge empty wilderness, or beside a herd of giraffes or ele-phants, and just yelp with delight.

I was having so much fun running around starting food-for-work proj-ects—water projects, agriculture projects, forestry projects—that I com-pletely overlooked the most obvious problem: I knew nothing about agriculture, forestry, road building, well digging, dam building, or any of the projects I was approving. But nobody seemed to care. Only once did any-one in authority at CRS ever go and look at a project. When I'd return to Nairobi every few weeks, my boss, who let me work completely unsuper-vised, had only one question: How many more recipients did you sign on? More recipients meant more government grant money, which meant we could buy more vehicles and hire more assistants.

When I slowed down for a moment to consider what was happening, it became clear: Aid distribution is just another big, private business that re-lies on government contracts. Groups like CRS are paid by the U.S. gov-ernment to give away surplus food produced by subsidized U.S. farmers. The more food CRS gave away, the more money they received from the government to administer the handouts. Since the securing of grant money is the primary goal, aid organizations rarely meet a development project they don't like.

All of this came into greater focus one morning at an office meeting. We were discussing a famine situation that was developing in Turkana in northwestern Kenya. I had recently returned from the area, where I'd been looking into doing some food-for-work projects. I wasn't very optimistic about succeeding in my efforts, since many of the people were too weak to work and it would be difficult to demand that some people dig holes and move rocks while others were getting food for doing nothing. A young woman who worked for CRS at the time and who was my immediate su-pervisor conceded my point but said we had to find some way to establish a program in the region. "We have to take advantage of this famine to expand our regular program," she insisted.

For her, and the organization, famine was a growth opportunity. Whatever the original intentions, aid programs had become an end in themselves. Hungry people were potential clients to be preyed upon in the same way hair replacement companies seek out bald people.

As ignorant as I was about development projects, there was no shortage of donors willing to hand over cash for me to spend for them. Within a few months additional funds were made available for the food-for-work projects. I now had money to buy pipes and cement and apparatus. I came up with an idea: to travel the deserts of northern Kenya drilling wells and setting up windmills to pump water. That, I had learned, was appropriate technology. Appropriate technology was all the rage. It meant anything but high technology, things that didn't run on electricity or require a lot of maintenance. There was money available for appropriate technology. It made donors' eyes light up. So I secured funds to purchase some windmills from a company in the American Midwest, as well as an electronic device that could be used to locate underground sources of water. I'd read some books about how people can dig deep wells by hand; we'd use food-for-work for that. And for places where they couldn't be hand dug, I'd use a not-yet-purchased portable drilling rig that I could drag around behind my Land Cruiser. I'd be the Johnny Appleseed of water. Soon the nomads in northern and eastern Kenya would be drinking clean water and taking showers.

As I was getting excited about the project, a friend suggested that I talk with an American named Andrew Clarke, who lived near Nanyuki to the north of Mount Kenya. Clarke had drilled some wells in his day and knew lots about Kenya's dry frontier areas. I went to see Clarke on his ranch and told him about my plans. I expected him to be excited. Instead, he told me to sit down.

He took out a pencil and drew a small circle in the center of a sheet of paper. "This is the desert," he said, waving his hand across the whole sheet of paper. Then he pointed to the circle: "Here is your well. During the rainy season this well will provide extra water for the nomads. It will allow them to have bigger herds. When the dry season comes, the nomads will begin to migrate toward your well or any permanent source of water. They will arrive with larger herds and begin to denude the land closest to the well. Soon they'll have to wander farther and farther from the well to find food."

He drew a large circle around the first circle. "Cows must eat and drink water every day. As soon as it's more than a day's walk from the water to the grass, the cows will die." He drew a third, larger circle around the other two. "Goats and sheep can go several days without water, but as soon as the food is consumed for a two-day radius from the water, the goats and sheep will die." He drew a fourth large circle around the other three. "And then there's the camels. The camels can go days without drinking water, but soon the walk will be too great for them. And when the camels die, the people die."

This was not a hypothetical scenario, Clarke explained. It had happened, and was still happening. Aid organizations were coming in and giving water to nomads, the gift of life, and it was killing them.

Then he asked me if I'd seen the windmill on the road to Moyale. I had. In northern Kenya just below the border with Ethiopia, beside a road, was a windmill tower crumpled like an aluminum can. The windmill apparatus lay on the ground. Clarke told me that some well-intentioned missionaries had ordered a top-of-the-line windmill apparatus from the United States and had hauled it to northern Kenya, where they proceeded to build the tower from local materials, held together with Kenyan-made bolts. Attracted by the water, a community gathered and prospered. After some time, the heavy-duty American apparatus began to weigh upon the flimsy Kenyan structure. The bolts sheared and the tower crumbled in the wind. The community disintegrated, and Clarke had heard that some members had died before they were able to find a place to relocate.

"You can put a water system in a community," he warned me, "but then you'll have to be there all the time as a policeman. You'll have to make rules: People can drink from the wells but animals can't. You won't really be able to explain to the people why their cattle can't drink from the water. For them, their herds are everything. A man's wealth and status is dependent on the size of his herd. So he won't understand why you're standing between his cattle and the water. Is that really what you want to do? The water will make you responsible for the community. And that's not why you came here."

Clarke had successfully soured my plans, but more important, he taught me to ask questions about so-called development projects. I still could have gone and drilled wells across the countryside. No one would have stopped me. I could even have gotten substantial grant money to do it. There was no one watchdogging the development business. There was no central authority curbing the ambitions of young people like myself. With my English degree and suburban upbringing and white skin, I could walk into an African village and throw money and bags of food around. I could do anything I pleased. I had, admittedly, enjoyed the feeling of power. Suddenly it scared me.

If my project created a disaster, no one outside of the village would ever hold me accountable. The missionaries who erected that windmill near Moyale, and other aid workers who bring destruction to communities, are probably still running around doing their "development" work in remote villages from where news of their failures will never emerge.

Kenya was a wonderful place to work and it attracted thousands of aid workers. The place was crawling with them. Aid organizations competed with each other for grant money and projects. Kenya's politicians loved it. They could give aid projects as gifts to their supporters. They weren't about to start asking tough questions or demanding long-term environmental impact statements. No one questioned the idea of aid. It was as if the good intentions alone were sufficient to redeem even the most horrific of aid-generated disasters.

This book is about aid and charity—aid and charity as an industry, as religion, as a self-serving system that sacrifices its own practitioners and intended beneficiaries in order that it may survive and grow. Much of this book is centered in Somalia, but it draws on my experiences with aid organizations over nineteen years around Africa: in places such as Kenya, Burkina Faso, Nigeria, Rwanda, Sudan, and Ethiopia. Like most people in the United States and Western Europe, I've heard the pleas of aid organizations and boasts of their accomplishments in the Third World, but the Africa I know today is in much worse shape than it was when I first arrived. The futures of Africa's children are less hopeful than ever before. The countries that received the most aid—Somalia, Liberia, and Zaire—have slid into virtual anarchy. Another large recipient, Kenya, inflicts unspeakable abuses of human rights on their own citizens while aid pays the bills.

In Africa, the people who are supposed to benefit from aid see what is happening. They hear foreigners talking about development, but they know development was a colonial policy. Development was a policy of subjugation. When colonials came ashore, they didn't say, "We're here to steal your land and take your resources and employ your people to clean our toilets and guard our big houses." They said, "We're here to help you." And then they went and took their land and resources and hired their people to clean their toilets. And now here come the aid workers, who move into the big colonial houses and ride in high cars above the squalor, all the while insisting they've come to help.

As in colonial times, the foreigners employ an elite cadre of locals to carry out their work. The elites are rewarded for their relationships with the foreigners. They enjoy higher pay than most. They have access to foreign goods, education and visas to foreign countries. And, just as in colonial times, the foreigners use this elite as their link to the rest of the population. They are regarded as the voice of the people and employed to speak on their behalf. In reality, however, the elite, with their vested interests in the system, tell the foreigners exactly what they want to hear: The system is good; the system works.

Thus affirmed, the aid establishment moves forward, as the colonial one did, ignorant of the widening rift between them and the supposed recipients of their beneficence.

In 1981, I left Kenya to take a job with USAID in Somalia. I knew little of what was going on in Somalia except that perhaps a million and a half refugees had entered the country fleeing the Ogaden war in Ethiopia. The world was mobilizing to help. I thought it was a good opportunity to try something new and get a fresh start in a different country. Alert to the corrupt and politicized aid business in Kenya, I felt ready to deal with the situation in Somalia.

I had learned to view development aid with skepticism, a skill I had hoped to put to good use to help ensure that aid projects, at worst, didn't hurt people. But Somalia added a whole new dimension to my view of the aid business. My experience there made me see that aid could be worse than incompetent and inadvertently destructive. It could be positively evil.

1

LAND CRUISERS

Charity creates a multitude of sins.
      —Oscar Wilde, *The Soul of Man Under Socialism*

The town of Baidoa in southwestern Somalia, it seems, will forever be called "the city formerly known as the City of Death." Aid workers attached the City of Death label during the famine of 1992. Before that, Baidoa wasn't really known as anything. It was a dusty little market town in the center of Somalia's agricultural region where nomads would exchange camels and milk for grains, cooking oil, cloth, and other items. In early 1991, after the government of dictator Mohamed Siyaad Barre was overthrown, Baidoa became a battleground, an arena of spectacular brutality. The dictator's retreating armies fled through the region, looting and killing as they passed, wrecking everything they couldn't carry off. They made a special point of pillaging farmers' traditional underground food stores in an effort to halt the advance of the pursuing forces of the United Somali Congress, who nonetheless managed to find more to loot and destroy. Before it was over, the armies would pass through the region four times, achieving monumental levels of destruction.

But Baidoa didn't become famous until the battles ended and people began to starve there. That's when the relief workers showed up with truckloads of food. That food along with everything else the outsiders brought were the only items of value in the area, so the relief supplies became the center of a new regional economy. It was an economy of theft. In the anarchy that followed the fighting, freelance militias, criminal gangs, ruled the roads and towns. They extorted money from relief organizations or simply stole the food. The nomads and others who fled to towns such as Baidoa expecting to be fed, waited and died.

After the relief organizations brought the media to videotape, photograph, and otherwise capture the death for the outside world, Baidoa became an international symbol of starvation. Then it became a symbol of liberation when the U.S. Marines rolled into town just before Christmas 1992, escorting a first symbolic shipment of relief food for the starving. The next day they escorted additional symbolic food shipments out of Baidoa to the hinterlands. Journalists crowded around to get the first shots of the first shipments arriving and leaving the City of Death. On New Year's Day 1993, President George Bush, on his final official trip, dropped into the symbolic city to meet the marines and tour an orphanage. He was greeted with banners and songs. "The marines saved us. Welcome, President, welcome," the orphans sang in Somali.

As he smiled and waved and grasped hands, Bush betrayed no sense that this site of his bold humanitarian act had once been the focus of intense American interest of a different kind. Under his administration and the previous ones, the same Siyaad Barre who delivered death to Baidoa was a friend and ally. Presidents Carter, Reagan, and Bush, in their campaign against communist influence in Africa, pumped massive amounts of military and economic aid into Somalia and kept the hated dictator in power. Fortress Somalia had been in part built from bags of food, relief food for the hungry refugees from an earlier war. The food fed the troops and kept the cadres in step behind the regime. It enriched loyal merchants in the capital and kept the president's family and friends awash in luxury. And though no one dared stain Bush's visit with questions of history, the Somalis who saw the convoys of food rolling inland toward Baidoa understood something that these relief workers and soldiers did not: The show unfolding before them was much more than a grand gesture of charity. Food was power, and so long as the food came in, the battle to control it would continue, as it had for years.

By the spring of 1993, people had stopped starving in Baidoa. American soldiers had come and gone, replaced by international peacekeepers. Aid workers by the hundreds descended upon the town to nurture the victims.

Many Somalis who had fled the city during more than a year of fighting began to return. And other Somalis, many of whom had never been to Baidoa, showed up looking for work with aid agencies, the United Nations, the Red Cross, and the so-called non-governmental organizations, commonly known as NGOs.

On a typically hot afternoon in June 1993, a young American aid worker climbs into the front passenger seat of his Toyota Land Cruiser. Beside him sits his driver, a nineteen-year-old Somali kid called Jiis. In the back seat of the vehicle sit two other young Somalis; one is Jiis's younger brother, and the other is a cousin of some sort. The trio are employed as security guards. Each holds a battered AK-47 assault rifle, muzzle resting lightly on the door frame and pointing toward the cloudless blue sky. With everyone in position, Jiis steers the car away from a massive tarmac airstrip and starts down a rutted, dusty road. Despite the weaponry, none of the gunmen appears particularly on guard. The American stares silently and grips a medium-sized package that he has collected from the plane. A white-on-faded-blue UN flag mounted on a little metal post crudely welded to the front bumper snaps in the wind. As the Land Cruiser rocks along, Jiis and his friends begin to talk to each other in Somali, softly at first, but the conversation soon escalates into louder, more adamant tones. The American doesn't understand a word, but it sounds to him as if they are arguing. He pays little attention; Somalis always seem to be arguing about something.

This time Jiis and the boys are really arguing. The two guards in the back seat are trying to convince Jiis that they should drive off and kill the American right now. Jiis insists they wait. He knows the package contains something important because the American seems nervous today—more nervous than usual. He was anxious earlier in the day when Jiis was late showing up at the compound where he lived with other foreigners. "Where the fuck is Mohamed," the American had said, using Jiis's real name. When Jiis arrived, he had to endure a lecture about the virtues of showing up on time. Jiis doesn't like the American. The American has complained about his work habits before, calling him lazy, threatening to fire him. Jiis isn't sure he wants to put up with anyone telling him what to do, especially a foreigner, a *gaal*, an infidel. As it turned out, they'd arrived in plenty of time to meet the plane.

When a silence finally settles in, the American speaks. The package, he says, contains food his mother has sent him from home, and when they get back to the compound he is going to open the package and share some chocolate.

Jiis translates for his colleagues and continues. "These people, they talk to us like we're children. They think they can make us happy with pieces of chocolate while they keep boxes of money."

"Thank you," Jiis says to the American.

"Let's kill him now," says Jiis's friend one more time.

"No. We have to have a plan," Jiis insists. "You boys are stupid. You can't just take all this money without a plan. We need to have a plan to take the money, and we need to have a plan to get away."

When troubles come, the Land Cruisers always follow. Airplanes and trucks bring bags of food and blankets, and Land Cruisers bring relief workers. They are young, earnest, healthy, clean, and tanned European and American kids in short pants, T-shirts, baseball caps, and sunglasses. They stride like an invincible force through the mass assembly of vulnerable, sick and dying victims of war, famine, and disease. In their Land Cruisers they glide over dusty streets in faraway, forgotten places, the flags of their aid organizations flying in the wind they make. The faster they drive, the more erect and firm fly their banners, bearing symbols that mean caring and helping to people thousands of miles away.

Now, in the middle of 1993, Baidoa is an aid workers' jamboree. There is food. People crowd the market. Children run and play and laugh. There are the sounds, generators from behind the walls of NGO compounds, and the grinding of tires on gravel. Only occasionally does the sharp crack of gunfire silence the clamor of normal activity. Land Cruisers are everywhere. The NGOs rent the Land Cruisers from their owners, their new owners, who looted them from the aid agencies that were in Somalia before the war. When things get more secure and their presence seems more permanent, the NGOs will buy their own Land Cruisers. Until then, it's safer to rent for $75 a day.

Each Land Cruiser carries one or two foreigners and three or four Somali kids. It gives the aid workers a thrill. And it gives jobs to the kids with guns. To most Somalis, the kids with guns are known as *mooryaan*, little bandits, punks, street kids. For the aid workers they are security guards. Most Somalis fear them and wonder why the helpers from abroad spend so much time with these *mooryaan*. These are the same kids who were looting the Land Cruisers before, and now it's not exactly clear whether they are paid to protect the vehicles or bribed not to loot them.

Mohamed Sheikh is a former looter who now has a job with the United Nations as a driver and gunman. He has a round, boyish, mischievous face, light brown skin, and sandy hair that appears streaked with blond when he stands in the sunlight. Mohamed was born with one leg slightly shorter than the other, and as a child he had walked with a barely perceptible limp. He had long ago learned to compensate for his imbalance, but the nickname he was given as a child had stuck. Everyone calls him Jiis, which means "limp." He had been living in the town of Beledweyne when the war to oust Mohamed Siyaad Barre began in 1989. Members of his Hawaadle clan had joined with the victorious forces of the USC, the United Somali Congress, and captured the capital of Mogadishu in January 1991. Jiis never fought with the guerrillas, but within days of their victory, he was in the capital, gleefully joining the festival of looting that had engulfed the city. He stole a rifle and began breaking into the abandoned homes that were once occupied by foreigners, NGOs, and members of Siyaad Barre's clan, the Daarood. He stole electric generators, televisions, and VCRs.

In Mogadishu in those days, a major cause of death was car accidents, as kids from the bush, former cattle herders, took to the streets in looted cars and Land Cruisers, driving on whichever side of the road they chose, not knowing any better and not really caring. In the new Mogadishu the *mooryaan* made the rules.

Jiis and his brother and a few friends took what they wanted and sold what they didn't need. They spent their time chewing *qat*, spending $10 or $20 a day on the stimulant, which even during the worst of the fighting and the peak of the famine was imported daily from neighboring Kenya. They watched looted movies on looted VCRs and televisions, all powered by looted generators. They particularly liked American movies, violent American movies. Jiis watched and worked on his English by listening to Clint Eastwood and Sylvester Stallone.

When there was nothing left to loot, the USC forces split into their clan and subclan factions and began to loot from each other. Mogadishu exploded again, and Jiis got out of town, first heading south along the coast to the port city of Kismaayo. Out of money and in need of work, he got a job there with the UN doing security, riding around in Land Cruisers, and protecting the occupants. He also made money on the side by running errands in the market for the foreigners who were afraid to leave their protected compounds. For example, a lot of them wanted to buy a *macawis*, the Somali sarong. Jiis would buy one for $8 and sell it to them for $25. Occasionally they would pay him off by letting him take bags of food, which he could sell on the market.

Not long after the Americans arrived in Somalia, Jiis was fired from his job in Kismaayo for being rude to his employers and not showing up for work. So he and his brother headed for Baidoa, where NGOs were setting up shop and work was plentiful. He had a gun. He knew how to drive. And he spoke English, after a fashion.

Several times a day in Baidoa the Land Cruisers congregate around the long tarmac airstrip. The aid workers talk quietly among themselves, exchanging news like African women at the village well. They complain about their Somali workers. They discuss the dangers of life in Somalia, or they pass along legends from the days before the arrival of the marines: the looting of the Red Cross warehouse, the hijacking of the CARE convoy on its way to Baidoa, aid workers who had been held hostage or murdered. They talk of the former Somali army major who ran the airport before the Americans came, how he charged landing fees and entrance fees and made a fortune from every relief plane that landed.

Their Somali escorts gather in their own group to complain about and ridicule the foreigners. They are certain the foreigners are getting rich in Baidoa. Why else would they have left their plush California mansions and English country estates to come here?

At first there is only the soft murmur of voices trailing away into the open air. Wind faintly rustles the thorny bushes. Heat rises from the tar. Most of the aid workers have walkie-talkies on their belts that occasionally squawk in unison. The landing lights of the C-130 Hercules appear in the distance long before any sound is heard. The plane emerges as a blurry white ball through the midday heat. Even the nomads gather just to watch. Sometimes they wander out on the runway and the aid workers shout and wave them off.

Then, instantly, in a shower of sound, the plane is on the ground. The Land Cruisers ring the hulking transport plane like suckling piglets. The ear-ripping rush from turbo props, and the toxic sweet smell of burning jet fuel fills the torrid air. The plane drops its rear cargo door and pallets are rolled toward a waiting forklift. There are crates of bottled water for aid workers and peacekeeping troops. There are cases of beer and boxes of medical supplies for UNICEF (United Nations Children's Fund). And there are smaller packages for individuals and organizations containing messages, personal mail, food from home, and cash for salaries. A wiry, gray-haired white man with no shirt stands in the back of the plane shouting in a colonial English accent at the Somalis who are unloading the packages. They don't understand and they can't hear anyway beneath the whine of the engines. Still, they respond to his directives. The white man's flesh is sticky with sweat, and flecks of grain, grains of sand and cardboard-brown dust from the boxes coat his body. Then the Hercules closes its door and is gone.

Most of the Somali security guards help their employers load the boxes into the backs of the Land Cruisers. But Jiis just watches. I'm not your fucking slave, he once told the American. The American is getting paid a lot of money, Jiis figures. He wants to be here. Let him load the boxes.

The American would like to fire Jiis, but he's afraid. He knows that labor disputes have led to deaths. A Red Cross worker was recently shot to death in the nearby town of Bardera by an angry former security guard. It's best to take these things slowly. It may be possible to make friends with the boy, make him understand that working with the UN is a big opportunity. He's already earning $300 a month in a country where annual per capita income is $150. Maybe he'll start to cooperate. But Jiis isn't going to cooperate. He's not impressed with the foreigners and their technology, the way they come and go in airplanes. They have their CD players, radios, and notebook computers, their Swiss Army knives, their running shoes and Gore-Tex clothes with Velcro fasteners. Jiis has seen this all before. The town of Beledweyne was full of them. They'd been there as long as he could remember, taking care of refugees from Ethiopia. As long as he could remember, the foreigners had been coming and staying for a few months and then leaving. There were always new ones walking wide-eyed through the market, staring at camels. But eventually they would become scarce, preferring to ride in their air-conditioned Land Cruisers, plowing slowly through crowds of Somalis as they passed on their way to work or to enjoy each others' company behind the walls of their compounds.

That evening, Jiis and his friends chew *qat* and talk. There are four of them now, as another security guard has been brought in on the plan. The *qat* keeps them awake and alert. The plan, a simple plan, is settled upon. The Americans have made the roads safe for travel at night. Buses will be going to Mogadishu before dawn. That is how they will make their escape.

In the very early hours of the morning, with everyone asleep, Jiis walks into the room where the American sleeps. He pushes the muzzle of his rifle against the sleeping man's head and prods him awake. Then, in the voice of a bad guy from one of the American movies he had once watched, Jiis says, "Open the fucking safe and give me the fucking money."

The American obeys. He is tied up and gagged and locked in his room. Then Jiis and his friends drive to the edge of town and abandon the Land Cruiser. Stealing the Land Cruiser would have brought problems. The Somali owner would have tracked them down or found a relative of his in

Mogadishu or Beledweyne. As dictated by Somali tradition, somebody would have had to pay. That crime would have trailed Jiis for the rest of his life. But stealing from the foreigners is something different. They would have no idea how to find him because they had no idea who he was.

The safe contained nearly $100,000 in cash. Jiis takes his $25,000 share and gives most of it to his ailing father in Mogadishu. He passes out more to friends and relatives and takes the last $5,000 and goes to the port city of Mombasa in Kenya, where he spends it on women and drugs. It is a glorious four months. Jiis, the limping kid from the Somali bush is a big man in the big city. The Mombasa bar girls call him the sheik.

When the money is gone, he moves in with family in Nairobi, where he is looking for another job with the UN. "The money was mine," Jiis explains a year later in Nairobi. He's wearing blue jeans and a U.S. Navy baseball cap, and looks very much at home slurping down a gin and tonic at the Serena Hotel. "You may say it's the UN's money, but what is the UN? This money comes to Somalia and people are taking it. I have just taken mine."

In the town of Galkayo, in the heart of Somalia's rangeland, I sit down to dinner with a group of aid workers at the United Nations compound. They are American and Belgian and Danish. There is a woman from India. The food is local meat with canned imported vegetables whipped up into a meal by a Somali cook who's learned to prepare food for Westerners. It is April of 1994 and Galkayo has been suspended in a tense peace for nearly a year despite its location at a point where two major feuding clan groups face each other.

The dinner conversation drifts over a number of subjects: negotiations with local leaders, information about supplies arriving on the next flight, the logistics of living in the middle of nowhere. Coffee is served. Electric lights pulse with the distant straining of diesel generators. A bottle of whisky is pulled from a cabinet, and the world slows. Cigarettes are lit. There is time to be thoughtful, and the conversation shifts from the daily details to the more general subject of aid, and the question arises: Are we doing more harm than good by being here? Nighttime discussions among aid workers always end up at this point. I've had this conversation with hundreds of different aid workers, on hundreds of occasions: with a Catholic priest in Kakuma, northwestern Kenya, during the famine of 1979; with the head of an NGO in Ouagadougou, capital of Burkina Faso, in 1986; in Addis Ababa, Ethiopia in 1995; in Kampala, Uganda in 1989;

in New Delhi, India in 1974. And nearly every night in 1981 when I was living in Beledweyne, Somalia.

Aid workers notice things: Food aid attracts people to refugee camps, where they die from dysentery or measles or other diseases they wouldn't have contracted in the bush. Is there really a food shortage when anyone with money can find all the food he wants, when the aid workers themselves enjoy meals that the locals could never get even in the best of times? And why does it always seem that a group of local elites finds a way to get rich from the disaster? Are we contributing to the problem by dealing with these businessmen-politicians who lease Land Cruisers and homes to the aid agencies and who provide trucks to transport food?

Someone offers history: Twenty-five years ago most of the countries in Africa had indigenous methods for dealing with food shortages. Somalia in particular had a well-established system for dealing with regular cycles of drought and famine. Farmers in the river valleys built secure underground vaults where grain was stored during the fat years. When drought threatened the nomads, animals that might die anyway were exchanged for grains. Though nomads showed very little respect for farmers, they were aware that their lives might one day depend on these sedentary clans. They were therefore generous with the bounty of their herds when times were good. The result was a mutual insurance system and a truce of necessity across the land.

But few of the aid workers here know anything about pre–civil war Somalia. Their only experience is with the beaten and anarchic society they see beyond the high walls of their compounds. Some of the more experienced aid workers can offer the wisdom that no country was ever transformed from being famine-prone to food self-sufficiency by international charity. In fact, as Harvard economist Amartya Sen has shown, famines always occur in authoritarian states, when the government mismanages the economy. Famines disappear when those countries become market-efficient. India, for example—the epitome of the famine-afflicted land when I was a child—no longer suffers famines despite its huge population.

And some targets of charity get worse. Today, after huge infusions of international aid, Somalia and all its formerly self-sufficient neighbors are chronically hungry and dependent on foreign food. It becomes increasingly difficult for aid workers to ignore the compelling correlation between massive international food aid and increasing vulnerability to famine. "Our charity does not overcome famine, and may help to prolong it," someone will always lament. Those who spend the time to study the local economies see that the people have now geared their own activities not to returning to their old lives but to getting their hands on aid.

And in the case of Somalia, the notion was beginning to dawn on a number of aid workers that the food aid was helping to prolong the war as well. Could it be that it was the food that was causing the conflict and the instability that was making it impossible for people to get their own food? Though the answers were never clear, the questions were always troubling.

While these doubts are often sent back to the home office in New York or Atlanta, they receive very little discussion beyond the walls of the relief agencies. To let that happen would mean having to consider the possibility of going out of business. Instead, the relief agencies advertise.

In America's intimate morning hours, television screens pulse with images of starvation. A typical television advertisement carefully scripted by an agency hired by Save the Children runs as follows:

VIDEO: SHOT OF NEEDY CHILD

A child's face collapsed around its pleading eyes.

The script calls for

SHOT OF MORE NEEDY CHILDREN

and then

EMOTIONALLY CHARGED CHILD SHOT

followed by

SHOT OF VERY MALNOURISHED CHILD

For sound effects, the script asks for

APPROPRIATELY HARD-HITTING, EMOTIONAL ORIGINAL MUSIC

The viewer might sink into helpless despair but for the interviews of a weepy actress who steps through the misery with a solution.

Voiceover: You've seen the frightened faces . . . heard their cries of hunger . . . watched their small bodies fall prey to sickness.

VIDEO: MORE HOPEFUL SHOTS OF KIDS—EATING, PLAYING, SMILING, ETC.

But you can help ease the pain—by becoming a Save the Children sponsor. It's so easy—just a phone call . . . then only pocket change—65¢ a day. Your concern can help stop horrible hunger with nutritious food . . .

Now is the time to rescue one fragile, weakened girl or boy . . . your $20 monthly gift will be combined with those of other sponsors . . .

Please—reach out . . . end this nightmare. You can do it, right now. With just a phone call, you can help stop a different kind of child abuse.

This is the extent of the public discussion instigated by the charity. The goal of the message is not to make us think about hunger and poverty. It is to relieve us of the burden of having to think about it. The charity provides this narrow portal into the world of hunger, a way to reach through the dark distances of space and culture to touch the child. This is real interactive TV. Pick up the phone. Pick up the phone. The deed is done. The child is healed before the viewer's eyes. The relentless message is that it is all so simple. It's easy. Just send money.

The $20 or $50 that the viewer has pledged now begins its long journey from his Visa or MasterCard account through the bank and bureaucracy of the charity, and into other bureaucracies of subsidiary charities. The funds appear as an asset on a series of spreadsheets and merge with funds from other donors and governments. Some is used to pay the $200,000 in salary and benefits for the president of the charity, and some is used for his $2,000-a-month housing allowance, which doesn't show up on public financial statements. Part of the money is used to pay the rents for the charity's offices and to buy airline tickets for the people who make the videos that are shown on television. Some of the money shows up in the ledgers of organizations in the country where the picture of the starving child originated. Some of that will be used to buy or rent a Land Cruiser or put petrol in the tanks of other Land Cruisers. Some will pay the salaries of expatriate workers. In Somalia, some of it will be used to pay the gunmen who protect the expatriate workers. And some of it will be stolen by those very gunmen. The bureaucracy is a hungry beast. It must be fed.

The donor doesn't really want to know any of this as he reads his credit card number over the telephone on that sleepless night. That's not the point. The aid is an offering, an act of compassion and sacrifice. Perhaps it will buy a good night's sleep and a feeling that from the dark interior fortress of America, a life can be touched 8,000 miles away. The charities count on that. They know that out in what they call "the field," the recipients of the charity are not exactly what they seem to be. The donors are amateurs. The recipients are professionals. The expatriate relief workers have been playing this game for a few months, or maybe a few years. The recipients have been on the dole and beating the system for decades.

For ten years before the famine of 1992, Somalia was the largest recipient of aid in sub-Saharan Africa, and in some years the third largest in the world behind perennial leaders Egypt and Israel. But most of Somalia's 6 million people never saw a penny. Much of what wasn't filtered out to pay the expenses of the relief agency was lost in the corrupt maze of the Somali government's nepotistic bureaucracy. Only the wiliest and most entrepreneurial of Somalia's people ever saw any tangible benefits from the aid. That money went to Somali bureaucrats whose primary skill was in earning money by dealing with foreign charities. And when money did drip down to the people it was used in ways designed by a government desperately trying to cling to its diminishing power. And in all these things, Somalia was only a slightly more extreme case of how aid works everywhere. The other big recipients of aid in Africa have fared no better than Somalia.

As Somalia stood on the brink of chaos in 1990, it was utterly dependent on foreign aid. It is little wonder then that when aid started pouring into the country once again in 1992, humble gratitude was not people's immediate response. Instead, another generation of Somalis prepared to get its share, to get rich by doing whatever it took to get as much as possible from the foreigners.

And it wasn't as if the foreigners weren't making out in the deal. The Somalis saw young white people in their mid-twenties with no recognizable skills driving about in Land Cruisers and living in nice houses for which their organizations were paying thousands of dollars a month in rent—rent money that was going to the biggest criminals in the country. The young foreigners didn't speak Somali and knew nothing of the history of the place. They always had plenty of money to spend and didn't mind paying absurd prices for what they bought. The people back home might have regarded what these people were doing as a sacrifice, but the Somalis saw them living high.

Few foreigners ever invested the time or effort to see aid from the point of view of the recipients. They rarely looked beyond their own idealized images of famine and charity. Into Somalia's nightmare world of warlords and forced starvation, they held aloft the image of the hungry child-God they themselves had created to justify their own actions. And they marched blindly into the mire.

2

FAR FROM SOMALIA

All domination involves invasion—at times physcial and overt, at times camouflaged, with the invader assuming the role of a helping friend.

—Paulo Freire, *Pedagogy of the Oppressed*

C hris Cassidy felt a rush of revulsion. Then a queasiness arose in his stomach. His life seemed to be unraveling all over again. He had tried to exile himself in eastern Washington State, as far away from Somalia as he could get, but now Somalia had come and found him. It appeared on the front pages of the local paper and on local radio and television stations. It wouldn't leave him alone.

Cassidy said from the beginning that the Americans should not have gone into Somalia. When he spoke, people were surprised to learn that the man who now lived alone in Yakima doing agricultural work on the nearby Indian reservation could become so enraged over what was seemingly a brave and charitable gesture from the United States government. Cassidy has always impressed people as the giving and caring type.

But then Cassidy would explain that he had lived in Somalia for six years. He had worked there with the U.S. government and with Save the

Children, and the United Nations Food and Agricultural Organization (FAO)—and he knew what he was talking about. Somalia was a trap.

It had been two years since he and his family had been forced to flee the violence of Mogadishu at the end of 1990. The rebels had been approaching the city, and the government troops had begun to terrorize the residents. Aid workers were particular targets, as government soldiers and the rebels began to commandeer Land Cruisers off the streets. All local authority broke down as the president hid in his bunker at the airport and his frightened, leaderless troops wandered the streets.

In this chaos, Cassidy guided his Norwegian wife, Tone, eight months pregnant, through the choking heat of the Mogadishu airport terminal, beneath the gaze of soldiers and police who must have known that they too would be fleeing the city soon. Cassidy held the baby in his arms. Little Christopher grasped his hand as the family climbed the stairs of the Kenya Airways plane. Gunfire cracked in the distance.

As the plane taxied away from the terminal, Cassidy should have felt relieved. But Tone's weighty silence told him that all was not right. For the first time he noticed how worn she was, how devastated. How long had she been like this? It could have been years. The look in her eyes petrified him. Below, in the northern part of Mogadishu, under a small stone in the Catholic cemetery, lay their eldest son, Bernie. There had been no time to remove the body, but Chris promised that he would do that in a few months, as soon as the fighting ended. Then Bernie could be buried in the family cemetery in New Orleans. But the flight to Nairobi would be the last thing the family would do together.

Later, in Yakima, Cassidy avoided talking about Somalia, and when it did come up he'd dismiss it. Where is Somalia? Never mind. Forget it. Nobody was really that curious anyway. Not in Yakima. He would tell them: "You know, it's in the Bible. The land of frankincense and myrrh. One of the wisemen was a Somali or something." Few knew what frankincense was and fewer could even guess about myrrh. But "frankincense and myrrh" floated like a familiar song and left people feeling some sort of connection.

Then, somehow, on this raw February night in 1993, Cassidy found himself preparing to give a talk about Somalia. He put on his best suit, climbed into his Toyota pickup truck, and drove along Route 82 from Yakima toward Ellensburg, some 45 miles away. The task should have been simple; the talk would be informal, relaxed. But Cassidy was not relaxed. He cracked open the window and cold, dry air filled the cab. And he thought one more time about what he would tell the audience.

As he sped through the early evening darkness, Cassidy knew he would not be allowed to get away with frankincense and myrrh. After the U.S. Marines landed, suddenly, people who had never heard of Somalia had opinions about it. It had been on television. Everyone knew it was a land where Americans had gone to rescue starving people from vicious warlords and drug-crazed thugs. They'd learned it all since the summer of 1992, when the picture of those beautiful black and dying people appeared on television screens across America. First they watched them starve and then they watched the marines climb over sand dunes. They watched blond-haired angels holding little black babies.

The crowd tonight is small, thirty or forty people in a small circular build-ing on the campus of Central Washington State University. They are mostly students and professors and a smattering of the liberal intelligentsia who gather around rural universities, people who reserve copies of the *New York Times* at the local drug store, listen to National Public Radio, and spend their evenings in meeting halls boning up on international affairs so they can offer knowledgeable critiques of current events. They are thoughtful people who once might have stated with certainty that the United States of America would send its soldiers to protect oil but never to help starving Africans. Now they are confused.

Before them on the stage they see two young and polished marines and Cassidy, a nervous man in a suit. Cassidy has a thick blond lumberjack beard mounted like a fuzzy wreath around a sharp, angular face with pierc-ing blue eyes and red cheeks. Some of the hairs from his mustache intrude upon his upper lip. He's thin, almost bony, and he steps up to the small stage with the cautious movement of a former athlete whose grace is haunted with memory of injury.

The soldiers speak first. They are polite and very persuasive. Their de-meanor radiates the "yes sir/yes ma'am" respect that has been drilled into them. They're reinforcing the rosy images that have come across the tele-vision. They're talking about the heroic effort to move through Somalia, secure towns, and open roads over which truck after truck now carried life-giving food to the mouths of starving children. The operation they describe is an unqualified success, a tribute to America and to people like you. They thank the people in the room for the opportunity to go and perform such deeds. The audience is smiling. They are getting into the spirit of Opera-tion Restore Hope.

Cassidy bends over in his chair, listening. These kids don't know what they're talking about, he thinks. They're public relations commandos who could put a feel-good patriotic face on a bloody massacre. Cassidy is feeling crotchety and angry. What the fuck do they know about Somalia? They've probably spent a week there. I'm the one who put six years of my life into the place. What are they doing telling me anything? What are they doing telling anybody anything, especially at a university. Save that shit for the American Legion, boys. Talk to me again when you've really experienced hunger. When you've lived with the people.

The soldiers' kind of charity, he reflects, is easy, like dropping a shiny coin into a grubby hand passing quickly in the hectic blur of the night. They want you to believe that's enough—for $20 a month little Pedro can have a hot meal and a place to go to school and new pajamas. Problem solved. If everyone gave money we could dispense with all these unpleasant pictures of dying children once and for all.

Cassidy is angry, not at the marines; he's angry at the stupid audience. These guys work for the government. Of course they're going to tell you the bullshit. You're a bunch of mush-minded guilty liberal assholes for believing them, for believing that money and guns can solve the problems of the poor.

"You know," Cassidy begins with a stammer, "you just can't send food and help starving people." You can't, he knows. But how to explain all of this? Why didn't he ever get around to actually writing a speech? "Well, you know, you just can't do that. It's, it's so really complicated."

And it's hard to explain. A better approach might be to sit and tell his story: Let me tell you what happened to me when I was in Somalia. But Cassidy isn't ready to tell this to anyone.

"Helping people is all well and good, but what's our policy? What is it going to do for our country? Why were those troops sent in there? I don't see a plan. You give a guy a bag of food today and you give him a bag of seeds and . . . There is no plan to end the relief. There's no phase-out built into the system." The marines are sitting erect and pokerfaced. Cassidy paces across the stage. His hands are shaking, though he's not nervous.

"You know," Cassidy begins again, reaching for something, straining to grasp the handle of an idea. Cassidy tells the people he's worried about sending troops without a mission. He's worried because this Somalia of TV and government propaganda, this Somalia crying out for rescue, doesn't at all resemble the Somalia he knows, and one day very soon the reality of Somalia will burst through and shatter the fragile media images. Then the world will punish Somalia for not living up to the manufactured mirage.

"Somalia doesn't need our help. Somalia can feed itself. The problems are political, and we don't have a plan for solving their political problems. In fact, we caused a lot of their political problems."

Cassidy looks again at the audience. They hate him. They hate his disjointed presentation, and if they think they understand what he's trying to say to them, they hate that, too. They prefer the modulated saccharine crap the marines are dishing out. They seem to be fading back into the distance. Cassidy has several friends in the audience, and they feel embarrassed for him. He's being inarticulate, almost a buffoon. They're not even sure what it is he's trying to say, and they've heard him before.

Then from the audience, one woman reaches out to him. She grabs hold of one solid thing Cassidy has said. "So are you saying these people were feeding themselves?" she asks seriously.

"Yes. Yes. Yes. Feeding themselves. And exporting it. They are perfectly capable of feeding themselves." Cassidy blurts out, thankful and exhausted. "They're smart people. They're grown-ups. They don't need your twenty-five bucks."

"How come we don't read this in the press?" someone asks. "Why is your version so different from what we see on television?"

"Because I lived there. I know. Why do you believe anything you read in the press?"

"They made me look like the bad guy out there," Cassidy told his friends Roger and Jane as he left that night. "When I was in school, Roger, the idea was to enlighten yourself. But people don't want to fucking hear about this stuff. They don't want to hear that we're hurting people while saying we're helping. There's no spirit of inquiry here. Fuck no, that's not what academia is about these days."

"Calm down," Roger counseled. "You can't just fly off the handle every time someone doesn't understand what you're trying to say about Somalia."

But Cassidy had been like that once. He was a believer who cared. He believed he could help, that it was his duty to help, so he joined the Peace Corps and went to Africa. His disillusionment settled into him over many years; the more he resisted it, the more deeply it seeped inside of him. The more his reality clashed with his idealism the more bitter his sense of betrayal became. He of all people should have been able to explain the gulf between the idea of aid and the reality of coming colonialism. It is a measure of his disillusionment that he cannot, and even the most sympathetic ear I could offer was barely enough to get his story out of him.

Chris Cassidy came to Mogadishu for the first time in August 1981. That Mogadishu was very different from the one he fled in December 1990. And it was completely different from the one the marines found when they landed in the early morning hours of December 9, 1992.

In 1981, Mogadishu was still a sleepy and forgotten whitewashed port town, not much different from the one built by Persian and Arab traders a thousand years before. Daily life in Mogadishu started off slowly and then ground to a halt as the midmorning heat settled like damp tissue paper on the city. The bold blue of the ocean and the dominant white of the buildings cut sharp lines and vivid contrasts in the clear morning air. Majestic Italianate villas, crumbling and peeling, loomed above the shoreline.

In the center of town, rising from the seawall, stood the Al Uruba Hotel, the most modern in Somalia, its arabesque portals stupidly out of place with the genuine Mogadishu architecture. It was built by the Soviets, and nothing worked. As with every sealed modern building in a tropical climate, the first time the air-conditioning went out, the place filled with mildew. After that, the stink never went away.

The American embassy was a small white building on a quiet main street. It looked like every other little building on the street. Outside the embassy, two Somali soldiers with AK-47s and blue berets always lounged peacefully against the wall, their uniforms slightly tattered, but clean. Inside, an American marine behind a glass partition handled security. There wasn't really much call for such a thing.

Beside the embassy stood shops that sold tea and other basic goods. There was a small book and magazine stand nearby that sold *Newsweek* and *Time* and the occasional copy of the *International Herald Tribune*, valued links to home in the days before CNN.

On each wall of the shops hung a picture of Jalle Mohamed Siyaad Barre, comrade Mohamed. The Somalis called him *afweyne*, big mouth. A little Hitler mustache connected his nose and upper lip. Most of the pictures were air brushed, softening the corners of the dictator's eyes and mouth, though the retouching did little to remove the dour, humorless gaze. In 1981, Jalle Siyaad still had a following, but it was fading fast. The dictator was rarely seen in person. There were few public speeches or motorcades. Somalia had no television in 1981.

At almost any time of the day, it was possible to stand in front of the embassy and hear the breeze in the trees and the surf pounding 300 yards in the distance. Voices drifted out of tea shops and around corners. Rolling Somali syllables cut the air with razor-sharp staccato consonants. Donkey hooves clicked by, towing grinding metal and wooden wheels on the pavement. Ancient red and yellow Fiat taxi cabs sputtered and spit plumes of black exhaust that vanished into the infinite clarity of the air.

Somalis walked slowly in the streets. Men wore the traditional *macawis*, sandals, and collared, vented shirts. Others wore tropical leisure suits of faded pastels with their short-sleeved tunic tops. Somalis with less to spend on new clothes wore combinations of local dress and used clothing imported by the ton from the West. These were drawn from clothes discarded in Goodwill boxes or Salvation Army depots. Garments not fit for resale as trendy vintage clothing in the developed world were sold to private companies that baled them like hay and shipped them off to Africa. "Who died?" one Somali might jokingly ask another who was sporting a new imported outfit. They soon became known as "Hoo-die" clothes, as the Somalis assumed that only the dead would part with a perfectly good pair of trousers.

The few people who had what could be described as a job got to work early and left early. They spent their days in offices that always seemed dark and stuffy. The higher the official the more carpet and fabric hung on the walls. And the more fabric in the room the heavier and more rancid the room was with mildew. Somali officials found comfort in the darkness.

In the old part of Mogadishu called Hamar Weyne, goldsmiths, direct descendants of the original Persian settlers, created intricate jewelry in thirteenth century buildings. The *reer Hamar*, as these people were called, had lighter skin than most Somalis. Some had blue eyes and sandy hair. They were regarded as a national treasure.

By the middle of the afternoon, the streets were quieter still, and everyone went home. There wasn't much traffic because there wasn't much fuel. Many Americans would be picked up in a blue van and taken to and from work at the embassy or USAID. The Somalis called the blue van the Russian bus, because the Soviets who had left recently used it for the same purpose.

The Somalis would retire to their homes or to tea shops for heated discussions about nothing in particular. Or they would chew *qat* with friends.

The life of the Somalis was utterly hidden to foreigners like Cassidy. In their offices they would come in contact with professionals who stepped comfortably into their roles as junior bureaucrats, administrative assistants, and secretaries. At the end of the day the Somalis would walk out the gates and disappear into the vast anonymity of Mogadishu, into neighborhoods such as Medina or Wardigley, where the streets became narrow and crowded.

The foreigners would get into their Land Cruisers and drive to one of the beach clubs. The Anglo-American Beach Club, the Italian Beach Club, and the UN Beach Club sat along the stretch of the Lido in north Mogadishu. People ate hamburgers and drank beer on patios overlooking the ocean. The company was cordial. Almost everyone in the small expatriate community knew everyone else. A few children played in the restaurants, running between the tables and chairs while their parents talked, usually about the business of development. And about the Somalis. Below, Somalis bathed and fished. Expatriates had long since stopped swimming there, since sharks prowled the shallow waters, eating the occasional swimmer. The expats drank their drinks and watched the fins in the waves and wondered who would be next. There were no hospitals in north Mogadishu, no ambulances. Open wounds drained until death.

In the last week of March 1981, three people died from shark attacks just off the Lido by the beach clubs. One was a fourteen-year-old boy who lost a piece of his thigh as he ran about five yards from the shore chasing a football. He bled to death on the way to the hospital. Two days later a man standing in waist-deep water had his intestines ripped out by a passing shark. Several hours later the corpse of another shark victim washed ashore.

Four years earlier the government had built a slaughterhouse just north of the Lido beach. Blood and guts drained into and floated about the water, attracting the great whites to the warm unprotected shore.

At the UN Beach Club someone drew a poster on notebook papers showing a panicked Somali bather watching wide-eyed as a great white shark swam off with his severed leg. Before this happens to you, we should get a pool, the sign said.

The people who sat around drinking beer and eating hamburgers were mostly young workers for private voluntary organizations. Today they are called NGOs, but in 1981 they were known as volags, a contraction of voluntary agencies, or PVOs, for private voluntary agencies. Neither one of these names was precisely accurate. Few of the people who worked for them were really volunteers. Most were getting paid, some quite handsomely, with prospects for advancement. And since most subsisted on government contracts, they weren't precisely private.

These years saw the dawn of the yuppie in America. Development work had once been the domain of good-hearted, globe-trotting, draft-dodging hippie types who enjoyed living and working in places where dope was cheap and life was easy. But by 1981, these people were being rapidly pushed aside by movers and shakers on a career track. Development work was being professionalized, which many saw as a good thing.

The people who started arriving to work in development were more and more young professionals with graduate degrees in nonprofit management from Yale or backgrounds in economic and political development from Columbia or the Kennedy School of Government at Harvard, the same people who were starting to take over Wall Street. They had new ideas about how to move all those bags and bags of U.S. relief food. They had ideas about how to feed hundreds of thousands of refugees and how to take a backward desert country where 70 percent of the people were nomads and where average life expectancy was thirty-nine years and turn it into a modern and more productive state.

But mostly they had ideas about spending money. And suddenly there was a lot of money available for Somalia. Fat contracts were floating about from the UN and the U.S. government to do things in Somalia. Much of that money was allocated to the care of ethnic Somali refugees who had fled Ethiopia in 1977 and 1978 in the wake of a short and brutal war between Somalia and Ethiopia in the Ogaden desert. Today the war in the Ogaden would be one of those African skirmishes lost on the inner pages of only the largest newspapers. In 1977, however, this border war became the vortex of American and Soviet power facing off in yet another test in the Cold War. The brief exaggerated importance of the Horn of Africa meant that arms poured in from the East and West, and along with these arms, to fight the battle for hearts and minds, came relief and development aid. For the new young professionals in the development industry, this Cold War aid race was a lucrative opportunity to practice their craft. Aid workers and military advisors splashed around together in the embassy swimming pool, but still the aid workers refused to imagine that they were all there for the same purpose, their funds coming from the same source to accomplish the same goal. In order for America to maintain a foothold on the Horn of Africa, they were all there to please one man, Siyaad Barre, to help the dictator stay in power, even if that meant supporting his broken dream of Greater Somalia.

The dream of Greater Somalia could be seen in the maps hanging on the walls of government offices. There were no borders where we're used to seeing borders, just uninterrupted stretches of brown and green reaching across through central Kenya, over into Djibouti, and across the Ogaden into the Ethiopian highlands, the area that Somali officials called Western Somalia. These were the lands inhabited by ethnic Somalis, one people divided by old colonial lines.

In the absence of any other forces uniting this nation of solitary nomads, the idea of Greater Somalia provided them at least with a common quest, some common enemies. The Somalis who live in these three other countries are represented by three of the points of the five-pointed star on the Somali flag. The other two points represent the regions of the former Italian Trust Territory of Somalia, that is, southern Somalia, and the former British Somaliland Protectorate, the northern region around Hargeysa.

The idea of uniting the five Somali groups has long been at the root of Somali nationalism. The former British region became independent on June 26, 1960. The Italian region achieved its independence five days later, and the two joined to form one country.

In 1963, as Kenya verged on independence from Britain, Somali Nationalists looked southwest to the part of Kenya known as the Northern Frontier District (NFD). Its population was more than 60 percent Somali, predominantly Muslim, and overwhelmingly in favor of unification with the Somali state. Their wishes were ignored in favor of those of Kenyan nationalists, who opposed partition of the colony. When Kenya became independent in December 1963, Somalis in the NFD began a long, futile war against the new government. The Somalis called them freedom fighters and the Kenyans called them *shifta*, a term applied to bandits and cattle thieves.

To this day, Kenya's Northeastern Province is a dangerous place to travel. *Shifta* still attack convoys and raid towns on occasion. And both the Kenyans and the Somalis are right: the *shifta* are usually bandits who call themselves freedom fighters, and occasionally freedom fighters who behave like bandits.

The situation in the Ogaden, however, proved much more explosive. For centuries Amharic Emperors had, through intimidation and agreements, controlled the Muslim lowlands of the Ogaden. As in Kenya, the freedom fight sputtered along, but the Somali military had little chance of any victory against the superior American-trained Ethiopian army under Emperor Haile Selassie.

In 1967, the elected Somali government of Prime Minister Mohamed Ibrahim Egal began a process of making peace with the nations that stood in the way of the pan-Somali dream. Egal realized that the dream was fruitless, that all of Africa, confronted with secessionist minorities, had lined up against Somalia. Though Egal's peace efforts weren't appreciated by Somalis, his coalition won the fraud-laced 1969 election. Yet in the process of assuring his own power, Egal had angered the military, which then overthrew him in October 1969. The coup leader, Major General Mohamed Siyaad Barre, ascended to the leadership of the country.

Several years after the coup, Barre announced that his government, led by the Supreme Revolutionary Council, would pursue the path of "scientific socialism." A loose military alliance with the Soviet Union became codified, and Barre began a massive military buildup with armored units, MiG-21 fighter-bombers, and Ilyushin bombers. Thousands of military advisors began to train the 20,000-man Somali army. The Ethiopians and Kenyans, with reason to be scared, turned to their American allies.

All of this might have turned into a typical Third World, Cold War arms race had it not been for the 1974 coup in Ethiopia that booted Haile Selassie from the imperial palace and installed a socialist government. The Soviets, seeing that Ethiopia was probably the most valuable piece of real estate in Africa, did a clean sweep on regional foreign policy. They stopped backing Eritrean and Tigrean rebels fighting against the Ethiopian government and began to arm the new military junta, the *Dergue*, while attempting to maintain their relationship with Somalia.

In 1977, however, the Soviets were forced to choose sides. A bloody internal power struggle in Ethiopia had left the regime vulnerable. Barre sensed his opening. The Soviet military buildup in Ethiopia hadn't gotten very far, and his own army was primed and ready. In July 1977, he invaded the Ogaden, rapidly capturing the region and driving the Ethiopians back into the hills. Elated Somalis decreed Barre the savior of the Somali nation. He was at the peak of his popularity.

What followed in Ethiopia was Jimmy Carter's worst nightmare, and it changed the direction of U.S. military policy. Midway through the war, the Russians, who had signed an "eternal" friendship treaty with Somalia in 1975, switched sides, airlifting 18,000 Cuban troops and $2 billion worth of arms to the Ethiopians. Barre turned to the Americans. The Carter administration promised him weapons but then, at the height of the fighting, decided to withhold them. By then it was too late for Somalia. By March 1978, the Somalis were run out of the Ogaden.

Shocked by the lightening Soviet response to the military and diplomatic crisis on the Horn, U.S. military strategists started feeling paranoid about America's ability to wage a "conventional" war, and the idea of a

Rapid Deployment Force took hold. The Americans convinced themselves that an abandoned Soviet naval base at Berbera, in northern Somalia, was critical to America's security.

The Heritage Foundation, soon to gain influence in the Reagan administration, spelled out the evolving mood concerning the Horn of Africa:

> The Soviet Military intervention in the Horn of Africa is the centerpiece of two new foreign policy initiatives: one in the Middle East and the other in Africa. The intermediate-range targets are Saudi Arabia, the world's largest producer of petroleum, and Kenya, the last pro-Western state from the Cape to the Horn.

Siyaad Barre had something the Americans wanted and were willing to pay for. For the next ten years he would use America's lust for the Berbera base to extract as much military and development aid as he could. By the time U.S. hostages were seized in Iran and the Soviets had invaded Afghanistan, the United States was scrambling to look tough. In early 1981, the incoming Reagan administration dispatched Henry Kissinger to Mogadishu, where he assured Siyaad Barre that America was behind him. "It is not tolerable that the Soviet Union and its proxy forces engage in expansion all over Africa and in the Middle East without opposition," Kissinger said in Cairo after a day with Barre in Somalia.

From Washington, the barren wastes of Somalia suddenly looked like the center of Berlin.

By 1979, within Somalia, the gloss had worn off the campaign in the Ogaden. Barre was becoming increasingly unpopular, and his secret police, the National Security Service (NSS) was stepping up its campaign of intimidation against his enemies. Previously, Somali governments had tried to maintain a broad base of representation from various clans. But as Barre began to feel less and less secure, he started to close the circle, increasingly employing his own clansmen and his own relatives in positions of power.

At the same time, Somalia maintained a low-level war against the Ethiopians in the Ogaden, arming a group of Ogaden Somalis called the Western Somalia Liberation Front, or WSLF. The WSLF attacks drew reprisals, and increasingly the Somali nomads from the region found themselves caught in the middle. Some of them sought safety over the border in Somalia. Barre began to pressure his Western allies for refugee relief, and they responded. There were big stakes placed on the table. Barre claimed a half a million refugees, then a million, and soon a million and a half. Journalists took pictures of the sick and the hungry, and the relief agencies arrived on the scene with the food. Siyaad Barre knew from the beginning that these foreigners, arriving in the guise of angels, could help him hold on to his flagging power.

Cassidy and the other Americans arrived in Somalia not exactly sure what they would find, but not particularly concerned either. U.S. government employees were housed in former Italian villas along the beach on the Lido or in other parts of town. The houses were luxurious by any standards. Floors were Italian porcelain tile. Their contracts specified that the houses contain refrigerators and huge freezers for storing their imported food. Likewise, under contractual agreement, the houses were air-conditioned. This all depended on the regularity and amperage of local electricity, which was beyond the control of the American government. When the air conditioner in an expatriate house kicked in, the street lights would dim.

Houses also included quarters for the help, verandahs, courtyards, and other niceties that made staying home infinitely more comfortable than venturing outside. Somali entrepreneurs were starting to catch on and build more and more homes to house the Americans, who were more demanding and had bigger budgets than the Soviets.

Those who needed more community were placed in the American compound at K-7, seven kilometers down the Afgooye road, which had a swimming pool, a number of bungalows, a five-story dormitory for the marines, a snack bar where hamburgers and other American treats were served, and a recreation room.

The entire compound was painted an industrial greenish blue. There the Americans would swim and gather for movies projected against a wall by the pool. This was for the American staff and their invited guests. There were very few invited guests, because few Americans knew anyone who wasn't an American, except for the Somalis who worked as assistants at the U.S. Embassy or USAID or the U.S. Information Service (USIS). There wasn't an actual rule prohibiting the Somalis who worked for the Americans from coming to the pool or the movies; it really wasn't necessary.

The town had a number of restaurants where the atmosphere was usually better than the food. There was a Chinese restaurant, which served spicy meat on spaghetti, not so different from Somali cuisine. Somali waiters in smudged white smocks served chicken and camel lo mein.

The Italian culture seemed to mix easily with the Somali. The breezy Mediterranean attitude that the Italian colonists brought meshed with the laid-back, urban environment of Mogadishu. On the other hand, sausage- and ham-loving Catholic Italian culture had little resonance out-side the city.

The restaurant at the Hotel Croce del Sud served passable Italian food but was most notable for the people who hung out there. The Croce had a telex machine, so it attracted the rare foreign journalist. It also had a book-store and a tea shop, and may have been the closest thing to Rick's Place in Africa. That feeling increased during the 1980s as the regime became more and more oppressive and the expatriate hangouts began to feel more and more like sanctuaries.

In the back of the Al Uruba Hotel the Club 57 disco overlooked the ocean. Somali rock 'n' roll and prostitutes mingled in the night air. At the Lido Club, sailors and prostitutes and aid workers drank as the surf pounded against the rocks below and the fragrant ocean breezes swirled magically around the room.

Open prostitution was frowned upon in Muslim Somalia. It was said that most of the girls were Somalis from Kenya, set morally adrift from time spent among the infidels. But that wasn't exactly true. In fact, many of the prostitutes in Kenya were girls from Somalia trying to earn a living. Some began to return to Mogadishu when the Western expatriates showed up there with dollars. The Somali police tried to keep a lid on the outward manifestation of lasciviousness. A police squad known as the *buona cos-tuma* enforced dress codes for women, arresting those who wore too-tight jeans or showed too much skin. The girls usually bought their freedom with small bribes or traded sex for the opportunity to return to the clubs.

Expatriates in Mogadishu invested vast amounts of their time and energy trying to live as normal a Western lifestyle as possible, which usually meant procuring food items that were not available in the local markets: fatty American beef, chocolate, butter. Once secured, these items would be used sparingly, mustered for maximum impact, such as when the boss came to dinner. Sometimes they would be hand carried from Nairobi. Sometimes Americans would stock up at an Italian shop at Fiat Circle that carried im-ported items. Often the embassy would provide them.

**Notice: 100 pounds of butter will be arriving on a government flight.
Those interested should sign up on a list at the K-7 compound.**

The American Embassy staff would flock to K-7 like Somali refugees lin-ing up for their rations of sorghum. Everyone signed up, and then the but-ter was parceled out among those with the highest ranks. It rarely made it down to the contractors and others who were actually doing the work in Somalia, remaining instead in the hands of senior officers.

Once in a while when someone would leave the country, he would hold a house sale. His kitchen would contain freezers full of butter and beef and turkeys, beer and whiskey, Rice-a-Roni and Hamburger Helper, and other rare goods, hoarded for some eventuality that had obviously not arrived. People talked about food, bragged about food, delighted in their goodies. Sometimes it seemed that it was all anybody ever did. Living the Western lifestyle became a game and an obsession with those who never left the capital.

In 1981, expat life was transformed by the arrival of the VCR, which changed the very nature of being at an overseas posting. Now there were movies and videotapes of month-old football games, that sort of thing. They provided escape and brought people closer to home. Where once an American foreign service officer might have decided to wander out into a local market, driven to such madness by sheer boredom, there was now the option of staying home with episodes of the Cosby show fresh from the diplomatic pouch.

A diplomatic shop in Mogadishu sold cheap whiskey and Dutch beer. Land Cruisers were always backed up to its gate, and expatriates stood around with checkbooks and ration cards in hand. So many bottles of whiskey and so much beer were allocated to each person. There was a healthy trade in unused ration cards that kept expats busy. Most bought their entire ration. It was impossible to know when the shop would be out of stock.

If one took the time to breathe Mogadishu in, to stop and watch it for a moment, one would have glimpsed a unique time fading quickly into history. The ancient charm of the city had withstood Portuguese invasions, Italian fascist colonialism, and ten years of Soviet-sponsored "Scientific Socialism." Now it was about to experience a seemingly benign invasion of young aid workers, people with money and a culture and lifestyle that was contagious. Nothing in Somalia's history had prepared it for this.

Two days after Cassidy finished a two-year tour of Peace Corps service in Kenya, he was ecstatic to be on his way to Somalia to work for USAID. After the Peace Corps, USAID was a giant step up the development ladder. The money and benefits were good, but best of all for Cassidy, he would get to stay in Africa doing development work.

USAID in Somalia was swamped and desperately in need of his help. Somalia had gone from being a socialist Soviet-aligned arch enemy to being an ally and major recipient of American aid in the space of a few years. There was aid money pouring in. Staff was arriving from all over the world. And there was no infrastructure to handle it. The sleepy little embassy was buzzing with activity. Refugee programs and development programs were bursting file cabinets at USAID, forcing it to move to larger offices. Cassidy was hired to provide logistics to development workers, to figure out how USAID could support all of its staff that was marching into the field.

Logistics is an important word in development. It's half the battle. If doctors are coming to work in a village somewhere, it's necessary to have someone handling logistics—making sure they get there, that supplies get there, that they can get out, that there's fuel for the vehicles, or whatever. These activities take more time in Africa than actual development work.

Cassidy was sent to northern Somalia, to Hargeysa, two days' drive from Mogadishu, where he was asked to look into the rehabilitation of Ogaden refugees. Do you settle them? Do you ship 'em back? And Cassidy was supposed to answer these questions even though he had no experience with refugees and knew little about Somalia.

But he was also answering questions of more immediate importance to the U.S. government. For example, if USAID opens a guest house in Hargeysa, who is allowed to stay there? Should USAID contractors be allowed to stay or just direct the hiring of employees? Cassidy, only a contractor, was asked to express an opinion.

He was also in charge of the field support unit, which meant clearing stuff at the port in Berbera. The only Americans who spent time with Somalis were people like Cassidy and other young former Peace Corps volunteers who were hired as personal service contractors (PCSs), to do the dirty work of going out into the bush and telling the career people what was going on.

Chris Cassidy seems to have few memories about that time long ago in Somalia. He remembers hanging around with his friend Doug Grice, another PSC who had been there for a year already when Cassidy arrived. Grice had been making a stink about something that was obvious to most of the aid workers in Somalia. The refugee programs, he said, were unnecessary. Instead of finding better ways to get food more efficiently to the refugees, someone might be looking for ways to get them back to their lives in the Ogaden. Everyone agreed that that was a good idea, but no one ever did anything about it. Instead, they designed programs to deliver more food to more refugees.

The Somali government wanted the refugees to stay. All the reasons for this weren't immediately apparent to the young aid workers. They did know that some government officials were getting rich stealing refugee supplies, but it had to be more complicated than that. The American government's motives were a little more transparent and could be summed up in one word: Berbera. If the Somali government insisted that 1.5 million hungry refugees needed relief food, why not give it to them? It was surplus anyway.

When he thought too much about it, the situation bothered Cassidy. He had really come to Africa to help people. It was a need hammered into him by a strict Catholic upbringing. Africa felt like his calling, development work his priesthood. But when he found the temple full of scoundrels, he couldn't find the courage to change it. So he did his job and drank his duty-free beer, went to parties, and traveled as much as he could, complaining sometimes. It was at one of these parties he met a quiet, serious Norwegian woman anthropologist. Her name was Tone (pronounced *tuna*) and she had a real interest in Somalia and its people. There was nothing cynical about her. For Cassidy, desperately trying to restore some meaning to an increasingly ambiguous experience, she was a stretch of dry land in an endless ocean of uncertainty.

3

FIXERS

There are men in the world who derive as stern an exaltation from proximity to disaster and ruin, as others from success.

—Winston Churchill, *The Malakand Field Force*

At the end of 1985, Chris Cassidy was on his way back to Mogadishu. Beside him was Tone, whom he had since married, and their six-week-old son, Bernie. Tone would have preferred waiting until Bernie was older before bringing him to so remote a place, but Chris had his dream job waiting for him back in Somalia. It was the job he had been preparing himself to take from the moment he had left Somalia the first time. Chris had departed Somalia as a well-meaning generalist and was now returning as an agricultural expert. Now he would be doing something real. He would be working with Save the Children on a project to teach refugees how to become self-sufficient farmers.

His first glimpse of Somalia from the plane was of the lazy port town of Merka, south of Mogadishu. Farther inland he could see the fertile Shebelle River valley. Somewhere along that strip of green, he knew, was Qorioley, the town that would be his home for the next five years. As the plane made its final approach along the beach into Mogadishu, he saw what looked to be about fifty Somali men, prisoners, stripped naked but for a cloth around their waists, hammering rocks in the brutal sun, black bodies shining on a field of rolling white sand.

There was a blast of thick warm air as the cabin door opened. The Cassidys were loaded down with baby stuff: a crib, a stroller, bags of disposable diapers, and boxes of baby food, as well as lamps and batteries and blankets. Just because Tone and Chris were willing to rough it in the African bush didn't mean that little Bernie had to suffer for one minute. He'd have all the advantages of a First World life, while understanding something about a world that didn't offer that life to everyone. Cassidy was determined that Bernie would learn a work ethic. He would understand life in a way that those TV-drugged kids in the States never would.

The family stepped slowly down toward the tarmac as the stairway wobbled beneath them. Below, Chris could see the plane surrounded by Somali police in blue berets lounging about the terminal, holding their automatic weapons as if they were as harmless as umbrellas. Fixers and greeters from various aid agencies milled among the police, smiling and patiently waiting in the hot sun for the Westerners they would usher through the erratic and intimidating Somali immigration maze. They would get the right stamps in passports and keep luggage from the grasp of customs officials seeking to supplement their salaries. Anyone who was not picked up by a fixer was at their mercy. A newcomer without an experienced escort would be like fresh carrion to the airport vultures.

Most of the non-Somalis on the plane were in the aid business, consultants and relief experts, development mavens, men and women of all ages and European nationalities. Flights in and out of Mogadishu were full of them, coming and going from Nairobi. Some were transiting from Europe. Most were on weekend rests in Kenya's consumer-friendly capital or game parks, fat from buffet dinners, relaxed from hours of lounging around glistening swimming pools and sipping drinks proffered by trained-in-the-art-of-service Kenyan waiters.

As they started the long walk across the tarmac to the arrivals building, it seemed like a mile away. Thick heat radiated from the sun-baked tar. The fatigue of a 12,000-mile nearly nonstop journey made their knees weak and left them feeling vaguely ill. Tone held the baby tightly as Chris scanned the crowd for a friendly face, someone to reach out and take some luggage and welcome him to Somalia. Each of the other passengers walked toward a Somali face, a warm glance, and a promise of efficient passage. Chris looked around nervously as he led his young family toward the sign that read Arrivals. The faces of the Somali fixers all looked familiar. He looked into their eyes hoping that one of them was there to meet him. There was no one.

Some years earlier, someone had described the Mogadishu airport to Cassidy as being like carnivale in Rio, except there's nothing to drink and there's no parade, just mass chaos. He remembered that now as the crowds and confusion thickened around him and sweat began to run down his forehead and into his eyes.

Inside the terminal the Cassidys struggled to produce passports. The baby stirred in his mother's arms. Cassidy kept looking for help but there was none.

"*Subax wanaagsan,*" he said, remembering a bit of Somali. Good morning. The official was unimpressed. Another family of foreigners coming; and this one is alone.

Vultures instinctively know how to work airports. Customs officials pounce like moonies or Hare Krishnas, delighted to find these people so close to the edge of despair and so ready to obey orders.

Tone held the baby while Chris wrestled with the luggage. Then a voice called out: "Chris." Cassidy looked up and saw a Somali he recognized from his days at USAID. The man waved and smiled, but Chris couldn't remember his name. Ali or Abdi or something. It didn't matter. The man was still working for USAID, fixing things at the airport. The Cassidys were rescued.

Cassidy was already disappointed in his new employer. He was no cowboy Peace Corps volunteer any more. He'd done that. He'd slept in sand crawling with scorpions. This time he had come with his family. His family. The concept was new to him, but he reveled in it. He was a man with his family. One kid now but Chris had plans for more kids, as many as he could have. His wife never expressed an opinion on this. But Cassidy was a man with traditional—some would say regressive—family values. He was the man. He would make the decisions and he would take care of the family as best he could. For now, Save the Children would have to help him. He had uprooted his family because the agency had said they needed someone like him to run an agricultural project for refugees from Ethiopia. They were being resettled on an irrigation project on the coast south of Mogadishu, in Qorioley. Cassidy had gone to Cal Poly and studied production agriculture. He'd gone to the Nobel Institute and the University of Oslo in Norway to study socialist development strategies. He was convinced that Somalia was a socialist state struggling to cope with Western capitalist development strategies. He'd done every damn thing he could. He was state of the art. He was a professional man with a family, and he expected to be treated like one. And he was prepared to take the project on, grow food, turn the refugees into highly productive farmers. That's what he was hired to do. They'd flown him all the way over here, but it was only luck that had gotten him through the trial of the airport. What other unexpected things awaited him?

After Oslo, Cassidy had returned to Cal Poly to teach and to look at other career options. There was plenty of work in Somalia, and Cassidy could afford to be choosy. The U.S. government had offered him a position in Erigavo, northern Somalia, but there was rebel activity in that area, making it an unsuitable place to raise his young family. Then Save the Children called.

"I was a sucker," Cassidy says about his decision to work for Save the Children. "Save the Children. What more could a bleeding heart liberal religious person want? I thought that the agency stood for promoting the health development and welfare of children. I bought that one hook, line, and sinker. I didn't realize it was a fucking government contracting business, you know, a bunch of cutthroat back-stabbing, selfish, greedy sons of bitches living off the fat of the establishment on the east coast of the U.S."

In May 1985, with his pregnant wife in California, he went to Westport, Connecticut, for three days of interviews. "They had an agriculture office and had agriculture people there, but I had just come from the best fucking production agriculture school in the United States. I was an experienced aid worker and an educated person. And it seemed to me that these people had a home gardening mentality with an environmental slant. They were good with the rhetoric but weak on the science." But he took the job anyway. He was restless teaching in California and longed to be out in the field doing the work.

Cassidy hated every moment of the training, but he remembers little of it, because he just ignored most of what happened. His friend, a former Peace Corps colleague and fellow trainee, José Ortiz, admired Cassidy's ability to just transcend everything.

"We felt embarrassed by the training," Ortiz remembers. "There was some woman, an ex-nun I remember, who hadn't done a lot of adult education, lecturing us in some condescending way about real remedial development stuff."

She'd say things like, "The Save the Children approach is not to give a man a fish but to teach him how to fish." Cassidy and Ortiz felt as if they were back in Catholic school and started rolling their eyes and kicking each other under the table.

The trainees, headed for different parts of the world (Ortiz was going to Sudan), were taught about Save's new and exciting approach to development called participatory development. The idea, as explained to them, was that PD would let the Third World beneficiaries of Western largesse have a say in what they were getting, ensuring that they really want what you're trying to give them.

The whole thing, thought Ortiz, was a scam. "They had us doing exercises on how to develop consensus, but in reality it was subtle manipulation in the name of participatory development. It was like law school or business school. Here's how you shoot down the other guy's argument. That's a game I refused to play. It was really distasteful to me."

"That's what modern business practices are today," said Ortiz, who now has an M.B.A. "It's no different from total quality management. In the business world you try to get employees to buy *your* strategic plan and make them think it's theirs."

This was the buzzword of the month. Experienced aid hands know that development concepts are generated at universities, accepted as profound by policy types in Washington, and then declared as gospel. In order to raise new money to do the same types of projects you've always done, you have to be sure to include the appropriate current jargon in your project proposal and in subsequent progress reports. And you have to be conversant with the jargon so you can use it when the academics who coined the terminology are sent by USAID on junkets to inspect your project. When you use their jargon, it makes the academics happy and they write you a nice evaluation and you can get more money.

While participatory development never really caught on, by the late 1980s, the development industry had found a new mantra it could use: sustainable development.

In a brief statement before the House Appropriations Committee in April 1994, Carolyn Long, vice president of InterAction (a consortium of NGOs), used the term *sustainable development* sixteen times. Not one representative asked her what she was talking about or requested that she define the term. Was it supposed to contrast with the "unsustainable" development that member organizations had been spending taxpayer money on for years?

In part, yes. Sustainable development emerged as a reaction to criticism that most development projects for the last thirty years fell apart the moment the foreign money was pulled out. So project proposals started referring to *sustainable* development. (In fact, the term is redundant; if it's not sustainable, it's not development.) What this novel approach meant, in essence, was that the designers of development projects would try to cook up projects that wouldn't fail.

Although nothing actually changed in the field, in the day-to-day operation of development projects, everyone now spoke about sustainable development. Every proposal to get money from the UN or U.S. government employed the term or even contained an entire section devoted to it. In Somalia, even the lower level employees on projects knew that sustainable development was somehow a good thing. If you used the term, it sounded as if you knew what you were talking about.

The beauty of the term "sustainable development" was that it could be manipulated for any purpose.

At the 1992 Rio conference on the environment, sustainable development was about ecology. Vice President Al Gore defined sustainable development as "economic progress without environmental destruction," adding: "That's what sustainable development is all about." (In the Third World, by contrast, there's been no economic progress and plenty of environmental destruction.)

But by the 1994 Cairo conference on population, it meant birth control. Leading up to that meeting, Nafis Sadik, executive director of the United Nations Fund for Population Activities (UNFPA) and secretary general of the Cairo conference, announced: "If we had paid more attention to empowering women thirty years ago, we might not have to battle so hard for sustainable development today." Her organization had just released a document declaring that fertility control was the key to sustainable development.

"This year, we must also do more to support democratic renewal and human rights and sustainable development all around the world," President Clinton said in his 1994 State of the Union Address. He didn't elaborate. Addressing Parliament in November 1993, Queen Elizabeth II said, "My government will maintain a substantial aid program to promote sustainable development and good government." She also chose not to elaborate.

In June 1993, Al Gore announced the formation of the President's Council on Sustainable Development. The council, he said, "can focus attention on issues of common interest. It can serve as a forum for raising ideas and plans. It can help resolve issues that arise as nations proceed in their sustainable development agendas. It can monitor progress. It can help shift the multilateral financial institutions and bilateral assistance efforts toward a sustainable development agenda. It can help revitalize the UN system to ensure that sustainable development is a central theme in each organization. Indeed, this commission, through its focus on sustainable development, can enhance UN efforts to maintain peace, stability, and prosperity in this post–Cold War world."

And it wasn't just heads of state who took up the sustainable development battle cry:

A paper industry journal noted, "Pragmatic environmentalists have also shown that industry, including paper, will be the major force for sustainable development in which the world's economic and environmental ambitions can best be met."

The 1991 annual report of the U.S. Army stated, "The Army possesses valuable knowledge about nation assistance, including expertise relating to health care, infrastructure rehabilitation, management and environmentally sustainable development."

The International Fertilizer Association at its 1993 conference pledged, "IFA will continue to communicate the importance of mineral fertilizers for a sustainable development of world agriculture."

This terminology emerged in the years after I entered the Peace Corps during the Carter administration, when the buzz was all about "meeting basic human needs." We were sent into villages at the grass-roots level. We were expected to live like the people in the villages; we were discouraged from buying vehicles for ourselves. When I went into the bush it was the late 1970s. I emerged in the 1980s, and the world had changed. The new wave of volunteers arrived as I was leaving. They had different music and punk haircuts. And the buzz was "women in development." A new group of women were given four-wheel-drive vehicles, and the woman who was the new Peace Corps director seemed to have little use for men or for any of those old development ideas. With this new development theory came a new rhetoric. "Teach a man and you teach an individual," people would say. "Teach a woman and you teach a family." The aphorism came in several versions depending upon the development project in question.

Cassidy, too, had been through "meeting basic human needs" and "women in development." In school he'd begun hearing about "sustainable development" and now this nun was pushing "participatory development." How does this help us do our jobs? Cassidy and Ortiz were asking. Tell us what all this means when you're standing in an African village knee-deep in cow shit trying to talk some local trucker into transporting your fertilizer, while at the same time someone is trying to steal your project funds.

Ortiz was insulted and decided not to cooperate. He raised objections in class and resisted joining the role-playing games.

"Ortiz, goddamn it, why don't you agree with us so we can all get the fuck out of here?" Cassidy would mutter.

Chris figured that he'd do what he wanted when he arrived in Somalia anyway, and he just wanted the training to end. Ortiz figured, "This is bullshit. We're professionals with advanced degrees being hired to do technical work overseas and we have to listen to all these little pieties like we're joining a church." Ortiz later recalled that he found the training "cultish and repugnant."

The worst thing about the training was that no one in Westport really knew anything about the actual projects. Both Ortiz and Cassidy wanted to know what they would encounter. Cassidy had been assigned to run a multimillion-dollar irrigation project. He wanted technical details, information on soil, availability of fuel, level of training of the participants, budgetary information, that sort of thing.

"They couldn't answer any of my questions about the projects or the country," Ortiz remembers. "We wanted nuts and bolts about what we would be doing, but they couldn't supply answers. The Sudan desk officer had visited the country only once and had never gotten out of Khartoum. When I asked him about conditions there, he said it was pretty awful and a lot of people were dying. Fucking great! That will help me solve the problem."

Both men were troubled throughout the training. What was going to happen to them in an organization that treated them with disrespect from the beginning, an organization that couldn't tell them what to expect, that didn't address issues of commitment to the country, the financing of the projects?

There was one practical thing taught in Westport: They were shown how to pose children for photographs to go into brochures and ads.

Both of them recall a sickening feeling when Save took them to a vegetable garden project they were doing in the Bronx. Amateur, they both thought. How can you hire an agriculture specialist to engineer a massive resettlement project and then expect to impress him with an urban tomato patch? Something was very wrong.

They were also taught to deal with controversies of the day.

• • •

In the spring of 1985, a young student in a public school in the small town
of Hughes, Arkansas, came home from school and dropped his knapsack on
the floor. Later, as his mother was going through the boy's belongings, she
found a photograph of a man and a woman and a letter addressed to her
son. The letter said that the man lived in New Hampshire and hoped
someday to come to Arkansas and see the boy and his family.

The boy's parents went to the school and then they went to an attorney.
Together they learned that the couple in the photograph were Save the
Children sponsors paying $16 a month for the support of their child. Not
only did the parents not know their child was being sponsored, they
weren't particularly needy. It was soon revealed that around 100 students
in town has been enrolled in the program without the knowledge of their
parents. Teachers at the school were being paid a dollar by Save the Children for each kid they recruited. The children were then "sold" to sponsors
for $16 a month.

In October of 1985, parents of twenty-one children filed a $21 million
lawsuit against Save the Children, the county director, and six public
school teachers, alleging that Save had used their children in advertising
campaigns without their permission. According to the suit, the teachers
obtained permission to photograph the children and collect biographical
information on them "deceitfully and without the consent or knowledge of
the students' parents or legal guardians."

"Not only did the teachers . . . fail to obtain the consent of the parents or
legal guardians of the students," the complaint alleged, "they knowingly
and deliberately withheld from the parents the fact that the information
was being gathered, and that the photographs were being taken and being
used by Save the Children Foundation [sic], Inc."

In addition, publication of the photographs and biographical information by Save the Children subjected the families "to ridicule, embarrassment and shame in the community as impoverished and oppressed
individuals."

The law suit was going on as Chris and José arrived for training. There had
been a few mentions in the newspapers, wire reports mostly, nothing really
big. But Save was focused on keeping the story under wraps. They wanted
their new trainees to know what to do if approached by a journalist. The
Arkansas business was just a small misunderstanding, nothing at all to
worry about. "Ninety cents out of every donated dollar goes to programs,"

they were taught to say. But both Chris and José knew enough about development to know that wasn't true.

Save the Children was also getting some bad publicity from the massive and massively televised Ethiopia relief campaign of 1984 and 1985. They were told to forget about that: All those good works and all those lives saved were certainly going to attract some criticism. You can't save millions of lives without making mistakes, can you? So what if Save the Children's trucks had been used to cart refugees off to concentration camps? There has to be some kind of balance sheet—lives saved versus lives lost. Not only Save, but other NGOs had been suckered into the Ethiopian government's war against its own people. The government had launched a cynical campaign: First you starve them, then attract them to central areas with food, then cart them off to where you want them. That had been the government's plan, carried out with the assistance, unwitting sometimes, of local foreign charities using monies donated by schoolchildren and old ladies and working-class families in church.

To Cassidy, it sounded an awful lot like what had been happening in Somalia.

On the short trip into Mogadishu from the airport, Cassidy noticed that the streets were more crowded, there was more traffic, and a sense of frenzy was discernible. Land Cruisers bearing the emblems of NGOs lined the streets and clogged traffic circles. There was new construction going on. White faces were everywhere.

The town was full of new restaurants, clubs, and hotels. None of it was on account of economic development really, but it was all supported by the aid business. The money was generated by Western governments and paid out in contracts to private foreign companies such as the New Jersey–based Louis Berger, Inc., which made millions annually in Somalia doing range management and construction. Other contracts went to NGOs from the UN or the States or the European Economic Community (EEC). All these people needed Western-style housing, so Somalis with close ties to the government borrowed money and built entire neighborhoods where they could rent homes to foreigners for $4,000 or $5,000 a month. Since the foreigners weren't paying their own rent, they didn't really care how much things cost. So, in Mogadishu, at least, everyone profited.

Just as there was no one at the airport, there was no one at the Save the Children office when the Cassidys arrived there. There was no house wait-

ing for them in Mogadishu. The office there was being run by the acting director, a man named Abdukadir. Abdukadir showed up about four hours
later and greeted Chris as if nothing were wrong. The two men had known
each other before. Abdukadir had worked at USAID with Chris before
moving on to Save the Children. He greeted Tone as if he had just seen her
earlier that morning.

Cassidy delivered a message from headquarters that they needed financial statements, but Abdukadir had heard that before. He laughed.

Abdukadir was doing what everyone did in Mogadishu, playing on the
black market. Organizations like Save the Children had to play it straight
and deal at the official exchange rate of 20 Somali shillings to the dollar.
But anyone who wanted could get 60 or more on the black market. The
only problem was that there were no bank receipts available. Abdukadir
made $2 for himself for every $1 that Save sent from headquarters. He
would invest the money or loan the hard currency to local businessmen,
who would use it to import consumer goods and repay Abdukadir a per-
centage of the profits. Abdukadir was getting rich. The financial reports
could wait.

Cassidy quickly figured out the game, and he might not have minded so
much if he didn't start having problems getting money to pay his workers
in the field.

"Don't worry about it, Cassidy," Abdukadir would say.

"He never hassled me about anything, but he never paid me any
money," Chris remembers.

Their first night back in Somalia the Cassidys slept in a storage room
above the Save the Children office. The room had just been emptied of
bags of relief food and the grain dust settled over the family as they tried to
sleep. Cassidy had expected a triumphant homecoming in Mogadishu. Instead, he felt within him a lump of anger.

But this was only the beginning. Cassidy, who had come to serve the
people of Somalia, the war refugees, was to learn that he had been unwit-
tingly employed in a cause, the cause of Greater Somalia.

Hassan Ilhan was one of the victims of the quest for Greater Somalia. He
was among those refugees who left Ethiopia in 1977 as the Somali armies
advanced across the Ogaden. An ethnic Somali, he was employed by the
Ethiopian government at their ministry of agriculture in the capital, Addis
Ababa. Hassan Ilhan was comfortable and could probably have gone on
with his life if not for the fact that most of his family was back home in an
area that had suddenly become a war zone. One day, he walked out of his

office and through the busy streets of the city. He collected his family, his wife and four children, and took a bus heading east toward the Ogaden town of Jigjiga and then on to the town of Dagahbuur, where he was born. There he collected other members of his family and they began to walk. They walked for more than 250 miles, joining with small groups of destitute nomads making their way toward the border with Somalia. For three weeks they shared food, water, and camel's milk with strangers.

As each day passed he began to look and feel more like a nomadic refugee and less like the urban bureaucrat he had been all his professional life. When they crossed the border into the Bakool region of Somalia, it was the first time he had ever set foot inside the country that was supposed to be his homeland.

Hassan Ilhan and his family waited quietly in a refugee transit camp, eating relief food and living in an *ochol*—a domelike Somali nomad hut made of grass, animals skins, and sticks. In the teeming camp, Hassan reflected on his flight. Why had he run from Addis? Fear. He was afraid the Ethiopian government would detain or harass ethnic Somalis. And what about the nomads? They, too, were running from fear as well as the Ethiopian army. As the victorious Somali troops had advanced through Ethiopia, they had sent the nomads behind the lines, telling them to go to Somalia to get away from the war. But then the direction of the war changed. With the help of Cubans and Soviets, the Ethiopians had stormed back, driving the Somali army back across its own border. The Somalis of the Ogaden were caught in the crossfire both times.

Hassan Ilhan was tall and husky for a Somali and stood out among the lean, wiry nomads. He had a big smile and his teeth were stained brown from chewing qat. One of his eyes would drift off in another direction and he usually wore sunglasses to hide it. It gave him an almost sinister look.

From transit camps, the Red Cross distributed refugees to thirty or so other camps throughout Somalia. Hassan Ilhan and his family were put on a truck and sent to Qorioley.

The Ogaden is sometimes called a desert, but in reality it is a huge savanna with scrub brush, a few trees, and rivers that run when there is rain in the Ethiopian mountains hundreds of miles away. It is oppressively hot and very dry. The people who live there travel with herds of camels, goats, and sheep. Other Somalis regard the Ogaadeen clan, Hassan Ilhan's clan, as the *true* nomads. They often wear the traditional white cotton robes and let their hair grow long and wild, and when they show up in the towns and markets of Somalia they are the objects of curiosity and respect. Other clans often speak enviously of how they live free under the warm, open sky, how a man can have 200 camels and four wives and not a care in the world.

Qorioley is very different from the Ogaden. It is located in a coastal plain where Somalia's two permanent rivers flow. It is humid and fertile with thick dark soil that sticks like paste to the soles of the feet. Herds of camels are a liability. At one time it was home to some of Somalia's agricultural clans, people who were looked down upon by the nomads. The camel herders would trade with them but wouldn't want their sons and daughters to marry them. Digging in the dirt was considered a demeaning way to earn a livelihood, and it made it impossible to collect enough camels to purchase wives.

No one really bothered the agriculturists, until the Italians came. There, in the soil of Qorioley, they cultivated their fortunes. Plantations were carved from the tropical bush; bananas were planted along with mangos and papaya and watermelon. These commodities were exported to Italy, and the plantation owners became rich. When Somalia gained independence in 1960, Somali leaders were aware that the despised and inferior clans inhabited land that could produce wealth in the modern world.

Since these clans didn't actually hold title to the land in any Western, bureaucratic sense, the people in power used the rules of their new government and deeded the land to themselves. The poor clans from the Digil/Rahanwiin families were pushed onto more marginal land. Still, there was plenty to go around, but in the late 1970s as the Ogaadeen refugees came in, some of the land was parceled out to them. (They received favored status because, like Siyaad, they were part of the Daarood clan family. In addition, Siyaad Barre's mother was Ogaadeen. Siyaad trusted them, and they regarded him as a savior.) The refugees were settled in areas near the most fertile land, areas that could produce food if there was irrigation. The foreign aid agencies were then asked to provide the money and expertise to irrigate the land. They happily complied.

By the time Hassan Ilhan got to Qorioley, he'd heard enough to believe that it was safe to return to Ethiopia and resume his life in Addis Ababa. And he could easily have gone, but he was surrounded by people who couldn't just leave. These nomads, now former nomads, were lost without their animals and had no way to support themselves on this land. Most had no way to get home except to walk. The Red Cross, which had trucked them in, wasn't offering return journeys. Whereas help and food were provided for them at Qorioley, nothing at all was waiting on the other side. They had no choice but to stay.

Hassan Ilhan knew his agricultural and administrative skills could be used to help these people. He also possessed the one skill that was the most valuable in the country in the mid-1980s: He spoke English and thus was a link to the great aid machine, a gateway of information that the people with the money needed to reach the beneficiary population.

Hassan thought himself fortunate for having had an education in English in Ethiopia. He felt like Moses, an intermediary with the powers that be and protector of the Ogaadeen people he had led through the desert. He feared his people would become prey to the Somali government as well as to the expatriates who said they were there to help.

During his few years in Qorioley, Hassan Ilhan witnessed frenetic activity. Foreigners in Land Cruisers came and went. They took notes. They talked with elders. They brought in Somali government officials. They poked the soil. They went away. Other foreigners brought food and handed out ration cards to the people. Foreign doctors came and set up clinics. More people came and poked at the soil. They would arrive in the morning and leave before dark. Then new foreigners would come and do the same thing. They always looked uncomfortable. They seemed anxious to leave.

Three years passed. The people were still eating from bags of food sent from America. Children were born in the camps. People died there. The nomads learned to wait in line for food. Some would take that food to the market and sell a bit to get money to buy other things such as clothing.

The foreigners kept coming, and finally they arrived with a plan. The land would be irrigated. People would be given plots. They would live there and make new lives for themselves. Hassan Ilhan knew that most of these people didn't want new lives for themselves. They wanted their old lives back, but they had run out of choices. They would plant or starve. The people from America and the people from the United Nations promised that the lives of the people would be wonderful after the project was finished in a few years.

After agreeing to help the foreigners with their project, Ilhan knew that he had become part of a great agricultural experiment. The Westerners wanted to show—needed to show—that nomads could become farmers. If they could teach these nomads to grow food, they could teach any nomads to do it. And there was a lot at stake here, especially funding. If nomads could successfully be guided into a sedentary lifestyle, there would be plenty of customers, not only in Somalia, but across all the semiarid areas of Africa, where governments were eager to turn troublesome border-crossing nomads into controllable tax-paying citizens of a nation-state.

And while governments were concerned with controlling people, NGOs were talking about preserving the environment. Nomads, it was widely assumed, were bad for the environment. Their goal in life was to collect more and more cattle wealth. If a man could gather 500 camels for himself, he would, just for the prestige of it, even if it didn't make sense economically. The cattle were destroying the fragile desert environment; the nomadic lifestyle was destroying itself. The nomads were killing themselves. For their own good, they had to be turned into farmers and fishermen.

Most African governments aren't worried about the nomads themselves, beyond the problem that pictures of starving people aren't good publicity. To them, nomads are pests, vermin. To nominally socialist governments like Somalia, nomads were a bigger problem than that. It's hard to impose socialism on people who can just walk away. In this battle, drought was an ally. It held them prisoners.

Attempts at turning nomads into farmers had met with spotty results at best. The nomadic ethos views farmers as inferior beings forced to live a life of toil. The nomad is a free man. Farming is a dirty job that is better left to the lower castes. A nomad whose cattle have died and who is left begging from foreign relief agencies is still better in his own mind than a successful farmer. This conceit is an important element in the Somali psyche.

Somalis' attachment was to cattle and clan. Second- and third-generation Somalis who've lived in North America all their lives still know their clan background, still derive their identity from that heritage, not from anything as temporal as a plot of dirt or a spot on the earth. Lineage is something that can never be taken away. It is this sense of belonging that allows Somalis to roam the world and still not feel they've lost anything. Home is something you carry inside.

As a trained agriculturist, Hassan Ilhan had transcended that notion and understood the value of agriculture and hard work, but he had no interest in the experimental nature of the Qorioley project. He didn't care about the principles involved. He worried about these nomads. These people. His family.

When Save the Children won the contract to implement the Qorioley refugee agriculture project, Hassan Ilhan had himself a full-time job and hoped to be put in charge of the project at some point. But he was confronted with a steady steam of new bosses, impenetrable layers of bosses, who came from America. Some of the bosses stayed in Mogadishu; others lived at the project site. They were always changing. Bosses never stayed around for too long. And it was always the same: They'd arrive full of promises, ideas, and enthusiasm. Then they'd leave, complaining about the corruption of the Somalis and the endless bureaucracy and an inability to get anything done. Hassan wasn't sure that any of them actually did anything. He'd watch them fumble around for a bit and then start spending more and more time in Mogadishu and less and less time working on the projects. Each one would kick the project a little further down the line, but in the end the refugees were still lining up for handouts of relief food.

Hassan worried that one day the relief food would end and that these people would once again have to start walking. For him, completing the project was a race against time.

By 1985, Hassan Ilhan once again thought he deserved a promotion—even though he knew it wasn't going to happen. He had in essence been running the project: He made sure the Somalis who worked for the project got paid. He got the pipes and the fuel and kept the books, handling the daily operation of the project. Still, the project never seemed to get anywhere. He blamed that on the foreign fuckups and on the Somali government, who, he had reason to suspect, didn't want the farmers to succeed. They would rather have people eating the food they could control, he figured out. If he could, he would lead all these people back to Ogaden today, but they had already stayed too long. There was nothing for them anywhere anymore.

Now, instead of putting him in charge of the project, he was informed that they were sending another foreigner, an American named Chris Cassidy, someone who had never farmed in his life, someone who couldn't possibly understand his people—and placing the lives of these nomads into this stranger's hands.

4

POTEMKIN VILLAGES

All ambitions are lawful except those which climb upward on the
miseries or credulities of mankind.

—Joseph Conrad, A Personal Record

The road south from Mogadishu passes through the K-4 traffic circle,
past the headquarters of the National Security Service, the Somali
secret police, topped with antennas and satellite dishes, past Benadir
Hospital, the USAID building, the American K-7 compound. After the
compound, across the street, is the site of the brand-new American Embassy, a $39-million project under construction, surrounded by high secu-
rity walls and protected by steel gates. A little farther down the road is the
university, the golf course, and the international school.

A few miles beyond this the landscape fades quickly into scrub and
sand. The potholes in the road grow larger until it becomes a dirt road with
deadly chunks of residual tar. For miles and miles along the road drivers
had chosen to plow through the bush rather than brave the tarmac. Every
vehicle moved in a massive cloud of dust.

One of those billowing dustballs contained the Cassidys and their
belongings. The Somali driver stared straight ahead and looked down occasionally to pull another twig from a small bundle of *qat* leaves that lay on

the seat beside him. The Land Cruiser rocked on the uneven trail. The driver chewed contentedly, the baby screamed, and Cassidy shouted at the driver to slow down. Cassidy wrapped his arms around the baby, who was belted into his car seat. The driver released the accelerator slightly, the dust overtook the car, and fine grains of Somali clay poured into the windows. The driver looked at Cassidy. Cassidy shielded Bernie's face from the dust, and the driver sped up again, outrunning the dust tail.

The town of Afgooye appears after about twenty miles and marks the beginning of an agricultural belt that extends along the Shebelle River southward along the coast. After ninety miles and some three hours down the road, one enters the rich agriculture lands of Shalambod and Qorioley. This is where the Italian colonists constructed their banana plantations and where rich Somalis built villas and plantations for themselves. It is Somalia's breadbasket, an area with enough fertile land to feed all of the country's seven million people.

And Cassidy was determined to see that it did.

Arriving in Qorioley, the family climbed down from the Land Cruiser and were directed toward a mud and wattle structure. Tone carried the baby and the three of them approached the house. Chris swung the door back to reveal a large empty room with unassembled furniture. In preparation for their arrival, the cracked cement floor had been swabbed with diesel fuel, to kill the chiggers and other little insects that lived in the dust. Diesel fumes hung in the air. Tone noticed immediately that there was no refrigerator, no cooker, no appliances of any sort.

This was not where Cassidy wanted to house his family. Again he fought his own anger, as his wife tried to make the best of it. It was primitive, she charitably thought. She wasn't going to make his work any harder than it was. But it was a point of honor for Chris. He was going to provide for his family within reason, given the fact that they were living in a country the World Bank considered one of the poorest in the world.

Cassidy might never have complained about the house had it not been for one seemingly petty thing: He soon learned that Save expected his family to share the place with a single woman, an American working for Save the Children. In the context of Somalia's problems, this was a relatively minor thing, but for the family getting settled, it proved to be a huge obstacle. This, after all, was their first family home, the place where little Bernie and his parents would spend the first years of their familyhood, a place to which he had made a five-year commitment.

It was this family's American dream, and it was a dump. They had trans-
ferred their whole lives to Somalia. His contract called for decent housing
and appliances. There were rats in the house, and the roof that was supposed to provide rainwater catchment was made of asbestos. There was no
electricity, no generator, no refrigerator for the baby's food. If Save wasn't
going to meet even these basic requirements, how were they going to handle the logistics of running a huge project?

Several months later when Cassidy would be in Mogadishu looking over
the project books he would notice a line item for the construction of his
house. The cost: $85,000. That was enough money to build a mansion in
Mogadishu and a castle in Qorioley. But by then he wasn't surprised by
anything. For nothing at the project was what it seemed to be, and he had
learned to assume his employers were as corrupt as the most corrupt Somali official.

Save the Children had one "impact area" in Somalia. That was Qorioley. All of their resources were concentrated there. All of their expatriate
personnel were there. Three of the American couples were what Cassidy
called dual-development couples, he-and-she aid workers. Tone was the
only spouse who didn't work in development. Cassidy didn't want her to
work even though in Africa it was easy to get nannies to raise the children.
For what African nannies get paid, any dual-development couple could
hire an army of them to take care of their kids. But Cassidy's ideas about
family prohibited it. He was one of eight children in a tight-knit family
group. He was going to reproduce what he knew. He insisted that Tone
take care of Bernie. "The others didn't approve of my family values," Cassidy says, explaining why he felt the other Americans shunned him.

They felt alone from the first night they arrived. During those early days
Bernie wasn't sleeping much. He cried all night as the three of them curled
up in a single mosquito-infested room.

When he awoke his first morning, Cassidy strapped Bernie onto his chest
and walked out into the muggy dawn of Qorioley. The damp, thick tropical air filled his nostrils with the smells of life; rotting vegetation, dung,
pollen. He walked a few yards from his house and there he encountered
the towering figure of Hassan Ilhan. Hassan looked at Bernie and grunted
disapprovingly.

"We don't do that here," he said.

"Excuse me," Chris said.

Somalis say what they think. In a culture where life is hard and short,
where any meeting with someone might be your last, you don't wait to get

to know a person before telling him his shirt is inside out or there's a piece of snot hanging from his nose. People with handicaps will quickly have them pointed out. A man with a limp will be called *Jiis*. A man with a hunchback will be called *Muluch*. No secrets, no shame.

"You can't carry the baby like that. People won't respect you. Only women carry babies and they don't carry them like that."

"You tell people that in my country, men carry babies like this. I'm going to do things the way I want. You tell them."

"Another arrogant American," Ilhan thought. "But he probably won't be here very long." He looked over the blond-haired foreigner. Then he asked, "Why did you come here with your wife and your child? Are you blind enough to believe you can help these people? Whatever happens, you will soon go. And we will be here. How long will you stay? Maybe you'll stay a year. You will write your reports and say the project is good and that's all that your people care about."

"What are you talking about?"

"You're going to boss some people around here. I know. I've worked for ten boys like you. You come here and spend money and get Land Cruisers. You dig holes. But what about my people? They have no land and no water. They eat your bags of food like beggars."

"We've got a saying in my country," Cassidy preached, "No free lunch. People have to get off their asses and grow their own food."

"Your people understand nothing," Ilhan shot back. "You don't even understand your own people, how they are stopping us from growing food. This land will grow nothing without water."

"What about the water from the irrigation canals?"

"What water?"

"The water from the irrigation project."

"Why are you telling me there is water when there is none?"

"Yes there is. I've seen photographs. I've read the reports. What are you trying to tell me?"

"Yes, there are irrigation canals. The people have dug them. But there is no water in the canals. There is no way to get the water from the river to the canals."

"But I saw pictures."

"Yes there is water in the pictures, but no water in the canal."

"What?"

In Westport Cassidy had seen photographs of happy farmers posing on the banks of flooded irrigation canals. Now Hassan Ilhan was telling him that land leveling hadn't been done and the water couldn't flow into the fields. And even if that work had been done, it wouldn't have mattered: There were no head gates on the river to control the water flow into the canals. And there were no gates on the irrigation ditches to drain the fields to keep them from being flooded if the water ever did reach the fields.

"Where did the pictures come from?" he asked Ilhan.

"They brought pumps to fill some of the canals for the photographs and the reports."

For the next few days, Hassan Ilhan showed Cassidy around the project. The two of them barely spoke. Chris asked questions. Ilhan provided concise answers. Chris learned that not only couldn't he get water into the canals but that most of the land still hadn't been divided among the refugee families, and there was no timetable for doing it.

"It was just a fucking scam," Cassidy recalls, "only I refused to see it at first. Nothing had been done. Sure, they'd spent money and bought some equipment. Pumps from Italy, engines from Japan, tractors from Britain. Everyone out there got a little piece of the money. There was lots of hardware. But that's not what you need to run an irrigation project."

Cassidy launches into lecture mode, explaining what it takes to get a self-sufficient irrigation program off the ground: "You need a schedule to get water on and off and have a maintenance program. Farmers have to be taught to farm and how to use the water and how much water. The project was years and years away from being completed. And here I thought I'd be coming in with the farmers ready to go."

"Any engineer can construct an irrigation system, but using the system to grow food is another matter altogether. In other words, if all it took were pipes and pumps to provide fresh, clean water to people, everyone in the world would have fresh, clean water. It's not hardware. It's systems and education. That's the hard part. Most aid workers are in love with hardware. You install the pipes and pumps and make them work. Then when the system breaks down you just blame the people. They're stupid, backward, and lazy. You did your job. You earned your paycheck. You can walk away, get your promotion, and talk about the dumb Somalis with your friends at the beach club or in your nice house while you're getting rich off taxpayer money being pumped in here."

Cassidy's project was called the Refugee Self-Reliance Project and was funded by USAID and the office of the UN High Commissioner for Refugees (UNHCR). In the world of aid, organizations like USAID only fund projects; they don't *do* projects. Organizations like Save the Children and CARE do projects with USAID money, the American taxpayer's money. Private companies like Louis Berger also do projects with USAID money. The big difference between Louis Berger and CARE is that CARE raises money from the public and doesn't have to pay taxes. Another difference is that as a private company, Louis Berger hires qualified and well-paid experts. Save the Children often uses college kids who work for little or nothing. And even Cassidy, with his masters degree and experience in Somalia, had agreed to work for $18,000 a year.

The project started in July 1983. USAID kicked in $473,000 and Save agreed to put up $79,000, much of which could be provided on an "in-kind" basis for administration. That means Save could just hire an accountant to write off a portion of the salaries of the secretaries and janitors and gardeners in Westport along with his own time and call it money spent on helping refugees become self-reliant. Cassidy's salary was paid by the U.S. government.

Another $550,000 was to be contributed by the Somali government, or the Government of the Somali Democratic Republic (GSDR), as it is referred to in official documentation. The agreement stipulates, however, that the GSDR could raise the money to pay for their share by selling off bags of U.S. surplus food donated to them by the people of the United States of America under a program known as Food for Peace, or less grandly as Public Law-480. Thus that part of the project was also in reality carried by U.S. taxpayers—at a cost considerably more than $550,000. Food was sold in Somalia for a lot less than the price paid to the American farmer by the U.S. Department of Agriculture, which made American farmers very happy. And since the business acumen needed to make a profit selling free food was nil, it made Siyaad Barre's relatives very happy; they were the ones who magically got all the contracts. In addition, $550,000 worth of food in a country of six million people where food was cheap, is a lot of food. The markets felt it.

Another $795,000 was to be contributed by UNHCR, much of which was also U.S. taxpayer money, bringing the total on the project to just over $2 million when all other miscellaneous inputs were computed.

USAID's partner in this was Somalia's National Refugee Commission, headed by a man named Mohamed Abdi Tarrah. Tarrah ran the NRC with an iron hand and sticky fingers and eventually became one of Somalia's richest men. It was his reward for being the caretaker of the refugee programs, the country's main earner of revenues.

The Qorioley project was fairly straightforward: 1,220 hectares of land would be prepared for irrigated farming and allocated to each of 2,500 refugee families. In order not to anger the local population, 400 local families would also be helped with land.

According to the project timetable, the primary irrigation canal was to have been completed by December 1983, with some 200 hectares of land distributed. By June 1986, all of the project's goals were to have been met: "The irrigated farm is self-sufficient financially and managerially. . . . All expatriate staff have been phased out of the project," the original project timetable said. In just three years, camel-herding nomads were to be completely transformed into self-sufficient farmers.

The rosy forecast bore no resemblance to the mess Cassidy found when he arrived at the end of 1985. No one seemed to care terribly. The project continued to receive funding, and Save the Children continued to get paid for administering it. The people from USAID, UNHCR, and Save who had designed and executed the project had long since moved on to other jobs in other countries. To their replacements, the Qorioley refugee agriculture project was a collection of file folders and a series of disbursements.

Most people who get a lousy $18,000 a year from the tax rolls consider it an insult and an entitlement. Cassidy considered it a sacred trust. He was angry about the plight of the refugees, but he was sincerely indignant about what was happening to the American taxpayers' money. The government could send millions of dollars over here and then pay no attention as it vanished into Potemkin villages. The modus operandi in Somalia, as far as Cassidy could tell, was keep your mouth shut, collect your salary, and keep the project going. That's what Hassan Ilhan expected from Cassidy.

By the time Cassidy arrived in Qorioley, Hassan Ilhan was thirty-three years old and had seven children of his own. Back in sedentary life, he had picked up some of his old urban habits, wearing Western clothes and carrying around documents in a briefcase. The project was *his*. Cassidy was an interloper.

In the early days Hassan Ilhan kept his distance from Cassidy. He mistrusted the frenetic and serious white man. Cassidy, Ilhan assumed, was untrustworthy. Why else would a *gaal* come to this place except to make his fortune, to steal his share of the money before leaving? Government officials were stealing money. Foreigners were stealing money. Everyone was getting a share.

Cassidy was oblivious, his mind occupied with making notes about what he needed to do to make the project work: He needed agricultural extension agents on staff to train people. He contacted USAID and the UN

Food and Agriculture Organization (FAO) and begged them to send some agriculture people. "Let's do some trials and demonstrations. Let's get some good seed out here. Otherwise you won't be able to pay for irrigation water. Let's get a few plots working so we can anticipate problems down the line."

In normal circumstances this might be considered initiative. In development work it's not appreciated. Cassidy was developing a reputation as a troublemaker. His gathering of resources for the project was highlighting its flaws. He was pointing out lapses in evaluation reports that had already been written saying that the project was coming along nicely. An expatriate who becomes a vocal advocate for the people he is trying to help is said to have "gone bush." And Cassidy's manner only reinforced that opinion.

"My thinking was this free lunch isn't going to go on forever. Eventually the free food will stop coming. The donors will get bored. They always get tired of it. They're going to leave Somalia hanging out there. The long-term outlook should be to develop the skills."

Cassidy demanded that the free food be phased out immediately. "How the hell am I going to convince these people to get out there and dig if they get more food than they can eat free from CARE?" No one was really interested in answering that.

The food wasn't coming only to Qorioley. Similar refugee projects dotted the country along the Juba and Shebele rivers in the northern areas around Hargeysa. Refugees from Ogaden were placed in camps, and convoy after convoy of food was leaving Mogadishu under the supervision of an organization called ELU/CARE. CARE, of course, was the American NGO; ELU stood for Emergency Logistics Unit. This hybrid agency was a tripartite cooperative run by CARE, Somalia's National Refugee Commission, and UNHCR. CARE and UNHCR were concerned with delivering as much food as they could as efficiently as possible. The NRC was apparently more interested in keeping cash and food flowing and with skimming as much as they could. The supposed beneficiaries of all of this, the refugees, seemed peripheral to the major issues confronting the logistics operation. Cassidy, too, might have forgotten why he was there, but Hassan Ilhan was always around to remind him.

Several weeks after arriving in Qorioley, Cassidy found he had an even bigger problem than dry canals. The staff wasn't being paid. They had no money for their families or even to buy food. The refugees at least had food. Cassidy knew this could spell disaster for the project. One way or the other they would eat. They would begin stealing from the project if they hadn't already. He would have to become a policeman. The project would devour itself.

Cassidy immediately dispatched angry letters to Mogadishu and Westport. He made deals with local shopkeepers to extend credit to the staff based on the promise that Save would pay the bills as soon as he straightened out a few things. As the weeks passed, he ran out of good will with the merchants. Cassidy spent his days walking the length and breadth of the project, meeting with the refugee farmers. And then he stayed up nights with a kerosene lantern going over the books.

The project had sixty-seven Somali employees. Some had degrees in engineering and agricultural sciences. The agriculture engineer was a Somali, Haroun Abrar. He had a master's degree, spoke perfect English, and was paid $40 a month. "Westport couldn't come up with a lousy forty bucks to pay his salary," Cassidy recalls. "Haroun worked anyway. I have no idea how he fed his family."

Cassidy hounded headquarters to come up with financial obligations. When letters didn't work, he started making the grueling drive to Mogadishu, banging on doors. People were stalling for days up there, and Cassidy knew that he was becoming a total pain in the ass. "They weren't giving us any money and they're advertising for funds with pictures of a starving Somali child."

Cassidy was spending more time hounding Abdukadir and calling Westport than he was working on the project. He'd march into government ministries and accuse them of trying to starve their own people. Cassidy's penchant for inflammatory rhetoric didn't help his cause. Expatriates thought he'd gone over the edge. Somali officials thought he was dangerous.

By February 1986, the family had settled in. Tone wrote a series of optimistic letters back to Cassidy's family in New Orleans. She noted that Bernie seemed to be thriving despite the heat, mosquitoes, and dust. He had grown to 12.5 pounds, not so big that she couldn't carry him around.

The Somalis would stare and laugh as Bernie was pushed around town in a stroller. They laughed harder when Chris carried him in the "snuggly" strapped to his chest. It was as if every time they saw him was the first time. Somali mothers, Tone noted, carry their infants wrapped in a piece of cloth on their backs. Carrying the baby up front is rare, and seeing the father carrying the child is unheard of.

Ilhan again warned Chris that people were talking. They'd lose respect for him. They'd lose respect for the project. Couldn't he just let his damn wife carry the baby? But Chris wasn't into this cultural sensitivity shit. He was there to teach agriculture. He accepted the Somalis on their terms and they had better goddamn well accept him on his own. He thought they could get used to it. It wasn't as if his wife was walking around topless. Eventually the people did come to accept the Cassidys. The people stopped laughing, though they still stared. They liked to come up and touch the little white baby.

While Chris struggled with the books at work, Tone was coping with the home life. For two months Bernie had been sleeping badly and waking up two to three times a night. While Chris was at work, Bernie and Tone remained inside the SCF compound. Tone wrote back that their house was adequate, but very primitive and very poorly constructed. It was full of one thousand and one different insects that entered through the cracks in the floor. She was worried that the plumbing wouldn't hold out, a problem because there was no water at all in the town of Qorioley. And because they had not received the promised gas stove from Save the Children, she was forced to cook on a charcoal grill in their small kitchen. It was unbearably hot.

On the surface, Tone was patient, reporting that things weren't great but she had faith that as soon as Chris got his job sorted out, things were sure to improve. He wasn't exactly working yet. Too much to clean up from the past, too much paperwork to be sorted out before he could get started on what he considered his real job, working on the refugee farm with the refugees.

As the Cassidys settled into a routine they began spending Fridays at the beach in Merka, about forty-five minutes from Qorioley. Tone would sit with Bernie on a hotel verandah overlooking the ocean. Chris purchased a wind surfer and would put on a show for his family. There was a small convent in Merka where a group of Italian nuns did medical work in the community. On Saturdays a priest would come from Mogadishu and conduct a Mass in Italian. The Cassidys never missed it. The nuns were always happy to see them and doted on Bernie.

Tone managed to forget about the hardships in Qorioley and eventually found life there peaceful and relaxing. She wrote of her contentment and reported that they had hired a girl to do some cooking, cleaning, and laundry. She wrote that she and Bernie were leading an easy, carefree life, and she expected that to continue as long as he stayed healthy, and she didn't see any reason why he wouldn't so long as she and Chris were careful.

As Bernie grew bigger Chris would stick him in the back of the bicycle and he and Tone would ride around Qorioley as if they were pedaling through an American suburb.

• • •

In early 1986, Siyaad Barre threw a little party. It was a dinner for hundreds of aid workers to let them know how much the GSDR appreciated their contributions. Chris and Hassan Ilhan went. The dinner was held in the parliament building.

After dinner Hassan and Chris wandered outside. There on a huge pedestal was a brass statue of a man on a horse. The horse was reared up and it reminded Cassidy of statues of Napoleon. From the little concrete park around the statue all of Mogadishu was visible, as well as the Indian Ocean all the way to the horizon. "Who is that?" he asked Ilhan.

"Sayid Mohamed Abdille Hassan. Your people called him the Mad Mullah. But he wasn't a mullah and he wasn't mad. He was a poet and a warrior who knew how to inspire people. And he knew how to use a gun. He nearly drove the British and Italians out of Somalia in the 1920s. Now the British and Italians are back, of course."

Hassan Ilhan looked up at the monument. Cassidy watched ships in the harbor. Most of the ships contained grain from the West. Behind him a row of Somali flags fluttered in the evening breeze.

Hassan Ilhan gave Cassidy a shorthand version of the story of the Somali nationalist hero. To be sure, it was not a story universally known in Somalia, and even today many educated Somalis know very little about the Mad Mullah. In the 1980s, there was only room for one hero in the country, and that was Mohamed Siyaad Barre. The story of Mohamed Abdille Hassan had to wait to be dusted off by Western journalists and piped back into Somali at the time of the U.S. intervention. By then, however, the statue was no longer a reference point. It had been stolen and reportedly sold off as scrap metal to feed the war of Somali upon Somali, a sad irony that once again seemed to have more resonance among Westerners in search of history than for Somalis rooted in the here and now.

Mohamed Abdille Hassan was an Islamic religious leader, a warrior, and a poet, who raised an army of Dervishes to confront the British colonial government in the first years of the twentieth century.* He is considered by many to be Somalia's foremost nationalist leader and a symbol of Somali pride. But, like most things in Somalia, the story of this hero ran up against the country's clan-based reality. The Mullah was a Daarood, descended from the Ogaadeen and Dulbahante clans. It was easy and natural for Daa-

---

*For a full account of the story of "the Mad Mullah" see *Divine Madness* by Abdi Sheik-Abdi (London: Zed Books, 1993).

roods to remember his war against British colonialism and honor him with the most prominent pedestal in modern Mogadishu, but others in the country regard him differently. Though the Mullah was a self-professed anti-tribalist, many of his victims were from the Isaaq and other non-Daarood clans. Some of his critics point out that his followers were little more than looters who ravaged their own people in the name of nationalism and Islam, charges that are identical to those leveled against the warlords who dominate Somalia today.

The two men stood before the statue in silence. Finally, as Cassidy recalls, Hassan Ilhan spoke. "Look at my people. What are they now? Beggars."

"We can make this project work," Chris said like a cheerleader. "We've got the skills. You can do the administration. There's nothing to stop us. We'll get the money. We've got the stuff here. We can make these people independent."

"They're wasting the money," Ilhan grumbled.

"No, man, this is American money, our taxpayers' money. They can't fuck it up. We can empower these people," Cassidy said. "I promise you, Hassan, they will be able to feed themselves. They will build something here."

Hassan looked back at the American. "You know nothing about power. There is only one power in this country, and that power doesn't want these people to feed themselves. That power wants them to eat out of the 'handshake' bags from America." Ilhan was referring to the symbol of USAID, two hands clasped in front of a stars-and-stripes medallion.

"Hassan. That makes no sense."

"You can't understand, because in your country things are simple."

"Well fucking explain it to me."

"They're screwing us." Hassan Ilhan said.

"Yes?"

Hassan Ilhan took a breath. "I can explain this to you, but you won't understand or you won't believe me."

"Just explain."

"The refugees are from Siyaad's mother's clan. They support him. They are grateful that he is feeding them."

"So?"

"So if he stops feeding them they will no longer be grateful. If they can live on their own they won't need him. Also, he has given them this land, but this land belongs to the Biimaal people and the Rahanwiin people. They will also need Siyaad to protect them from the people who want their land back. And the land he has given them isn't enough to really live on.

It's nothing that a man can pass down to his sons. Siyaad has made them his slaves, and he has you here to help him."

"So why are you helping him?"

"What can I do? I have to say that this is better than nothing. This is all we have."

Back in Qorioley, Cassidy sank back into frustration. He wasn't doing the project. He'd spent months just trying to figure out what was going on, trying to make the books and records reflect reality. And he still couldn't get money from the Mogadishu office.

So he began to pay his staff from his own salary. When Tone heard about it she exploded. There was barely enough money for them to live on as it was. It was expensive to import things for Bernie. Chris was still paying college loans back in the States. And now he was paying salaries.

Chris argued that it wasn't much money.

But soon it was. Before long he had invested $3,000 cash into the project. And now a second baby was on the way. Chris was drinking heavily and Tone wasn't far behind. He'd come home evenings hauling work with him. Hassan Ilhan would often stop by and the two of them would shuffle through reams of paper. Tone didn't know what they were up to. Her anger grew, but she and Chris rarely spoke of problems. On the outside she expressed confidence that everything would pass. Inside she was sinking deeper and deeper into despair.

On top of his problems with Save the Children, Cassidy was running up against the corruption and indifference of the Ministry of Agriculture. Resources and field support that were supposed to have been funneled through the ministry never arrived. Cassidy suspected they ended up in the hands of private farmers with connections to Siyaad's family. When ministry officials did show up at the project site it was always to deliver bad news: Land originally slated for allocation to refugees is no longer available. Hardware or fertilizer in the project warehouse has to be be "reallocated" to another project somewhere else. Expats were helpless to do anything about it, and most just grumbled quietly to themselves. Cassidy shouted to anyone who would listen. Part of him really thought he could change things.

Not long after Cassidy and Hassan Ilhan's conversation by the monument, Siyaad Barre was traveling back to Mogadishu from an inspection tour of the southern Lower Shebelle region. The car in which he was traveling overturned in heavy rain. The president was injured in the crash and flown to Saudi Arabia for treatment. Radio Mogadishu tried to downplay the incident, but Barre was seriously injured. The president was described as being sixty-seven years old, but in truth he was probably ten years older. Things would never be the same in Somalia again.

In early 1986, some of the Somali shillings that made their way to Qorioley had an extra symbol hand-stamped on them. It stood for the Somali National Movement, a northern rebel group that had begun fighting to overthrow the regime. Panic set in among the refugees. They didn't want to touch the money. It was as if each exchange of the currency slowly eroded the foundations of the regime that had invited them to Somalia and made them the wards of the state. Even those refugees who despised Siyaad knew that other Somalis regarded them as his allies. Their fate was tied to that of the dictator.

In late 1986, nine months after Cassidy arrived in Qorioley, a new Save the Children director was finally appointed in Mogadishu. His name was John Marks, a former Peace Corps volunteer who was in Somalia when Siyaad threw the Peace Corps out in 1969. Marks spoke Somali fluently, which was an impressive trait. Few of the foreigners who came to Somalia in the 1980s ever learned the language. For one, it was tough to learn. For another, the government didn't encourage Somalis to teach the language to foreigners. A Somali-speaking foreigner was a danger to the system.

Marks had been working for CARE in Hargeysa, where he had a reputation for being too friendly with government officials who were orchestrating a campaign of terror against the Isaaq clan in response to their support of the rebel Somali National Movement. In Hargeysa Marks's name still elicits negative reactions. He was said to be friendly with General Gani, the military commander who later was responsible for bombing the city into rubble, and he was there to feed Ogaadeen refugees, people who moved into Isaaq land and soon started supporting Siyaad's government in its campaign of extermination against the Isaaq.

Save the Children wasn't going out of its way to hire a director; they saved a lot of money by not having one. But the absence of a director was endangering the project. A German NGO, GTZ, was prowling about Qorioley and drooling. They saw the potential of the project, its possible impact, and its potential for attracting money. Qorioley was a pilot. Make it work and rich contracts are yours. Hundreds of refugees could be made self-sufficient. Anyone would want to sign on to that team. "Frankly, I think the Germans would have done a good job," Cassidy says.

• • •

The first thing Marks did was to get a new director's residence in Mogadishu. He rented a former USAID guest house near Villa Somalia, the presidential palace, with a view of the city. The second thing he did was throw a cocktail party. Chris came for the free booze and to be polite and meet the new director. The place was full of every NGO representative in Mogadishu plus Somali government officials, the same ones from the Ministry of Agriculture who had been stealing from the project.

At the party, Abdi Mohamed, the project's farm manager, had been drinking heavily. He kept staring at Marks. Finally he walked over to him: "How is it that the first thing you do is rent a mansion and buy alcohol for all these white people?"

Cassidy walked over and grabbed him from behind and dragged him out of the party.

Despite the confrontation, Cassidy returned to Qorioley optimistic that once Marks came down to the project site, they would get things straightened out. Chris assured everyone that Marks would be there to clear up the salary situation. And when Marks didn't show up, Chris made excuses. He's busy. He has to set up the office in Mogadishu. He has to be in contact with Westport. In reality, however, Cassidy was fuming mad. Since Qorioley was the only place Save was working in Somalia, he had no idea why they even needed an office and a big house in Mogadishu.

Months passed and no Marks.

The bush telegraph operates fantastically well in Somalia. If you punched someone in the nose in Beledweyne and then drove nonstop four hours to Mogadishu, the news will have arrived before you and the family of the aggrieved victim would be there waiting at your doorstep to settle the matter.

So when John Marks started spending weekends at a friend's house on the coast in Brava, word hit the project very quickly. Brava is two hours south of Qorioley, and to get there you have to drive within a few minutes of Qorioley. As soon as Marks showed up at his beach house, everyone in Qorioley knew it.

After several weeks, Cassidy walked into a staff meeting and overheard an angry conversation. He understood enough Somali to get the gist, but waited until after the meeting to ask Hassan Ilhan about it.

"These guys are pissed off. He's renting a house and driving by here every weekend. He's spending money using our vehicles and our fuel but we're not getting paid."

If you want to insult someone in Somali you say, "fuck your sister." It's not a phrase to be taken lightly, and a Somali might use it five or six times in his life. Words are important. Words kill. Before a Somali says something, he usually considers it carefully.

Hassan Ilhan was insistent that Cassidy should confront Marks with the problem: "You're a *gaal* and he's a *gaal*. You both work for Save the Children. Do something, goddamn it," Hassan shouted.

Chris finally confronted Marks. "We're taking the money and not delivering the work and pissing people off. We go over there and tell everyone we're committed to the project. Then we just disappear when it's time to pay the workers."

"You're getting paid. Keep your mouth shut," Marks said.

Cassidy never thought of resigning. His commitment was to Somalia, not to Save the Children. There was nothing they could do to him, no discomfort was too great to bear. He was going to stay. He was going to prove to the refugees, prove to Hassan Ilhan, that this *gaal* was different. This one was going to throw his lot in with the people of Somalia, not with the government, not with the aid agencies, but with the refugees. Cassidy felt that he would have to redeem the image of the West in Africa. He would erase the legacy of a hundred years of colonialism and deceit.

He would make Hassan Ilhan his ally. The two of them would make the project succeed. If Ilhan were doing up a résumé, he might put down that he had people skills, at least compared to Cassidy.

A system was developing between the two of them. "We could always come up with something. He was good with the numbers too. It's rare that you find someone who complements your strengths."

Although Cassidy complained about the bureaucracy, he relished the fight. His trips to Mogadishu became more frequent. Together he and Hassan Ilhan stormed government ministries and began demanding resources. They accused Save of corruption. They accused the Ministry of Agriculture of corruption. The Somali government, Cassidy charged, was not living up to its end of the bargain.

Then there was a visit from the new Africa director for Save the Children. He arrived in Somalia telling the organization's staff that there were negative stories about Save in the press back in the States. Reporters were investigating the organization. He was concerned that some of the reporters might show up in Somalia, might start asking questions about projects and project funds. "Don't talk to the press," the assembled Save staff was told. "All queries must be directed through the public relations office in Westport."

Cassidy raised his hand. "What are these rumors that we're not supposed to talk about?" he wanted to know.

"Since you're not supposed to talk about them, you have no need to know. It's not important." Cassidy persisted but only succeeded in alienating the regional director and everyone else in the organization. (Ten years later, when I was doing my own investigation of the organization, they likewise sent out word to their worldwide staff that no one was to talk to the press without the presence of the public relations staff from Westport.)

Cassidy wondered if there was any relation between the investigations and the problems he was having in Qorioley. Everyone knew Save wasn't paying bills. People with jobs support hundreds of others. Local refugee leaders came to Cassidy and accused *him* of stealing the money. In turn, Save's Mogadishu office said they weren't getting money from Westport.

"We are committed," headquarters assured Cassidy. "Don't worry about funding. Save the Children is here to stay. We are a community development agency."

At a meeting in Mogadishu, Chris discussed the financial situation of the projects with Marks and his financial officer. Chris remembers, "I was basically saying, Here's my budget for the year, here's the disbursements that we've had, and when are we going to get the disbursement that we need to cover the project expenses? This money has been allocated, earmarked, obligated, and we need to get it into those accounts to run the projects. When you're having difficulties making payroll, it puts management in a bad position, and I wanted this situation corrected.

"On the books we're carrying this money, and in reality it's nowhere to be had and, like I say, you're basically being corrupt. I want an answer to this. I want the money that is allocated in the project according to the project documents."

"Is your salary being met? Are your needs being met as an individual?" Cassidy was asked.

Marks finally showed up unannounced in Qorioley one day. It was a Friday, the day of rest in Muslim Somalia, and Cassidy had some visitors for whom he had just roasted a goat. Why the hell couldn't he show up on a workday, Cassidy wanted to know. This is, after all, work. This is the only work we're doing in the country. Yet he can only find the time to come here when he's passing to his weekend recreation.

Cassidy lit into Marks. "Dammit, that is U.S. taxpayer money that Save the Children is using. We have a responsibility to the taxpayer too, to be sure they're getting a positive result from that. It's a rip-off. Everybody is losing on this deal except a couple of individuals at the headquarters level."

Looking back on it, Cassidy is even more bitter. "We took their lives away. We stifled the opportunity for them to have a life and raise their kids and have a future.

"Whatever we did for them, they were still damn refugees, captives in the refugee camp. They were learning to be different people, learning to act in ways that they were never trained to act. They couldn't rely on themselves any more. Essentially, we were telling them, You want to eat? Get in line. No food today? Maybe next Tuesday. Maybe next week. We'll tell you what to eat, how much to eat, and when to eat.

"It was a question of control. What happens if there's civil strife and the donors run away? You starve to death. Look. If you've got the skill and tools and knowledge you can be a man. You can march the fuck out of that camp and set up on your own. You can take care of yourself."

By May, the rains made the ramshackle house unbearable. Insects swarmed through the walls and floors. They crept into the food and wandered across the baby's crib. Water dripped from the ceiling and through the walls. Bernie cried. He'd come down with a fever. So Tone and Bernie had moved to Mogadishu to get away from the rains.

After three weeks in Mogadishu Tone wrote back about conditions in Qorioley. Her mood, for the first time, was gloomy as she related her hardships. The house, she wrote, had become unbearable, full of insects and leaks. The laundry never dried. Tone was pregnant again and morning sickness compounded her discomfort. She was, she wrote, unable to face another meal of spaghetti covered with camel meat stew. The baby was due on November 22, and she wrote that they were thrilled. They had decided that the child would be born in Norway or the U.S.

She wrote that Chris was starting to relax a bit more and had begun to read novels, which she had been begging him to do since they'd arrived in Qorioley. The rains had kept them from the beach, but they had made plans to drive along the coast road the next day. Bernie loved the beach, she wrote. And he would sleep some after spending the day there. In general, however, he rarely slept through the night. His sleeping problem was growing worse. Whenever he awoke, she would nurse him, but now not even that was helping.

Since Bernie didn't have his own bedroom it meant that she and Chris were awake most nights.

Tone's letters always promised the Cassidys that Chris would write soon.

In April of 1986, the press investigation that Westport so feared was published in *Forbes* magazine. The shocking revelation was that Save wasn't exactly hand carrying donated money to recipient children but was instead pooling it into community development projects where the children lived. Nonetheless, the sponsorship program was still marketed as a way to establish one-on-one relationships with children in the United States and the Third World.

Save tried to make it all sound like a misunderstanding, but in reality the deception was quite deliberate. *Forbes* reported: "SCF staffers find such revelations particularly embarrassing. 'Many have asked that the ads be more representative of what we're actually doing,' says one field director. We even recommended that we get away from child sponsorship and just sponsor communities. But headquarters doesn't address our questions."

The *Forbes* article led to an NBC television exposé, and the firing of one employee who spoke with the network. Then, in September 1986, in response to a threatened lawsuit from the Connecticut attorney general, Save the Children agreed to follow new guidelines in advertising.

Under the guidelines, SCF agreed that its advertisements would not state or imply that money is given directly to any particular child or that it will be used to help only one particular child, but was instead pooled and sent in one batch to a community.

The announcement of the agreement between Attorney General Joseph I. Lieberman (later a senator and chairman of the Democratic Leadership Committee) and David Guyer, then president of Save the Children, had an old-boy feel to it, as if it was all a small misunderstanding about fine print. Both men said they were pleased with the agreement.

"I am confident that adherence to these guidelines will allow the public to be fully informed about how this charity operates, and will enable Save the Children Federation to continue its good work in communities around the world," Lieberman said.

"We are dedicated to preserving public confidence in charitable giving, and the guidelines we intend to follow allow us to accomplish that goal while fulfilling our organization's desire to save the children in economically distressed regions of the world," Guyer said. He went on to state that Save was happy that concerns raised by Lieberman's office had been resolved by the guidelines, which, by the way, Save the Children had voluntarily changed already.

In truth, the advertising barely changed, and the agreement received little publicity. Even today, Save's ads, but for a grammatical nuance, seem to imply that the money is going to help *your* child. The first question asked if you phone them for information still is: "Would you like to sponsor a boy or a girl?"

By late 1986, the project, despite all its problems, was 75 percent completed because Cassidy was able to mobilize the people and use what he had. If he'd had the resources on time, it would have been finished. The civil engineering was mostly done. The agricultural engineering canals were 50 percent done. To Chris's mind it was starting to look like a successful project. "We were kicking some ass out there. We had a vision. Some of the farmers were getting into it. Now was the time to really teach the farmers, to teach the management how to run the projects, how to open the gates to irrigate everyone. The training component was the key to making it all work. That was the next step, the important one."

Cassidy and Hassan Ilhan had nearly made the damn thing work despite the problems with payroll and management. But his story—of a man "going bush," fighting the system, refusing the bribes, writing checks out of his own pocket—would have a price beyond simple disillusionment with local governments and Connecticut charities. The more time he put into it, the more he reveled in his triumphs, the more fanatical he became, the farther away drifted his family. Tone began to drink more and more and Chris never noticed.

Chris and Tone and Bernie went to Norway for a month at the end of the year for the birth of their second child, Christopher. The birth had been traumatic. Tone had undergone a cesarean that resulted in minor complications but left deeper psychic scars. While in Europe, Chris spent a lot of time on the phone to Westport. They had him running errands to buy things that were hard to get in Somalia: computer paper, ribbons for printers, a Swedish electric typewriter. Chris packed everything up and took it back with him to Mogadishu, where he arrived—this time—with two babies. Again no hotel arrangements had been made for him, no guest house was provided. No one met him at the airport. "No common courtesy for human beings," was how Chris summed it up. He dropped the equipment and the receipts at the office and found a hotel for his family.

The next day the family hauled itself to Qorioley. They hadn't even un-
packed when Chris found a letter waiting. It was dated from when he was
still in Europe. The letter said that funding had dried up and the position
was eliminated.

Cassidy had been fired.

$$5$$

DEATH IN MOGADISHU

For there is nothing heavier than compassion. Not even one's own
pain weighs so heavy as the pain one feels with someone, for someone, a pain intensified by the imagination and prolonged by a hundred echoes.

> —Milan Kundera, *The Unbearable Lightness of Being*

Willie Huber had always admired Chris Cassidy. He admired his work
ethic and his straightforward and honest way of dealing with Somalis and Somalia. So he immediately offered Chris a job.

He promised that his organization, SOS Kinderdorf, would be different
from Save the Children. SOS was an Austrian-based organization that set
up children's villages and practiced integrated development policies in restricted environments. The villages included schools, hospitals, teaching
farms. They took no money from governments and stayed highly focused
on improving the lives of the children within their project. Huber figured
that the difference between SOS and Save was that SOS supported its
people in the field. He was confident that he could close his project at his
own discretion at any time.

When Huber first moved to Somalia in 1982 to set up an SOS village,
he was immediately shaken down by assistant government ministers and

their relatives. Rent my land. Rent my house. Use my vehicles. Hire my nephew. Buy my food. Huber saw things were getting off on the wrong foot and demanded and received a meeting with Siyaad Barre.

They met at 1:00 A.M. in Villa Somalia. Barre was an insomniac who stayed awake at night chain-smoking Benson & Hedges cigarettes and insisting that people meet him on his schedule. Huber walked in angry and delivered a quick ultimatum.

"I don't want to get into a fight with your ministers," Huber told the president, "but we have to do our project our way. If in a year from now you don't like what we're doing, we'll leave." Huber half expected that Barre would toss him out of the country. There were some ninety other NGOs in Somalia at that point. The government could pick and choose. They didn't need this arrogant German-speaking Italian from the Alps having his own way. But Barre just smiled. At 2:00 A.M. he summoned some of his ministers. "When the wheel is turning fine you don't put a stick in it," he lectured. Huber had his year.

"You have to be firm," Huber told me later. We were sitting in his high-rise office in Nairobi talking about Cassidy. "And to be firm you have to know exactly what you want to do. You have to be prepared to walk away. Most important, you need your organization to back you. The Somalis know this. If an organization just wants to work, and doesn't know or care what they do, they'll make any kind of compromise and the Somalis will eat them alive. They want new people who will not cross them. There is a history here of driving away NGO directors until they find someone who won't resist. They want a puppet. Most NGOs oblige them."

Cassidy refused to be a puppet; Save the Children was all too willing.

"The first things the Somalis will do is find out your weaknesses and then exploit them," Huber said. "You have to admire them for that. They are the world's greatest entrepreneurs."

Just north of Mogadishu, in Balad, SOS had a 500-hectare farm where Huber wanted Cassidy to work. Cassidy flew off to SOS headquarters in Innsbruck to get the details. And then, to Huber's surprise, he turned the job down.

He wanted something bigger. He wanted to make a huge difference and wasn't interested in a small project. Huber figured that after his experience with Save the Children, Cassidy wanted to prove something. He wanted a project to shove in the government's face, and to show up Save the Children. He needed to succeed on a massive scale. He wanted revenge. According to Cassidy, Save the Children should have had $400,000 on their books for the Qorioley project when he took his home leave. How could they not have the money to pay his measly salary? How could they have let him run around busting his ass doing errands in Europe for them when they knew in advance that he would be let go? How could they have let him return to Somalia with his recovering wife and infant son and then tell him they had no money to buy him air tickets home? Cassidy would never have brought his family back had he known.

Back in Mogadishu, Cassidy rented a small house and started teaching English at night and got a day job managing the International Golf and Tennis Club near the site of the new U.S. Embassy compound under construction. Playing the nine-hole golf course was more novelty than sport so it attracted many nongolfers who wanted to whack at golf balls in the exotic setting of Mogadishu. It was one huge sandtrap. The "greens" were really "brown" surfaces where the sand had been tamped down and oiled to allow for putting. Keeping them smooth kept the Somali caddies busy. The rough was truly rough, full of wildlife and glorious birds and dik-diks, tiny antelopes.

The club had been around since the 1960s, when the Somali government had given the Americans (as well as the Italians and British) a big chunk of desert out on the far edge of town in the hopes that they'd build an embassy there. The American ambassador decided to use his parcel to build a golf course. Eventually, tennis courts and a clubhouse were added, and much later the embassy was relocated there. (The Italians built the University of Mogadishu on theirs; the British sold theirs to a private entrepreneur.)

When Siyaad Barre seized power, the club became a sort of subversive hangout for the regime's more patrician opponents. Later, in the 1980s, when the aid agencies and Americans started moving back in force, the incumbent ambassador persuaded the Department of Defense to fund an expansion of the club—swimming pool, showers, snack bar—for R&R purposes. The place became less "international" and more strictly American. As one former American diplomat recalled, "We had redneck DOD contractors all over the place who couldn't bear to see foreign children, never mind Somalis, swimming in the same pool as their own kiddies— their U.S. Defense Department–built pool."

In the 1980s, a running and walking course was cleared with the help of the military and the CIA. "Just strolling in the early evening was a delight," the diplomat remembers. "At the end, we had problems with herders running cattle onto the course at night and kids throwing stones at the golfers and joggers from beyond the fence."

The good life in Mogadishu was coming to an end.

It was early in 1987 and Somalia was going through some changes. This was the time of Siyaad Barre's car accident, and there were rumors that he had suffered some sort of brain damage. What else could explain the way his closest relatives were snatching up all the government ministries and having their way with the country? Family members took over the Central Bank, the Ministry of Defense, foreign ambassadorships, and the director-ships of state-owned enterprises such as Somali Airlines and the petroleum agency. Wholesale looting of government coffers kicked into high gear, and people were taking actions to protect their own turf. Aid workers who challenged the corruption were being threatened and occasionally beaten up.

Somalia's political prison, Labatan Jirow, about 190 miles down the coast from the capital, filled up with dissidents and others who had displeased the president and his buddies. There they were tortured and kept for years in solitary confinement in tiny cells. And in northern Somalia, the guerrilla war against the government intensified. The streets of Mogadishu grew tense with fear as those who were "in" with the regime now had, or feel they had, carte blanche to pursue their own interests and deal with their enemies.

Chris Cassidy never spoke about the events that followed. Many of his friends knew vaguely what had happened to Bernie and the rest of the family, but no one ever asked Chris about it. He had constructed a solid wall around the issue.

In the winter of 1994, I went to Yakima, Washington, to see Chris. It was a year after his "debate" with the marines at Central Washington State University and he was still too shaken and embittered by his Somalia experience to really discuss it. We'd spoken on the phone a few times since the Somalia intervention, but Cassidy's comments were general and political, never personal, not a word about what he himself had been through.

I met him as I came off a flight from Seattle at the Yakima airport. We drove back to Cassidy's tiny one-room apartment. We sat and talked, but he said little. Each time I'd ask him about his experiences in Somalia, he would quickly digress into development theory and what he was doing in Yakima, about his plans to build an airstrip so Japan-bound cargo planes could take off with fresh apples and peaches from the reservation.

Cassidy seemed more comfortable talking when we were in the car, so we drove around the reservation, where he kept interrupting his narrative to point out various sites. Finally, on my fifth day in Yakima, we went up a road where we could go no farther.

"This is as far as I can take you, Mike. You can see we're getting into a timber area. This is paradise, man. You go through the commercial forest, the closed area, where it's just old-growth forest—the sacred religious area for the Indians—I mean it's just . . . you get there and you feel inside . . . I've never been so moved by anything. The elders tell you the legends, and I can't go to the sacred areas with anybody, but we're here on the edge of it. This is a special place up here."

Cassidy pulled the car off the road where we sat in silence looking out at the cloud-shrouded Cascade range. And he started to talk about what had happened after he was fired by Save the Children.

"I mean, I didn't have any . . . I had no fucking margin. I had debts, I had no money in the bank, no cash in reserve, because Save hadn't paid me and I had no way to get back to the U.S. I was stranded. Shit, what does a guy do?

"Goddamn it, you put a roof over your family's head, and you get your ass to work, and then you take care of the emergency and then we'll start figuring out the short-term and the long-term plan from here.

"When I was down grabbing my shit from Qorioley, those guys are really pissed off. It's just like, Hey, why the fuck is agriculture getting shut down? Why are you getting kicked outta here when we have all this money on the books? Our project's supposed to be ongoing, we have these agreements. The project people were pissed, all kinds of rumors were floating around.

"'Why didn't you take your cut?' they kept asking me. 'Why don't you go back and negotiate with them?' Shit, tell me who played the game. I just said fuck it guys. I gotta eat, you gotta eat. Sorry, that's the way things worked out. Yeah, they didn't follow the plan, they're not fulfilling their agreements. It's a raw deal all around.

"I had to forget about others for a change and concentrate on my own family situation, because we were fucking desperate, man. A newborn, a guy who had just come back, shit, he was just a month old, a month and a half, something like that—and a toddler. Anyway, I was trying to keep my rage from being known. I didn't want to have a reputation in that town as being, 'Oh, Cassidy gets the ax and now he's going around badmouthing Save the Children.' I needed a job.

"So I went to USAID, the private consulting firms in town. I'm a talented guy, I had a good reputation for work, people are . . . you can't fuckin' walk in a door and get a job overnight. You gotta see what projects are on the drawing board, who needs what help, where your skills match. So I was working on that. We're living down there in Lido . . . had to deal with the same old shit: no appliances, no cooker, no refrigerator, no fucking generator. We had mats on the floor, we had cribs for the kids and mosquito net, but I mean it was . . . we were roughing it, and shit, I went for an interview for a job at FAO [the UN Food and Agriculture Organization]. It was a high-pressure thing. They had the boss-man there, and the representative, the project manager, some other technical experts. I had applied through the headquarters, the headquarters had sent a telex to the field office, and hey this guy's available, he has really interesting credentials, can you call him in and interview him?

"Just like everybody else, you gotta family, you gotta big fuckin' time job interview, you're a bit nervous, it's stressful, it's a difficult time in your life, and still recovering from this childbirth thing, you know, normal shit.

"I came back from this interview, like everybody's starving and say hey, let's go down to the Anglo-American Club. It was a short walk down from where we had rented this house and I thought it was a safe area. People knew us. People knew the kids. It was in the time of the day when it's quiet."

Cassidy paused. The dry January wind whistled over the hood of his truck. And then the distant clouds began to lift, revealing the magnificent snow-covered peak of Mount Adams. Cassidy pointed out a fox that had strolled across the road. He asked if I was warm enough. Should he turn on the engine and warm up the truck.

"No. Continue," I told him.

I thought about the Anglo-American Club and long afternoons drinking beer on a verandah feeling the steady, warm ocean breeze. White noise, wind, and surf enclosed each little group of expatriates in a den of silence. I could picture Chris there with his family laughing and enjoying the afternoon.

The club was private. Membership was restricted to British and American citizens and their invited—usually European—guests. Some of the tables were outside on the deck, and others were under the roof of a wide open room. A Somali bartender served drinks, and waiters came when called upon. I'd spent a year living in a house just down the road, but I preferred the UN Beach Club, which was just up the road. The crowd at the UN Club was a bit younger and more international. The Anglo-American Club attracted families like the Cassidys.

Off the club's main dining room there were several doors to rest rooms and the kitchen. Cassidy now remembers one of those doors in particular. "There was a door with some kind of latticework covering it. I hadn't noticed it before, but we sit down and the next thing you know, the oldest guy

[Bernie] disappears. A second later we start looking around. I mean, it was just the staff of this place and one other couple with a child there, looking around.

"Where's Bernie, where's Bernie? Anybody seen Bernie? The gates are closed, so he can't get out. All the doors are closed. There's no way for a small kid to wander out. I looked over the wall down to the beach. There's no way down. No way he could have climbed up and over.

"I run over to the road, but everything is blocked off and gated off. There's an eating room and a verandah there and two rest rooms, and the guy's nowhere to be found. And then somehow, behind this latticework that has always been there, there's another door. I'd never even seen that door before in all the times I had been there, all the years I had been in that country, never even . . . never even knew. Inside, there is a cesspool. I removed the lattice and pulled open the door. I could barely get in there myself. No way a two-year-old could open that door. I looked in there. Nothin'. Kids don't wander into dark rooms, and not dark, smelly rooms. The place smells like shit. I went back outside, looking around.

"One of the staff there says, Oh, I think he's in there. No, Cassidy says, I already checked in there. He says, No, I think he's in there. He's really insistent this time—really saying, I *know* he's in there.

"So I go in there and shove my hands into the cesspool and sure enough, there's something in there. I know what it is. I pull out a body."

Cassidy, drenched in shit and crouching in a dark room, began breathing air into his son's mouth, while outside the wind muffled all sounds and waiters served beers.

"I thought I could still get a pulse. I tried reviving him. I thought I could do this. It was as nasty and ugly as you can possibly fucking imagine. He wasn't conscious, but I had a pulse going there and I thought I could revive him. And after, I don't know, shit maybe twenty, thirty minutes, just decided, shit this is really touch-and-go, better fuckin' scream, get some help, throw the guy in a taxi, haul ass down to the embassy.

"Those guys know you at the gate, jump out with this kid, they let me in there. The marine guard took me to one of those back rooms. They started their emergency type thing. They get on the horn, get some other guys down there and I don't know, worked like hell trying to revive that guy, and finally after what would seem to be some hours, something like that, they really get a nurse down there and say it was all over.

"It was one of the strange things, I've never been able to . . . the guy had his head smashed in, Mike. And the cesspool wasn't just out in the open. It was under a three-inch slab of concrete. And how a fucking tiny toddler kid that age could move this latticework that has plants hanging from it, open up a fucking door, get through that cement, with a smashed head, and end up in that thing when I didn't see him the first time through there, but he was there the second time . . . he was there."

Cassidy slumps slightly behind the wheel of the pickup truck and crosses his hands tightly over his chest. His eyes fill with tears. He's sobbing.

"I knew that Save was pissed. I knew there was gonna be some government guys pissed that I was hanging around looking for jobs. You know, when you get fired you're supposed to fucking go home. You're not supposed to hang around looking for work. I mean in hindsight, it's easy to figure that out."

Was Bernie murdered? It's difficult to imagine that even the most evil Somali security officer would kill a child. Why not just kill Chris? But Cassidy is convinced that Bernie's death was no accident.

"At that time, it's a typical kind of killing," Cassidy says. "You go through the list of the violent activities that have happened in that country over time . . . I mean, that's a pretty standard calling card, giving some guy a subtle warning.

"Next time I was in Qorioley, guys come up and say, Listen, we wanna fuckin' get those guys that did that to you, to that child. I mean I was really well liked there, that family was really well liked, I mean Jesus, this kid . . . Anyway, as I was saying, you know, this is God's will and try to deal with it.

"That night I was completely fucked up . . . You can't even fuckin describe what the hell you go through with an ordeal like that, and it was . . . that was my fuckin life, I mean, that little guy named after my daddy had passed away. That was fuckin tough, and I just couldn't deal with it, you know, I was completely . . . that's the way you work through problems—just go to fuckin work, man. I just keep working even harder and I just wasn't prepared, I couldn't understand. I wasn't trying to figure out a reason for this, and that kind of shit'll drive you nuts. I was really questioning my religious convictions and spirituality. I was cursing God and the human race and everything, and everything I stood for and believed in had just been . . . the harder you work, trying to do good things for people and you just get, I really got fucked. Anyway, the Somali guys and the Ethiopian refugees are friends and everybody is really pissed off and the other, the American guys, some of the other expatriate guys, they know how sensitive I was to this.

"I wasn't one of these fuckin guys who say it's the old lady's job to take care of the kids. I was a diaper-changer, waking up in the middle of the night to get those kids so they could be breast-fed. I baby-sat, bathed them.

When I wasn't at work, that's what I was doing, taking care of those guys, and that was my life. Jesus. I didn't really care to dwell on Save the Children and this and that. It's get yourself up by your bootstraps and get on with it and try to deal with this as best you can.

"Then Hassan Ilhan came back from his training in Kenya and he was just shattered about this whole thing, about what happened to my employment, what happened to the project when he was gone. Because I was still trying to take care of his family when he was out, throw 'em a little money, make sure that they got transportation, that the kids were okay. He was a committed guy, he was going out for his training and coming back and was gonna stay with the project. We had some long heart-to-heart talks and he said, 'I've heard certain things and I can check into it further. Do you want me to do anything?' And I would say no, and he said, 'You know the rest of these guys are really pissed and they wanna go after these fuckers and they wanna settle the score. You know how we do things in the Muslim world, eye for an eye.'

"Then it was some months later we heard reports that Somalis who spoke English, who associated with foreigners, were being harassed by the intelligence people. They were shaking them down for information. And there was a guy associated with that club that had some security force come to his place one night and interrogate him, and when he wouldn't provide the information, they raped his wife and a couple of his daughters. Some other male member of the family that resisted was killed and this guy was hauled off, being accused of supplying arms and information to the rebels."

I tried to pin Cassidy down. What did he think happened? Was the man who worked at the club terrorized into taking revenge against Cassidy's family? That's possible, Cassidy seemed to say. He clearly didn't want to talk about it anymore.

We were driving in the truck again, down from the hill, away from the Yakima sacred forest. Cassidy seemed scattered now, unable to focus. He wasn't looking for answers any more. He had them. His commitment to development work had killed his son.

Bernie was buried at a Catholic cemetery near the headquarters in Mogadishu of SOS Kinderdorf. Willie Huber helped with the arrangements. A service was held in the capital's central cathedral, presided over by Salvatore Colombo, the bishop of Mogadishu. When Chris and Tone and little Christopher arrived home from the funeral, they found that their house had been ransacked.

Two years later, the bishop of Mogadishu would be shot to death on the steps of that very cathedral by gunmen acting for the government. The bishop had been speaking about human rights and about helping the poor. Like Chris and hundreds of others, he had realized that charity and development work are political, that doing relief and development work in the context of oppression is counterproductive. Any real commitment to development requires political action, speaking out against the powers that keep populations from developing themselves. In the Somali context, doing *real* development work was a truly subversive activity. During the late 1980s, at least a dozen aid workers were killed in Somalia. In 1988 alone, there were over 200 acts of violence *reported* against aid workers. Some of it was robbery and general harassment, much of it was directed against activities that the government viewed as against its best interests.

Aid groups were left in peace so long as they didn't cross the government. Most kept working through the violence, though their activities were kept to a minimum. In essence, they were allowed to stay and work so long as they really didn't do their jobs.

In 1989, Hassan Ilhan was gunned down outside of Qorioley after he protested that government soldiers were looting supplies from refugees.

In this context, it doesn't seem that farfetched that the government would want Cassidy to leave. But Cassidy didn't leave. He was offered the job at FAO and accepted it. Now his determination to succeed with an agricultural project was more single-minded than ever. If the people who killed Bernie thought it would drive Cassidy from the country they couldn't have been more mistaken. It never occurred to him that he should leave.

When Cassidy took the FAO job, he and his family stayed in Mogadishu and he commuted southward to the town of Afgooye. Every day, six days a week, he left at dawn and drove to the project. By this time, things started to become dangerous. Soldiers appeared on the roads and began collecting "tolls." Cassidy noticed military vehicles cruising around his project sites and following people working on the project.

"Soldiers started appearing at the project site, fucking with the irrigation system," Cassidy told me. "They vandalized it to prevent people from getting water. Then they started raiding warehouses, stealing fertilizer and tools. Military trucks rolled in and took vehicles and fertilizer. The roads were so dangerous we couldn't move things from the port to the project anymore.

"It was a terrifying situation. I was being constantly threatened. People carrying automatic weapons were demanding rides. It was hell. I was scared for my wife and kids at home in Mogadishu. The UN hired armed guys with machine guns to watch our house."

Once when Cassidy was driving his kids (another child had been born) to the embassy swimming pool, a car chased him down and passed him. Inside the car a group of men stared back at him, and one drew his finger across his throat making the universal sign for "I'm going to kill you."

The men in the car were not common thieves. Common thieves in Somalia did not have cars. Over the next months, the stealing of Land Cruisers from NGOs would become the most common crime in the country. They were stolen by rebels looking for vehicles to turn into "technicals" and by government soldiers at the direction of their superiors or on their own.

"The worst part was that we didn't know what was going on," Cassidy said. "There was no public information. The UN didn't offer any. We just heard things by word of mouth, stories about nerve gas and mercenaries doing bombing, but we never knew what was really going on.

"Because of the security situation, I'd stay in Mogadishu for a few weeks. Then I'd come back and find everything destroyed.

"On the project site, farmers were suddenly afraid to deal with the foreigners. 'The white people are working for the people who are oppressing us,' was the way they saw it. The aid workers were caught in a cross fire. The peasants said we supported the military, and the military said we supported the peasants. Men started disappearing from the project sites. One of our drivers was shot to death at a road check."

Some of the looting was carried out by Siyaad's personal "red beret" security forces. "They just came there in hoards and took off with tractors and pumps and vehicles," Cassidy said. "Then they hit the seed multiplication center. What are the military doing stealing seeds? They're not going to plant them! They want people to eat in the refugee camps, where they can control the food. It was a blatant politically motivated attempt to prevent people from growing their own food. There was a campaign to destroy agriculture."

"Why did you even stay there?" I asked Cassidy.

"You bullshit yourself. It all comes down to why you're there in the first place. Adventure? Sure. Money? Sure. Some people got raises to stay in the danger zones. Development work? If so, well there wasn't much development work going on there. All those who want to do development work can go home now because there isn't any development work to do."

At one point Cassidy protested to Somali authorities and heard from one of the Somali officials involved: "I'm in charge of your security. Are you worried about being the next foreigner to die here?"

As it turned out, the next foreigner to die there, in March of 1990, was Peter White, a British agricultural consultant. White was approached by a gang outside his home in Mogadishu and, according to the British Embassy, they demanded the keys to his Land Cruiser and then killed him when he resisted. He had lived in Mogadishu with his wife and young daughter since the start of a two-year contract in July 1988. The Somali police claimed White was the first casualty in a series of robberies by armed gangs intent on stealing four-wheel-drive vehicles and smuggling them across the border to Ethiopia.

Cassidy never believed that it was really about the car. As an agricultural consultant, White had seen what Cassidy had seen. Cassidy believes that White was silenced, and the Land Cruiser was the payment by the government to the killers.

At the end of 1990 the Cassidys fled Somalia with hundreds of other expatriates. Development work in Somalia had ended, at least for the immediate future. The family went to Nairobi and then Tone took the kids back to Norway while Chris looked for work once again. He ended up in Rome at the headquarters of the FAO where he was told another job would soon be offered to him—another development challenge in another country. He phoned Norway with the news and told his family that he would soon be there.

There was a cold silence at the other end of the line. Tone was direct. She never wanted to see him. She was keeping the children, and he would not be allowed to see them until they were old enough to decide for themselves if they wanted to see their father. Divorce papers written in Norwegian showed up at the Cassidy homestead in New Orleans. His family, everything he thought he was working for, was gone. Cassidy first begged, and then tried to use the courts. Nothing worked. Norwegian law left him with nothing.

In the Spring of 1995, I walked down the Lido, pausing for a moment at the house where I had once lived. It was as I remembered it except that it was full of bullet holes. A refugee family was living there. A woman sat weaving a mat on the front verandah. A goat wandered around on what used to be the front lawn. Children quietly played in the yard. I waved to the woman on the verandah and told her that I'd once lived in that house. She said nothing. A man came out of the house and stared. Then I realized he was looking past me to my Somali guard, Nur, who was chewing *qat* and had an AK-47 strapped around his neck.

Nur shadowed me everywhere, even though guards were not needed in this part of Mogadishu at this time. Northern Mogadishu, north of the "green line" that divided rival factions, was enjoying the fruits of *Sharia*, Islamic law. Thieves were hauled before Islamic courts, tried, and then had their hands sawed off. After several months people got the message.

(Things were different in south Mogadishu, where Mohamed Farah Aydiid was more or less in charge. There, walking on the streets wasn't a good idea, even with a phalanx of bodyguards.)

I continued walking down the Lido. It was a wide avenue with a slim median strip. Street lights hung over the street, but there was no electricity here, though the Ali Mahdi faction that controlled the north had managed to restore electricity in some of the more commercial areas. For a moment I could almost imagine the Lido as it was. At certain angles I could make the destruction disappear, but only for a moment.

I walked on to the Anglo-American Club. The building was destroyed but the wall around it was still standing. The gate had been blocked off with pieces of scrap metal, so I climbed over the wall. The verandah overlooking the beach and the Indian Ocean was still intact. No one was on the beach. I walked into what had been the dining room and imagined Chris and Tone and the kids sitting there with the other aid workers eating their hamburgers. Then I imagined little Bernie wandering away. I looked to where the bar used to be. The place had been used as a fortress recently. Stones had been placed on the walls as gun rests. The floor was covered with rubble, probably the remains of the roof, but someone had cleared an area for sleeping. Several fires had been lit on the floor.

I walked along by the rest rooms, looking for the doorway—there were no doors—where the latticework was. But the floors were covered with too many layers of rock and metal and wood. I thought for a moment about digging through to find the hole in the floor, but Nur, who was standing behind me, looked concerned. Then it occurred to me that this might not be a good idea. Landmines or other unexploded devices could have easily been under any stone. Nur relaxed when I finally turned to go.

6

CRAZY WITH FOOD

Very few policy makers understand what famine is. They think it means there's no food. . . . Famine is a failure of the market. And you can't fight an economic problem by giving away food.

—Fred Cuny

Chris Cassidy wasn't like most young college graduate aid workers who want to do good, give it a shot for two years, see some of the contradictions of aid but decide to get on with their lives rather than deal with them. For them, aid is a phase to be passed through, a rite of passage on their way to law school or business school, something to be forgotten except for those stories that can be told over and over again over beers in evenings far away. And Chris wasn't like the ones who fall in love with the aid life. They stay in it, become part of the system, and only resist it on occasion. They cling to the idea of aid. Aid redeems their lives and uplifts the lives of the poor. To them, the contradictions all stem from the West's not understanding or helping enough. Their answer is always *more* aid, bigger budgets, another project.

Cassidy identified the problem. It was political. He kept pointing to it. His tragedy might have been avoided, but his entanglement in local politics and the local authority's resentment of him would not have been otherwise. He was dedicated to his job, not to his career.

My story is different from Chris's in many ways. Both of us still wrestle with the contradictions of aid. I sometimes write about it; he still practices it. I once thought I might have a career in the aid business, but Somalia changed all that for me. It made painfully clear to me the full extent of aid's failure.

When USAID hired me to go to Somalia, I felt that I'd been called up by the big leagues. For a young man looking for advancement in the development world, this was as good an opportunity as ever came along. In the scheme of the development universe, USAID was a donor, up there with the World Bank or Britain's ODA (Overseas Development Administration). All the NGOs received their funding through the big guys. In Somalia USAID was calling the shots. The UN was there with all its agencies—UNICEF, UNHCR, UNDP, WFP, FAO—and all the European countries were represented, but everyone knew who was in charge. I was playing a minor supporting role in the organization as a personal services contractor, PSC. I had no diplomatic status and was on six-month contracts.

I was a food monitor until my title was upgraded to food assessment specialist. But I was only twenty-five, and I had time. The money was great. I had my own four-wheel-drive vehicle and a house on the beach in Mogadishu. Most of the time, however, I was in Beledweyne, a town on the Ethiopian border about 200 miles from Mogadishu. I was in the middle of a group of refugee camps that had been set up along the banks of the Shebelle River, where it was all happening in Somalia. The future looked bright.

My job was to make sure that the food sent from the docks of Mogadishu reached the refugees in my region. When the food didn't arrive, I was supposed to find out what had happened to it. Most of the time I felt like a cop. People were actually afraid of me. I could sit down with military men and accuse them of stealing food, and there was nothing they could do about it. I worked for USAID. A food monitor working with Save the Children, on the other hand, was badly beaten by thugs in a refugee camp.

The job didn't require a lot of detective work. On my first few days in the region, I saw military vehicles leaving refugee camps loaded down with bags of food. I saw merchants' warehouses filled with bags bearing the USAID handshake logo and the words "Donated by the People of the

United States of America, Not for Sale." Over the next few days, I saw military warehouses packed to the ceilings with refugee food.

After checking ledgers at refugee camps, I figured that most of the relief food being sent to the region—probably about two-thirds—was being stolen. Some disappeared from the docks in Mogadishu. Some disappeared from the trucks along the way to the camps. Sometimes entire trucks would leave the port and vanish forever. Most of it, it seemed, disappeared from the camps, sold by camp commanders, who were usually Somali military men, or were just taken by the soldiers or by the guerrillas, who were members of the Western Somalia Liberation Front (WSLF). Along with the food, the WSLF also raided the camps for able-bodied young men, unwilling conscripts for their murky guerrilla war across the Ethiopian border in the Ogaden desert.

Soon after I arrived in Beledweyne, the town began to fill up with NGOs. Each group rented a walled compound with plenty of room to park Land Cruisers, and with houses large enough to house the expatriate staff. Everyone hired a watchman and a cook and a maid.

I rented a room at the UNHCR compound. It was a small stone house surrounded by a wall. The dining area was outside on a patio covered with a thatched canopy. A second patio served as an outdoor living room. The shower was also outdoors. A 55-gallon UN-blue drum was mounted on a platform above a shoulder-high stall. Water would be hand-pumped into the barrel in the morning. After baking in the sun all day the water was perfect shower temperature.

Behind the compound was open desert. Peering above the wall in the evenings provided magnificent sunsets and the sight of camels moving in and out of town as nomads came across the Ethiopian border to trade animals and milk. Across the street was a German NGO primarily doing water engineering. Oxfam and a religious British group called the Tear Fund, which did medical work in the refugee camps, were a short walk away. Save the Children moved in, along with two separate teams of Italian doctors. In a refugee camp outside of town was an American group called Medical Volunteers International. The French group Médecins sans Frontières (Doctors Without Borders) showed up eventually.

Why so many NGOs? There was money available from donors, so they came. The Somali government loved it as well. More NGOs meant more headquarters in Mogadishu. Most of the major landlords in the city were relatives of the president or other high government officials. Even in towns such as Beledweyne, homes were rented from government officials at preposterous rates. The government was pleased to have all the NGOs they could get. So, in addition to the NGOs permanently camped out in town, we had a steady stream of itinerant charities that came through looking for projects and things to do.

A Canadian group arrived one day looking for orphans. They checked into the local office of the National Refugee Commission and were given permission to collect whatever orphans they found. Of all the problems that had sprung up in the refugee camps, I was never aware that orphans was one of them. The tight-knit clan structure meant that every child had a relative around somewhere. If no one closer could be found, a third cousin would gladly take and raise a child. But nonetheless thirty or forty children were gathered together and loaded onto a truck and carted off to an orphanage in Mogadishu, while their clan's elders protested.

Other NGOs came prospecting for projects. They would spend a day and then submit a project proposal to USAID in Mogadishu. When I'd get back to the capital, my opinion would be solicited. I always recommended that the projects not be funded. They were never well thought out. For example, one NGO sent a recent graduate from a forestry program to look into planting trees in Somalia. She had no practical experience in Africa yet submitted a proposal for more than $100,000. Later I brought her out to the site near the Shebelle River where she proposed to plant the trees. I pointed out to her that in much of the area the subsoil was limestone, and even if trees *could* be made to grow in part of the area, nomads normally brought their cattle to that spot, and the trees would be munched up in no time unless she proposed stationing armed guards around the area for the next four years.

And it wasn't as if the refugees were urbanites forced to live in tents. These people were nomads who'd spent their entire lives outdoors. For the most part, they could handle themselves.

In the evenings, when I could stand it, I'd get on the radio and talk to Mogadishu to find out what trucks had left and how much food they were carrying. The reception was so bad, nearly every word had to be spelled out using the Alpha-Bravo-Charlie-Delta alphabet. Passing along information could take hours.

My days were spent looking at registers and counting bags of food. I'd walk down to the local NRC office and sit down with the head, Abdullahi Jama. It was obvious that he was mucking with the books to hide the food. The numbers never matched. Abdullahi would shrug and smile. He was about thirty, and well educated. He had a bearded face that was marred by his crooked, *qat*-stained teeth when he smiled. Abdullahi Jama had a career in front of him. The NRC was becoming a powerful organization in

Somalia by virtue of its control of the programs that were bringing foreign money into the country.

Then I'd go and try to find out if the right amount of food had come in. Monitoring was impossible. I'd do spot checks at warehouses in the camps. If bags were short, they'd tell me that they had distributed them. Unless I stood there for an entire distribution, there was no way I could tell where the food was going. In addition, there were many camps with multiple distribution sites in a vast area to keep track of. I was sure that a lot of theft was going on, but I couldn't rule out every excuse for missing bags of food.

My trips to the NRC office became a bit of theater. I'd barge in and demand to see the books. I had to be forceful without humiliating Abdullahi in front of the people who worked for him. Sometimes I had to let him throw me out of the office. Usually he would instruct someone to fetch the ledgers, and I'd complain that records weren't being well kept. Abdullahi would blame it on the infrastructure. They didn't have chairs or desks or pencils, he'd complain. Then he'd ask me if he could borrow some of my pencils.

Most of my time was spent wandering around the camps and talking to refugees: They would tell me that everything was fine. If I asked where the boys and men were, I was always told that they were around or would be back soon. (In fact, they were back in the Ogaden with their herds.) I was regularly told how the Cubans and Russians bombed their cows. The stories were identical and clearly untrue. Obviously there was a movement afoot in the refugee camps to make sure that the refugees presented a united front to the foreigners. By my side on all these trips was my translator, a nervous man named Abdi, whose English wasn't very good. At first I kept him on because I felt sorry for him. Later I learned that Abdi reported every day to the National Security Service in Beledweyne. When I confronted him, he told me that it was true. He had no choice. He told them who I talked to and what I'd learned. Abdi apologized and begged me not to fire him. I fired him. A feisty young Somali woman named Faduma replaced him. I thought she might help me get information from the women in the camps.

There was a great deal of surplus food; even with the amount being stolen and disappearing, there was plenty of surplus food. Food was everywhere. Despite this, journalists still seemed to find emaciated children to write about. They'd hear from NGOs in the capital about how many lives they were saving, then they'd come out to the bush and probably not see much. Sometimes NGOs would lead them to hospitals and small pockets where children were suffering from dysentery or other debilitating diseases.

But they got these diseases from being in the camps in the first place. And back home NGOs continued to raise money by advertising that people were starving in Somalia.

At the center of the problem was this: The million and a half refugees who were allegedly in Somalia didn't exist. The Somali government liked to say 1.5 million. Journalists liked to say 1.5 million. It sounded good and added a weightiness to their stories. Several press reports even took the liberty of pushing the figure up to 2 million. I saw official reports from UNHCR and USAID that put the number at less than 400,000. And my own rough estimates from time spent in the camps made me suspect that even the 400,000 was generous. The camps were filled mostly with women and children and old men.

While I was monitoring the situation in Hiran District, my colleague and friend, Doug Grice, was doing the same job farther south in Bardera and the region along the Kenya border. Once a month, I'd make the five-hour drive to Mogadishu, and we'd meet in the house we shared on the Lido, across from the beach clubs. We were given a week or so to prepare our reports, maybe meet with the ambassador, get a hot shower, catch a movie or a videotape at the American compound. We'd sit on our roof deck and cut into our rations of whiskey and beer from the diplomatic shop. We'd chew qat and watch the ships in the harbor, or try to spot sharks off the coast. And we'd exchange stories about the refugee camps. Separately, we'd arrived at the conclusion that the relief program was probably killing as many people as it was saving, that Somali soldiers were supplementing their income by selling food, and that the WSLF was fueling their attacks into Ethiopia.

We'd then dutifully submit our reports and head back to the countryside to start monitoring the food all over again. At one point a State Department delegation came to Somalia because (I presumed) of all the reports back home about stolen relief food. In the field I spoke with one of the delegates, who started asking me questions, questions that I and other food monitors had answered a hundred times in our reports. "Haven't you read the reports?" I asked. She'd seen reports, she told me, but they were not mine. They were executive summaries compiled by the USAID mission. The detailed reports I'd written had remained in the files in Mogadishu. It was then that I became aware of what my real role was: I was writing reports because the Food for Peace program regulations said that reports had to be written. The food monitor was a requirement built into the law, but what I actually reported was meaningless. No one really cared what we had to say.

In June of 1981, CARE, the American NGO, was hired to distribute food. They were experts at it. In fact, it was practically all they did. Even today, nearly half of CARE's budget comes from the distribution of surplus U.S. commodities. USAID had insisted that CARE distribute the food in order to keep track of it. They entered into a contract with UNHCR and Somalia's National Refugee Commission. The resulting organization was called ELU/CARE (Emergency Logistics Unit).

To run the program, they brought in people from India—hard working, meticulous, efficient, and most of all, cheap. They seized the ports and began trying to keep records.

Within a few months the record books looked better. The reality, however, was that the WSLF and the army still ended up with the food. The National Refugee Commission was still pocketing millions of dollars, and there were still far fewer refugees than food was being supplied for.

I was no longer concerned with where the food was going. The more time I spent in Somalia, the less it seemed to matter. I was more concerned with what the food was doing.

In Beledweyne I spent more time talking with Abdullahi Jama. I stopped pestering him about the records and the food. I figured CARE could worry about that now. The streets of Beledweyne became more and more crowded with Land Cruisers as more NGOs showed up.

At night the expats would gather and drink whiskey and smoke cigarettes. The conversation was monotonously the same. Talk was about the refugees, the stolen food, the corrupt camp commanders, and the idiotic projects. Oxfam was teaching refugees to grow onions and cabbages and peppers in the refugee camp. The two Oxfam agriculturists discussed their dilemma nightly: The idea behind their project was to make refugees more self-sufficient. But if the refugees were going to return to their nomadic way of life, these skills wouldn't be very useful. And if they were going to settle down and become farmers, they'd need to know a lot more about agriculture than how to grow just a few cash crops. And there was very little incentive for them to learn. They could eat fine on their rations and sell the surplus for whatever pocket change they needed. The Oxfam team drank their whisky every night and wondered aloud why they were doing what they were doing every day.

One evening during the Islamic month of daytime fasting, Ramadan, I went to Abdullahi Jama's house to chew *qat* and break the fast. We talked about the refugees. He didn't seem to care much about them, but he was starting to feel that things might be turning against him politically. Then he started telling me about the food being stolen. The conversation was strictly off the record at that time. It was two friends talking.

He explained to me that the people around Beledweyne were from the Hawaadle clan, related to the large Hawiye clan that dominated the area. The refugees were mainly Ogaadeen, from the Daarood clan, relatives of Siyaad Barre. At first the Hawiye welcomed the refugees, but now they'd been there for three years. The refugees were getting rich. They were getting rations. (The word *ration* is now part of the Somali vocabulary. It refers to any kind of free food.) The local people were getting nothing and starting to resent it. And many people were starting to say that the purpose of the refugee camps was to replace Hawiye with Daarood.

Abdullahi Jama didn't buy that, but the talk scared him. He was from another Daarood subclan, the Majeerteen. After the Ogaden war, a Majeerteen leader, Colonel Abdullahi Yusuf, had split with Siyaad Barre and, with the support of the Ethiopians, had begun a low-key guerrilla war against the Somali government. His group was called the Somali Salvation Democratic Front, or the SSDF. Jama wasn't sure who his friends were anymore. He knew that much of the stolen refugee food went to the Western Somalia Liberation Front, which claimed to be fighting the Ethiopian government for control of the Ogaden. In reality, they were fighting the SSDF. And as an employee of the National Refugee Commission, he was feeding them—feeding people who were killing his own clansmen.

Abdullahi Jama was not a man inclined to view the world through the lens of clan. He was a modern Somali, a nationalist. But suddenly he was thrust back into the clan-centered world of his ancestors. Siyaad Barre was using foreign aid to manipulate ethnic rivalries, and Abdullahi Jama was being forced into the dangerous politics of clan.

Many years later, I would learn that Abdullahi Jama had been somewhat naïve about clan politics. Siyaad Barre was indeed using the refugee crisis to displace clans whom he viewed as his political enemies.

I was in the town of Boosaaso in 1994 at the Hotel Ga'ate, where I thought I might find some answers to questions I'd had in 1981. The Ga'ate could almost be a motel in Miami Beach. Low, white buildings perched on the edge of the sea surrounded a courtyard where old men, retirees, sat and drank tea. The sand was pure white and the ground was covered with small, round white stones. But these weren't any old men. The first person I met in the parking lot was Mohammed Jibril, former head of the feared NSS, now an overweight and sickly man who leaned heavily on an intricately carved cane. I approached him and asked for an hour of his time. He told me he'd be happy to talk. We set up an appointment, but I never saw him again. A few yards away I ran into General Gani, the man who bombed Hargeysa to dust. It struck me that Hotel Ga'ate was a rest home for war criminals. It also became the unofficial seat of the Northeastern Somali government in the years after the fall of Siyaad Barre. In the hotel lounge a group of men were glued to CNN watching *Larry King Live*. One of them, a large man with crooked teeth and an imposing beard, was Abdullahi Boqor Muusse. Boqor is a title meaning king. Abdullahi Boqor is widely known by his nickname, King Kong. As king of the Majeerteen, Abdullahi Boqor was also king of the Daarood.

In traditional terms Abdullahi Boqor's father, Muusse Boqor, would have been considered Siyaad Barre's king. Siyaad didn't always appreciate this and alternated between tossing Muusse Boqor into jail and inviting him over for dinner. Siyaad always tried to stay on good terms with his political prisoners. Abdullahi Boqor spent three years in isolation in one of Barre's prisons from 1976 to 1978, where he was beaten and tortured. Barre tossed him into jail eight other times on various offenses.

One time was punishment for something his father did. Abdullahi Boqor explained: "In 1983 Siyaad called the Harti* elders together at Villa Somalia in Mogadishu and told them about a plan for the Daarood to control the country. 'If we put half a million Ogaadeen in Beledweyne the Hawaadle will be a minority,' he told them. It was his plan to move the Ogaadeen into all the strategic areas. The Warsangeli and Dulbahante agreed to go along with Siyaad, but my father refused.

"He refused because the Majeerteen are friends with the Hawiye. We do business with them. The Warsangeli and Dulbahante don't have anything to do with the Hawiye. My father had many meetings with the elders of the Hawiye. He wasn't going to betray them."

Siyaad was furious that a traditional leader would so brazenly rebuke him. At the time, Muusse Boqor was old and sick. Putting him in prison wouldn't have been very satisfying to Siyaad so he took his revenge on Abdullahi, Muusse's eldest son and heir to the leadership of the Daarood. Once again Abdullahi Boqor was tossed in jail and tortured.

Boqor Abdullahi wandered back to the CNN room. General Gani squeezed over on the couch and made room for him. There they were, the torturer and the tortured. Gani, the ultimate Siyaad Barre loyalist, and Abdullahi, his victim, sitting and watching NBA highlights on CNN.

---

*The Harti are a subgroup of the Daarood which includes the Majeerteen, Dulbahante, and Warsangeli subclans. The Marehan and Ogaadeen clans—Siyaad's family groups—are not included. The Harti are considered by some to be the upper classes of the Daarood.

The scene reminded me how little I had understood in 1981. But Abdullahi Boqor's brief explanation put a lot of what I had seen into perspective. And it showed me how the events placed into motion thirteen years earlier had resulted in the present chaos in Somalia.

I had seen young toughs starting to throw their weight around, a foreshadowing of the role the *mooryaan* would later play in Somalia. Under normal conditions, survival for Somalis is a precarious and delicate balancing act, requiring the wisdom and guidance of the elders. The society was solid and intact. But with food arriving on trucks every day, traditional wisdom and guidance were no longer needed. Kids with guns were king.

I thought it was my job to report these developments, but I soon learned that this was exactly the type of information my bosses in Mogadishu did not want in field reports. They wanted the tonnage of food received, and the tons missing; plate numbers of trucks seen driving off with food and names of camp commanders who weren't cooperating. Still, every month Doug Grice and I would write the reports and tack on our observations about the state of the refugees and of our growing doubts about the wisdom of the relief program.

Our boss, Robert J. Luneburg, the Food for Peace officer, would storm back with the reports and say, "You guys know you can't write this stuff. Stick to the facts as you observe them." So we'd retype the reports and head back to the bush.

Thus confined by the USAID report format, I sat down at my typewriter in the dusty heat of the afternoon in Beledweyne and wrote a personal memo to Luneburg. It would be my last memo to USAID:

At the risk of being labeled politically naïve, I submit the following. I cannot in good conscience leave Somalia without expressing these opinions to the U.S. government in writing.

My experience in Beledweyne during the last few months has confirmed my growing suspicion that the Somali government is deliberately taking part in the diversion of refugee food, has deliberately inflated refugee figures in order to facilitate these diversions, and is now simply humoring donors by submitting itself to the impotent inspection and monitoring of the donors.

Our involvement in the refugee relief operation is participation in a political ploy to gain support for an unpopular military government. I do not presume to influence the policy of the American government in this regard, however I believe that the situation should be recognized for what it is. Our continued support for the refugees makes possible continued activity of the WSLF in the Ogaden, which in turn results in more refugees.

I realize that you have much more information than I do about the actual situation in the Ogaden, however I have made a point of speaking with refugees about the situation there until I was "warned" by the NRC early in July to desist. When I didn't, I was confined to my house for four days and denied access to the records of food deliveries.

I believe that the refugees have been coerced as to the manner in which to answer questions pertaining to the Ogaden. I know that there are individuals living in the camps known as "politicians" who instruct the refugees in political rhetoric and in how to answer these types of questions. I have been struck by the consistent similarities of their answers to the basic questions of "Why did you come here?" and "What was life like under the Ethiopians?" They all report that Cuban and Russian pilots had bombed their cattle and killed their relatives.

There is a festering resentment among the general population toward the expatriates and the refugees. An old man stopped me on the streets of Beledweyne and demanded to know why he was not entitled to rations and health care just because he had decided to settle in the town instead of in a refugee camp.

A man with four children working in Beledweyne for 800 shillings a month (an extraordinarily high salary) could not supply his family with the amount of food the refugees receive for free.

Many of the town people have solved that problem by keeping a residence or a part of their family in the camps. Sigalow camp [near Beledweyne] is indistinguishable from the mud-house back streets of Beledweyne which have now reached the borders of the camp and are joining it to the town.

There are other issues that make our involvement questionable. Such as the recruitment by the WSLF and Somali Army in the camps. This activity takes place in all the camps in Hiran. Some of the camp commanders are WSLF officers.

PVOs are now submitting hundreds of proposals to improve services to refugees. Expanded services to the refugees will only aggravate the problem by encouraging them to stay, and more refugees will arrive. It will spread more thinly the resource base, leaving the door open for a real emergency situation in the future.

The future for refugees in the camps holds only years of relief. The efforts of the international community should be aimed at solving the problem—getting the refugees out of the camps.

USAID and the U.S. government weren't interested in what I had to say, and, for the most part, neither was the press. Reporters seemed content to write about stolen food, starving babies, and heroic aid workers. I handed some of my memos to the only reporter who seemed interested in what I thought was the real story in Somalia. The story by Richard Ben Cramer was published in the *Philadelphia Inquirer* in the fall of 1981. It wasn't until fourteen years later that I heard of any fallout from the article.

I was in Nairobi visiting with Mohamed Abshir Waldo (not to be confused with SSDF leader General Mohamed Abshir Muusse). Born in the bush and a camel herder, he ended up at Columbia University during the student uprisings in the late '60s.

He became Information Minister for the SSDF and briefly head of the organization in the 1980s. From his home in Nairobi he was still active in the SSDF and in the running of the Majeerteen area in northeastern Somalia. He was explaining why the SSDF had turned down food aid from the UN. Though the 1992 famine in Somalia did not affect the northeast region, food and aid were still offered.

"If 10,000 tons of food arrives it will be sold on the black market and the proceeds used to buy arms," he said. "It becomes an arms race. It means war. If food comes we lose our ability to control the peace and the stability of the region. Everybody will want to have a share, but that's not possible. It's been three years since there was any food aid and three years since there was the hijacking of a truck. The only trucks that are hijacked are the ones carrying food aid. No private truck with private cargo has been hijacked.

"We had meetings about this in Djibouti and in Garowe," Abshir continued. "I met with Mohamed Abshir Muusse and with a number of elders and we discussed how any form of aid whether it was food or tents would cause problems. For example we had about 300 family-sized tents to be used exclusively for people who were living in public premises after the war: schools, hospitals, regional, administration offices, ports, shops, police stations. They were a Swedish church donation. They caused problems the moment they arrived. Those who were off loading the plane wanted to take some for themselves, and people immediately began fighting over them. The Red Cross also supplied quite a substantial number of people with kitchen utensils as an incentive for them to leave those places. The people took everything and never left the houses. This created a conflict between the administration and the people. And our relationship with the donors also gets spoiled because we've taken the gifts and haven't done what we were supposed to do.

"So if we had accepted the food we knew it was going present these problems of instability in the region and attract bandits. There was very good trading going on; livestock, hides, and fish were exported. Commodities were imported. People were trading. You know, things were normal. Nomads were breeding the animals for sale, but if you have the food even the nomad will leave the animals to have a share of this food.

"On the other hand, we could not say we did not want food. We wanted the food to buy arms. The donors were giving food to our enemies and they were buying arms. We did not even dare not to protest very loudly for aid because otherwise the population would say, why are we not getting our share of the food? And secondly, what do you do about the liquidity that the food will bring in, the selling of the food, realizing money, and then buying arms?"

"It's like a mini arms race fueled with food. If your enemy does not buy arms you don't have to be armed yourself. Or if you rearm and get the finance and so on, then you need to rearm also, to balance. Just like the big powers were doing.

"So we decided to minimize the damage. What we actually did—why we had peace—was to give 90 percent of the food straight to the militias. That was not what the donors intended, but the donors were giving it to our enemy. What would you do?"

Abshir left the room and returned with some pamphlets from when he was in charge of propaganda for the SSDF in the mid-1980s. He showed me that the SSDF leadership had come to terms with the military uses of food aid from watching the Siyaad Barre regime manipulate food aid for years.

"We've known for a long time about the damage caused by food," he said pointing to a pamphlet entitled "Somalia Under the Dictatorship of General Siyaad Barre." At the bottom the pamphlet it said Printed in Mogadishu, August 1994. In reality it was printed in Ethiopia, but Abshir explained with a laugh that they were just trying to piss off Siyaad. I flipped through the pamphlet until something caught my eye.

Feeding on the Hungry of Somalia

"Profiting from misery" From "Good Intentions gone sour." a series of reports published in the Philadelphia Inguirer, USA by Richard Ben Grammer, the staff writer, in 1981.

They hadn't gotten the name of the paper exactly right, and the writer's name was misspelled. Close enough. I read on.

Famine is not the issue in Somali Refugee camps. The huge international relief effort has succeeded to this extent: Food has poured into Somalia . . .
The relief effort was spurred by a fraud. The theft, the false population count,
the fraudulent nature of the emergency are all common knowledge in Somalia. The army of relief workers talks of little else. But nothing is said publicly
because the relief business is big business, and no one can afford to derail the
gravy train—not Somalia, not the donors, not the relief workers, Specially
not the refugees because they are hungry.

A food monitor for the US AID programme, Mr. Michael Maren said,
"sixty percent of the food for the refugees is stolen. Sixty percent or two
thirds. A third of the food that is loaded on trucks never gets to the camps,
and half the food that does get through is stolen in the camps."

I showed it to Abshir. "You were quoting me before you knew me," I said.

"As a US civil servant, I am not free to criticize the UN agencies. You can do
what you like, of course, using this information . . . I am not surprised it's all
screwed up out there, food going every way," pointed out Mr. Michael
Maren."

I looked at Abshir. "I didn't say this. You guys just made it up. I never
said anything of the sort."

"The theft was not possible to be the work of a certain individual. He had to
have certain support within the system. We shared our reports with the Somali Government. Relief business is like other business: there are careers and
organizations to protect," concluded US relief expert Mr. Michael Maren.

I hadn't said that either, not exactly, though it was inferred from other
comments I'd made to the paper. All these years, unbeknownst to me, my
name was being used against the government of Siyaad Barre. Abshir
smiled mischievously. "Thanks," he said.

The refugees never left the camps. The "temporary" camps, set up allegedly to shelter refugees from the Ogaden war are still there, more than
ten years after that war ended. As I and many of the other critics of the
1981 relief effort predicted, the residents of those camps are still dependent on relief food and still have no way to earn a living on their own.

Several months after I sent my final memo, Grice participated in a study
of the Somali economy. It found that the relief industry accounted for two-
thirds of the country's economy. There was no way Siyaad Barre could afford to let the refugees go.

And the private relief agencies couldn't let them go, either.

When I was back in Mogadishu in 1993 and 1994, I decided to try to find out what happened to the Ogaadeen refugees from the camps in the Hiran region. I found groups of them in Mogadishu, where they had settled in open spaces, on the grounds of deserted public areas, in school compounds. They were in the same thatched huts living, it seemed, much as they had lived in the camps. The difference now was that there were no NGOs there working with them and supplying food and medical care. The children whom I had seen running around in the camps in 1981 were now young adults, and there were hundreds of children who had known nothing except refugee camps in their entire lives.

In Mogadishu in 1993, these Ogaadeen were nonpersons. The city was controlled by various factions of the Hawiye clan, who were fighting among themselves for power and loot. The Ogaadeen hadn't had any particular problems with the Hawiye, since they had nothing worth stealing. The young Hawiye gunmen were not looking to avenge the wrongs of the past. So the Ogaadeen in Mogadishu did as they had been doing for the past fifteen years: They sat. They waited.

A small group of men quietly gathered around me, looking almost embarrassed at their predicament. We met under a tree just outside their encampment, but as we were making our introductions, children came over and began shouting. Unable to hold the discussion, we moved indoors to what was once a Save the Children health center. It was a cavernous cement structure with cartoonish drawings on the walls showing fat, healthy children, children being weighed, inoculated, fed.

Then one of the elders spoke: "We are known to respect and welcome our visitors. If we had the resources we would have killed a goat. Since you came here, we have been trying to obtain even some cups of tea. But poverty does not permit us."

They were surprised that I was interested in history, and shocked that I knew anything about the refugee camps at Beledweyne and Jalalaqsi. Everyone in this group had been in those camps and fled to Mogadishu ahead of the advancing rebel force. They fled toward the protection of a government that was crumbling, a government that had long before deserted them.

Did they know they were being used? I asked. A young man named Ahmed Sheikh Osman spoke up. "I was told that as a refugee I would have the opportunity for further study. It was a program through UNHCR. I filled out the documents. But then I realized there wasn't any chance of that. It was the children of government officials who were getting those scholarships; they were claiming to be refugees. How could these foreigners possibly know the difference?"

An older man, Mohamed Mohamoud Aden, joined in. "We are putting the blame in UNHCR. They didn't care who used the food and the money for the refugee children. Food was diverted and so were the funds the government was getting for the refugees. Refugee children were supposed to study but couldn't. So we wanted to go back, back to the Ogaden. We had our documents ready for repatriation [in 1988], but the civil war came. The rations grew less and less. When the fighting started, they left us holding our forms for repatriation. We hear UNHCR is supposed to help people. They just abandoned us. Now they don't think about the people they left behind in Jalalaqsi."

Two men left the room and returned with six blue plastic ration cards on a dirty string: a big hole punched in the middle of the cards for the refugees who chose to stay in Somalia; three little holes in the middle for those who wanted to be repatriated. They regarded those three little holes as a promise, Mohamed explained, and they are still holding on to those cards in the hope that something will come of it. But those cards are from 1988, another era. They are from another humanitarian crisis ministered to by a different group of NGOs spending different funds from long-expired government contracts. Those cards mean nothing, but they are all the refugees have to hold onto now.

Ahmed Sheikh Osman said, "I would have gone back to the Ogaden in 1986 if I had been given the chance. As a student willing to pursue studies, I sent a letter to UNHCR. What happened to the letter for scholarship? They never replied. That's when I wanted to go back."

As we were talking, the children once again gathered around and started shouting. Some of them came into the room and ignored the demands of the adults to leave.

"When a child has been a refugee, he loses his manners," one of the men offered. "He has no loyalty to his parents. We were seated under a tree; why did we have to leave? Before, children would never come to where the elders are. We are living so close together here. If you send them somewhere, they object. They refuse." He shook his head and then looked up at me as if to apologize.

Abdi Ahmed Yusuf is a small, wiry man of fifty-nine with a tight gray beard, pasted unevenly across his face. He was a herder in 1974 when the first famine hit the Ogaden. His cattle died and he went to refugee camps established in the Ogaden by the government of Ethiopia. I met with him later that afternoon in another part of Mogadishu. He and his family had found a structure that looked as if it had once been a garage. It had three walls and a corrugated iron roof that kept the sun away. Every day he went around the hellish streets of Mogadishu and somehow returned with scraps of food for his children.

We sat on a pile of rubble beside his shelter. "Once I had a good life," he told me. "I had seven children and a wife, fifty cattle and forty goats. I was eating *ghee* and meat and drinking milk. I didn't need to ask for permission to sleep anywhere. I was not asked Where are you going? The children went to Koran schools. There was peace in the bush, and Somalis never wanted to kill one another. Water was easy."

Then came a drought in 1974.

"My animals started dying. I didn't sleep for many nights. Hyenas would eat them. I had to run around trying to put more energy into the goats so they could escape. Sometimes I would take just their skins and sell them. I would bring a few animals into the *boma* [compound]. I saw my wife holding both hands to her face; the woman was demanding some things I could not afford. We began to ask Allah for rain.

"I would take the prayer boards with the Koran written on them and put them over my head and pray for rain. We called that the 'cow death' year. Twenty families lost all their cows and goats. When there were only seven cows left, it was time to move to town. I put the *hori* [shelter] onto a donkey. I put children who were well onto the donkey. I had one camel for transporting water in the *haman* [intricately woven water-carrying containers]. We started trekking. I was very strong and I could carry some of the children on my back. It was the worst time in my life. On the way to the town we saw people dying. People shit their rectums out and died on the path.

"We settled in a camp near Korahey, a baked, dry place with no trees. The Ethiopian government took us there and established shelters. We were given food by the Ethiopians. The government encouraged us to learn agriculture. We were brought to a project and taught to farm. The government would take the produce and bring us money. We didn't mind because we were hungry. We started growing fat again. We got blisters on our hands until we got used to the hoes."

Then, in 1977, Somalia invaded the Ogaden.

"We were having a good life until the bullets started coming," Abdi said. "First the Ethiopian troops were there. Then the Somali army came with tanks. I captured three Ethiopian soldiers who were not armed and brought them to the Somali commander. I told him that they should not be killed. The Somali commander was a good man, brave and understanding. But we were sad at the loss of so many Ethiopians."

While we were talking, a friend of Abdi's wandered over and sat with us. His name was Aden Farah Mohamed. He was in his late fifties, and had a long beard dyed red with henna. Together they looked like two respected elders of the Ogaadeen clan, and under different circumstances they might be enjoying the fruits of their years, relaxing with other elders and presiding over the affairs of the clan. Instead, they were scavengers in the urban wasteland. He listened as Abdi told me how some of the Ogaadeen had fought alongside the advancing Somali troops. Then he added, "Many of us helped the Ethiopians. Many of the Ethiopians had to come to the Somalis for water. They wanted to flee back to Addis Ababa with their families. We helped them because they were our friends.

"Then the Somali troops came to us with trucks and sent us to Beledweyne. We were told, 'you will get medical care, food, and water.' Some of us were taken to Jalalaqsi, down the road from Beledweyne. Others were put into camps near Beledweyne. People were given knives and pots and kettles. The food was very little but we were told that we would get farming land."

I stopped him. "Do you mean that you were sent back to Somalia before the Ethiopian counteroffensive drove the Somali army from the Ogaden?"

"Yes," they told me. The Ogaadeen had been sent back across the border into Somalia even as the Somali soldiers were advancing.

I had been under the impression that the first wave of Somali refugees had crossed into Somalia fleeing the Cuban-Ethiopian counteroffensive. The truth was that the Somali government intended to settle at least some Ogaadeen in Somalia from the beginning. It was ironic. Somali culture is deeply rooted in nomadic culture. Nomadic lore is venerated by people generations removed from that existence. And most Somalis say that the Ogaadeen are the keepers of the true culture.

Abdi told me how from Beledweyne they were asked to move to camps in Jalalaqsi. At first they refused, but the government took him and some of the elders to the campsite there and showed them around for four days. "We saw the river and the farming area and everything. It was good. Then they said, 'Sign here and say it's good and you can live there.'"

Aden ended up in Qorioley. "I had no choice. I wanted a place to live in peace and we were just taken there," he said. "I opposed the Somali government encouraging the people to come this way. 'We promise you we are taking you to a land where there is a big river and good pasture. Food. Shelter. Medical help.' I said No! But we were taken there in government vehicles."

Abdi picked up their story in Jalalaqsi. "First the Somali government was bringing the ration, and then CARE came with cards and started giving rations.

"We were made crazy with food. I became rich from food. I was able to marry another woman, a second wife who I call CARE wife, and then I married another woman, a young one who has many children who are starving now."

"How did you get rich on the refugee food?" I asked.

"We were getting too much food so we would take the food and sell it to buy soap and cloth and kerosene. Several refugees opened shops in Jalalaqsi town and started selling the food. It was cheap, so the people were buying it. And it was cheaper than in Mogadishu, so merchants from the city came to buy the food.

"I was an elder on the committee in the refugee camp. Because we were respected, we were given a bonus in food from the camp commanders. So I could sell that food and with the money I would buy the rations from others in the camps. I opened a big shop in Jalalaqsi. Wife number one and daughter took care of the business. I was buying food from the refugees at a good price and selling it in Jalalaqsi town and returning with food, fuel, and watches that I would sell back to the refugees. Soon I was bringing food to Mogadishu directly and making a lot of money. Then I married CARE wife. I was happy.

"One day I woke up and said my prayers. I was sitting on my mat when I saw a group of people coming carrying the Koran. They came into my compound.

"'Salaam Alechem.'

"'Alechem Salaam,' I said. We shook hands. I knew the first man. He spread mats. We were talking about the Koran and life. I told CARE wife to prepare tea, and quickly. She was eighteen years old and a beauty.

"'What can I do for you?' I asked the men.

"'We are here to propose that you marry the daughter of this sheikh.'

"This was the biggest honor. I had earned this. A man would not have offered his daughter if I was a bad man.

"I said, 'Thank you. I want to be engaged now,' so it took place there and then. A goat was brought and slaughtered and we had a feast of rice and goat meat. I gave the elders a gift of an *imamad*, a cloth turban. And then I paid the bride price of 2 million shillings."

I was astonished. That was a lot of money in 1986. But Abdi was proud. "She was the daughter of a sheikh," he told me again. "And that is nothing compared to the camels and guns and horses that would be expected of me when I was a nomad. I would have given 100 camels.

"I had three wives and life was blessed. Later the NGOs came and advised people to farm, but there was no reason to. When the NGOs would tell us this or that, we would try to make them believe we were serious. When they would leave, we would just laugh at them.

"Anyone who was seen doing that work was seen as someone who is poor, someone with no camels and no goats. A man of that sort cannot marry a girl whose father has camels. A man of that sort cannot marry the daughter of a sheikh.

"We became richer than the Hawiye people who lived in the area, and they used to approach us for food help.

"At first we had good relations with the people. We were sharing and helping each other and doing business. Then the Siyaad Barre disaster fell on us. Around 1985, he started saying, 'These people are Hawiye and these people are Ogaadeen.' We started getting the first ideas of what Siyaad Barre was up to.

"First there were the rumors," he said, tugging on his ear. We'd start to hear that this person was from this clan and this person is that clan. There were people in the camps who were watching and listening. We were afraid."

Abdi paused for a moment. We could hear the sounds of children crying in the distance. He looked around at the broken buildings. "Every problem that takes place in this world comes from top officials from the big city," he said softly. "Our problems started when Siyaad started handling his own people with his right hand and the others with his left hand."

Siyaad Barre had succeeded in turning the Hawiye and Ogaadeen clans against each other. Young Ogaadeen, convinced that the Hawiye, Isaaq, and other clans were their enemies, began joining the armed forces in record numbers.

"Do you think Siyaad Barre was using the refugees to protect his clan against the Hawiye?" I asked Abdi.

"First we were ignorant about it. Later we discovered that it was the intent of the Siyaad Barre regime to use refugees for his selfish ends." He paused. "I never thought a foreigner would ask that question. . . . We discovered that when the war started. Had I discovered it earlier, I would have done something."

"What?"

"I would have been the first to leave."

"And you didn't know."

He looked at me sternly. "You are a foreigner. You are writing many pages, but I trust you. You will go abroad and you may go and publish anything. What you are writing may harm me. If I know now that you are going to harm me, I would not talk to you.

"If I had known earlier, 2,000 lives would not have been lost in the Shebelle River. Women and children were put in the river to flow with the current.

"I myself was rescued by a Habar Gidir [Hawiye] man. I buried my brother and my daughter with my own hands, in Jalalaqsi, 1990. This is the foundation Afweyne [Siyaad] laid. Now I have the whole picture.

"There were people in the camps who said they were 'politicians.' They would lecture us: 'This is your government; the leader, Siyaad, is your relative. Without him you wouldn't have gotten all these opportunities. He has brought CARE with the food. We expect you to follow the way of the government.' Then they would leave and give the elders more money and tell them to talk to the younger ones. We were afraid."

I had known some of this from Abdullahi Jama and learned more when I was working with Faduma in the refugee camps, but overall, they seemed to have kept it all hidden very well. "Were you told how to deal with the foreigners?" I asked Abdi.

"Siyaad Barre planted some people in the camps called *the eyes of Siyaad Barre*. We knew who they were. They were armed with pistols, and they were everywhere in camp. If foreigners came to the camp and wanted to speak with refugees, the guys from the government would arrange a meeting of stooges. And even if you don't give the answers they want you to give to the foreigners—if you raise your voice or go away from the point—you will be jailed.

"If foreigners come and ask if we have trouble with local people, we were to say, 'We don't have a problem with the locals. We are brothers.' If they asked about government propaganda, we were to say, 'This is a refugee camp; we are free from politics.' If they ask about tribes, just say, 'We are all Somali.'

"If foreigners asked about rations being stolen, we had to say, 'Nothing has been stolen. We get our fair share of what has been given.'"

It was true. I'd heard all those responses thirteen years before.

I turned to Aden Farah, who had been listening silently. He had been sent far away to Qorioley. "When we first got to Qorioley," he said, "Save the Children gave us hoes and seeds. We were told that we should go and plant and then eat the food. The people were angry. 'What are we, slaves?' we asked. There was a big confrontation. How can you ask us to dig and plant?

"'We know you're not slaves, but don't you want to be self-sufficient? Now you have to be given food. We've done everything for you.' We said that we were living on meat and milk before. They said, 'You have left the milk and meat behind. You are refugees. How do you expect to survive now?'

"The people who knew about farming started to plant. The nomads waited to see what would happen."

Aden Farah recalled how an American man with a blond beard stood before them one day after the harvest and, pointing to the farmers, said, "This man is rich and you are poor. He was not too proud to work in the soil."

"People started going toward the farms. Everyone turned toward farming. I planted onions, and soon I had some money and bought a plot of land from another refugee who didn't want to farm.

"I still own the land," he said, quietly, plaintively. "But now all the land that was allocated to the refugees, including the land I have bought there, has been taken over by the people who were living in Qorioley, and I can't use it anymore."

As it turned out, some of the land given to refugees in Qorioley actually belonged to other people. When the government of Siyaad Barre fell, some of those people returned to reclaim their land. And some of the land was taken over by General Mohamed Farah Aydiid's militias. Most of the Ogaadeen refugees fled. Aden said he thought the ones who stayed had been killed.

"There are none left now," he said. "It's too dangerous. If people know you have land there, with documents, they will kill you. The people there take everything, and if you say that you have documents, they say, 'We don't care about the former government and the documents.' They say, 'The government was wrong to settle the refugees here in the first place, and we will not listen to anything you have been given unlawfully.'"

In 1990, the Hawiye-based United Somali Congress, led by Mohamed Farah Aydiid, started fighting its way from the center of Somalia toward Mogadishu. Their route to the city took them through traditional Hawiye areas along the Shebelle River southward from Beledweyne. It was along this very route that the Somali government had located the refugee camps, including Jalalaqsi.

Siyaad Barre expected that his Ogaadeen relatives in the camps, grateful for years of relief food and assistance, would help him battle the rebel army. In some cases they did help. But usually they fled. Barre had failed to terrorize them into loyalty. They feared him as much as they feared the rebels. The camps at Jalalaqsi were the closest to Mogadishu, and by the time the rebels were approaching, most of the inhabitants had heard stories from other refugee camps: Those who resisted were killed.

Abdi and the elders at Jalalaqsi decided not to resist. But then word came to them that Siyaad was sending a shipment of arms to the camp and they were expected to mount a defense against Aydiid and the USC army. The NGOs fled, and the rebels learned that the refugees at Jalalaqsi were armed—even though very few weapons had actually reached the camp. Most had been seized en route by the rebels.

With the Jalalaqsi camp in a panic, the local population from the rebel-allied Hawaadle clan began to attack in advance of the rebel army, which was composed mostly of fighters from the Habar Gidir clan.

"They came through the camp and slaughtered people like goats, and they were thrown into the river," Abdi said. "There was one month of serious fighting every morning.

"One morning after prayers, while I was just having my cup of tea, the Hawaadles came toward the camp." Abdi began to halt. His eyes moistened. "They were using APCs [armored personnel carriers] with big guns that they were firing. We had only light arms, but bullets from an AK are nothing compared to the big guns. There were casualties, and we were all rounded up. We were told to surrender the guns, and we gave them up. And they went to each and every house and looted everything—men, women, and children herded like animals into the town center.

"The Hawaadles knew the refugees well and vice versa. The bad people were known. Those who sided with Barre were known. Some people were put on trucks by the USCSNA [United Somali Congress rebels] and taken toward the Ogaden, taken out of town. Some were massacred on the river in Beledweyne.

"I stood with my arms folded while they took everything from me— clothing, mattresses, beds, 1,000,710 shillings. A married daughter of mine was trying to stop one of them from going into the house. I saw her shot to death in front of me, and I could do nothing.

"I had a Haawadle friend who was a driver. He rescued me and my family and brought us to Mogadishu, where I am today. I lost everything. Everything. Even now I'm afraid."

• • •

I spoke with Abdi and Aden over a period of days, while Mogadishu rocked around us with clan violence. After every night of fighting, I went back to visit them, and they were glad to see me. I met CARE wife who apologized again and again that she had no tea for me.

Abdi understood what the aid had done to him. He knew that it had made him greedy and enticed him to abandon the life he would give anything to return to now.

7

GENEVA

A man tries hard to help you find your lost camels.
He works more tirelessly than even you,
But in truth he does not want you to find them, ever.
— From the Somali poem, "The Fire," by Ali Dhux

In 1985, eight years after the end of the Ogaden war, six years after the refugee crisis began in Somalia, CARE reported that their food delivery systems were running smoothly, their ration card system was mostly in place, they had cut down on the theft of commodities, and refugees were getting fed. By 1985, however, the reasons for the refugee crisis had been long forgotten. In Ethiopia a massive and telegenic famine was dominating world headlines and mobilizing rock 'n' roll stars. The Ethiopian government was busy using the famine to eliminate their own ethnic problems and wasn't worrying much about Somalia. Siyaad Barre had long since abandoned the dream of greater Somalia and was instead obsessed with the rapid rise of militant resistance to his regime.

Some relief agencies had reported as far back as the middle of 1982 that the crisis was over. In February of 1984, Red Cross officials announced that 150,000 refugees had returned home on their own during the previous six months. When the world responded to the famine in Ethiopia, word had spread among the refugees that better relief and aid programs were available across the border.

The Somali government routinely rejected plans to repatriate the refugees, and then they rejected plans to resettle them. Either option would have meant an end to their "refugee" status in the eyes of the UN and therefore an end to the more than $80 million in annual refugee aid. Aid workers complained but continued to administer the relief programs.

A 1982 Associated Press report summed up the common perception:

> "There are strong political and economic reasons why Somalia wants the refugees to remain refugees," said a top relief official in Mogadishu. . . . Refugee aid has become so big a source of foreign exchange that it has become an important component of the Somali gross national product, he said, asking to remain anonymous because of his position.

This "top relief official," like hundreds of others, continued dumping aid into what he knew was a scam, yet he fled from the consequences of his action in order to protect "his position."

When the first refugees from the Ogaden war crossed into Somalia in 1977, other Somalis welcomed them as family returned home. The war and Somalia's brief victory had set off a rush of nationalist fervor. After seven years, however, the welcome had worn thin. The refugees were receiving favorable treatment from the government and were prospering. Many kept decrepit huts in the camps in order to continue collecting rations but had managed to buy houses in the towns. In some cases the camps were in better shape than the towns.

Around Somalia, refugees were getting government jobs. They were joining the army in increasing numbers. In a country ruled by a military government, it meant a tidal shifting of power from the local clan to a group of outsiders who were totally indebted to Siyaad's government for their food and livelihood. Add to that the fact that the Ogaadeen had a clan relationship with the rulers, and Siyaad Barre had a loyal armed cadre firmly entrenched on the land of his enemies.

Throughout the early 1980s, Siyaad Barre had been faced with an uprising by rebels of the Somali Salvation Democratic Front, made up predominantly of members of the Majeerteen clan. The SSDF leader, Colonel Abdullahi Yusuf, was a hero of the Ogaden war who, along with his colleague Mohamed Farah Aydiid, led a failed coup at the end of the war in April 1978. Barre's troops hit back against Abdullahi Yusuf's Majeerteen subclan in the early 1980s, executing hundreds. All of this took place far away from the expatriates, the refugee camps, and the press. Western governments said little to Siyaad Barre, who continued to gather more and more economic and military assistance.

The SSDF operated predominantly out of Ethiopia. Barre couldn't use his own troops across the border, which is why the "rebel" Western Somalia Liberation Front became so important. And since the WSLF was composed of Ogaadeen refugees operating out of refugee camps on the border, the camps were a key strategic consideration.

By the mid-1980s, the aid-fed militias of the WSLF had succeeded in tying down the SSDF (which eventually neutralized itself because of internal squabbles), and the Majeerteen were rehabilitated in the eyes of Siyaad, who figured he could count on them if the government were challenged by the Isaaq or Hawiye clans.

Increasingly, the Isaaq clan in the north became the biggest threat to Siyaad's government. Siyaad had a deep and personal dislike for the clan. The real reasons can only be guessed at, but in part it was due to his inability to control them. As accomplished business operatives, they had built a society that was not dependent on government largesse. The Isaaq had traditional trade relationships with the nations of the Arabian Peninsula that continued despite the attempts of the government to center all economic activity in Mogadishu. Siyaad did what he could, however, and Isaaq traders were forced to make the long trip to Mogadishu for permits and licenses.

In addition, the Isaaq definitely had an "attitude" about the southerners. In part, it came from their disparate colonial experiences. The British-colonized north had a more efficient civil service and better system of education than the Italian south.

In 1981, Isaaq dissidents in London formed a rebel group to overthrow Siyaad Barre. It was called the Somali National Movement (SNM). Like the SSDF, they set up their military bases in Ethiopia, and though they didn't cause any immediate problems for the government, they appeared to be growing into a threat. Barre sent two of his most trusted generals to the north to keep things quiet. As military governor, he sent his son-in-law, Mohamed Hersi "Morgan." Morgan, who was at first referred to simply as the son-in-law, would soon earn a third nickname, the Butcher of Hargeysa. To command the government troops in the area, he sent his cousin, General Mohamed Hashi Gani.

Among other things, Gani directed the refugee-camp-based WSLF in a campaign to terrorize Isaaq civilians and loot food convoys.

As in the south of Somalia, by 1985, the refugee crisis in the north was no longer a refugee crisis. It was status quo. A report from the human rights organization Africa Watch documented some of what was going on. Hargeysa resident Safia Ali Mataan told Africa Watch,

> When refugees from Ethiopia flooded the north, they expressed surprise to find so many Isaaqs living there, as they had been led to believe that the land was more or less empty. . . . [T]he government would appeal to us [Isaaqs] to "help our impoverished countrymen" and we gave extravagantly. . . . They would come to rely on the refugees both as spies and soldiers—at the same time using them to get massive aid from the world.
>
> Everyone who had a business was ordered to hire refugees or to train them for work in the camps. After six months "training," their minimum wage was 1,300 shillings, going up to 3,000, while the average local citizen earned about 500. Every Isaaq in a prominent government job was seconded by a refugee who, after a short while, would take over and be in command. Land in Hargeysa was given to some of them free and we had to buy it back from them.*

It is possible for groups of expatriate aid workers to live and work in places while having not even the smallest clue what is happening to the general population. They rarely speak the language or socialize with the objects of their benevolence, but in the Somali situation it was glaringly obvious that the aid was being manipulated and abused.

The Africa Watch report quotes a Swiss national who worked in a Hargeysa orphanage:

> The refugees in the camps were better off than the local population, which was a great source of tension. The government made a huge profit out of the substantial food and other aid given for the benefit of the refugees. This was resold by the government openly in the markets of Hargeysa, not in the front stalls where foreigners would see too easily "NOT TO BE SOLD" signs. But if you knew your way around the market, you could see all this for yourself. The fact that the government was using the refugees both to get aid and to weaken the Isaaqs politically was a major problem.

Why did CARE and other humanitarian organizations continue to feed the "refugees" when their partner in the project, Somalia's National Refugee Commission, pursued an agenda that created misery? I suspected I knew the answer.

---

*The report, A Government at War With Its Own People, was published in 1989 and provides detailed testimony about government activities in northern Somalia during the 1980s.

Back home after a series of trips to Somalia during 1993, I received a call from a woman who had worked for CARE in New York. She had a few internal documents she wanted to show me. Mostly she was vaguely uncomfortable about CARE, suspecting that their decisions had more to do with business than humanitarianism. Her documents shed little light on the situation in Somalia, but she told me about a memo that a CARE administrator in Somalia had sent back to headquarters sometime in 1984 or 1985. The memo outlined the political situation in Somalia and questioned why CARE was still working there. According to her, the reply was blunt: CARE had a huge contract in Somalia. They couldn't afford to walk away from it.

How much was the contract worth? What were its terms? I called CARE. No, they wouldn't like to show me their contracts. That was the end of that.

As a private charity, CARE is not obligated to disclose the details of where their money comes from or how their funds are spent. Their only obligation is to make available their IRS 990 tax forms, which show aggregate inflows and expenditures. There is little useful information to be gained from such documents. The UN system is even more impenetrable. Only the U.S. government, under the Freedom of Information Act (FOIA), has an obligation to tell me how CARE and other charities spend their money. But CARE's Somalia contracts were with UNHCR, and the National Refugee Commission, not with the U.S. government. And even though a large part of UNHCR's budget was covered by American taxpayers, I had no official channels through which to explore where the money went. There was no way to trace a path of accountability.

No one ever called on CARE to answer for its shipment of food to armed fighters. If the consequences bothered anyone at headquarters, it was never made public. CARE continued to raise money from the public and to collect hundreds of millions in publicly funded contracts without anyone investigating a connection between their projects and the deaths of thousands of people in the Horn of Africa. The organization was, and is, allowed to define its own success. The sad truth is that CARE and other NGOs are never held accountable for their actions. And when U.S. troops went into Somalia in 1992, CARE was right there, collecting millions in new contracts.

At the USAID office in Nairobi in 1994, I asked an administrator who had just overseen a multimillion dollar grant to CARE why the organization continued to get money from the government. "It's because they keep good books," she said. "When we give money to CARE, we always know where it goes."

And that, in reality, is the limit of accountability in the world of development and relief. NGOs are accountable to accountants, not to their individual donors, who have no way of judging the organizations' work, and least of all to the victims, the recipients of their aid, who have no voice and who are expected to look grateful when the cameras are pointed their way.

On my way back to Somalia in the winter of 1994, I made several stops in Europe, including Geneva, headquarters for UNHCR, on the long-shot possibility that I could talk someone into opening the files for me. I had several friends there whom I'd met working and reporting from Africa in the past. Perhaps one of them would help.

My connections got me past the guards and through the front door.

At that time, UNHCR was in the process of moving from their lakeside art deco building to more modern and spacious headquarters. It was obvious why. The organization had been growing wildly in the last decade. The little commission had become a powerhouse UN agency. File cabinets, bookshelves, and copiers spilled out of office doorways into corridors. Desks were crowded into tiny rooms. Inside the offices were secretaries typing documents into word processors and other people running around with stacks of papers in their hands looking busy. "They think they're saving refugees, but they're all just worried about rescuing their careers," my friend Marco commented.

Marco had been with UNHCR for a long time, serving in both Geneva and perhaps a dozen overseas assignments, including Somalia. His cynicism wasn't unique among UN employees. He was just noting the obvious. The UN is as hierarchical a bureaucracy as exists anywhere. UN employees grouse endlessly about salaries, benefits, and their all-important ranking: "This guy is a P-4 and I'm only a P-3, and I've been here for two years longer. It's because his brother-in-law is the assistant deputy minister of finance in Ecuador." That sort of thing. Rank is everything and often has little to do with performance and everything to do with politics.

Marco turned me loose in the corridors, and I found my way to the Somalia desk and asked if it might be possible to see some records going back a few years. The desk officer, a Mexican, said he'd see what he could do and picked up the phone. He flirted a bit with the woman on the other end. I took this to be a good sign. Maybe they'll do each other a favor and I'll be the beneficiary. He asked her about going out to dinner, and seemed pleased with the answer. Then, replacing the receiver on the phone he asked me, "What did you want again?"

"Somalia. Records."

"I don't know. I don't think we have records that far back. I think they're stored in a warehouse somewhere else. I don't know where they are."

"Is there anyone else here who deals with Somalia?"

He sent me down the hall and into an office where a friendly looking man sat at his desk, doing nothing, surrounded by large stacks of paper. The man appeared to be from Asia, somewhere in Indochina I guessed.

"Excuse me. I was looking for some information on Somalia. I was wondering if you could help."

"Of course," he said. "Somalia became independent in 1960, when the former Italian Somaliland merged with the British Protectorate of Somaliland."

I stopped him. That wasn't really what I had in mind. I was looking for archives. Did he know of any? No, he told me. He hadn't been on the job for very long, had never been to Somalia, and was just starting to study the history. He hadn't yet reached the Ogaden war of 1977 or the refugee crisis in the 1980s, and really had no idea where records might be.

I went back to Marco's office and we went to lunch in the cafeteria of the main UN headquarters at the Palais high on a hill overlooking the lake.

The UN was neck deep in its peacemaking role in Somalia at that time. UNHCR was actively working with Somali refugees in Kenya. The entire UN organization had committed huge amounts of resources to various humanitarian projects. Marco and I sat down over our trays of food, and he started to speak about the mess in Somalia, and his colleagues at the UN. "No one here has the courage to say that Aydiid is a criminal. They'll be the first to criticize a Western power, but they're available to accept any kind of crime to stay in a country and show the world they care about starving children." He paused to look around the room full of smartly dressed UN bureaucrats who were eating their lunches and drinking wine. "It is just a big masturbation," Marco said in English heavily spiced with his Italian accent. "UN bureaucrats are people too stupid to get real jobs with their own governments but too powerful to be disposed of. I can't stand them. They should disappear, all of them." Once more he paused. "These are the people who decide the future of Angola and Somalia."

After lunch we went back to the UNHCR offices and started trolling around once again. This time Marco stayed with me. Several more people told me that there weren't any records. Another may or may not have known anything but said he wouldn't help me. There wasn't much else to do, so we wandered around the halls talking. Marco continued to disparage the UN but also seemed resigned to spending the rest of his career there. He was well paid and had a good pension to look forward to. He had maintained a degree of distance from the bureaucracy and thereby kept a grip on his sanity.

We walked past the mailroom, where a young kid was distributing envelopes into rows of pigeonholes. We strolled in, and Marco asked the kid if he knew whom we should contact to get to the UNHCR archives. The kid put down his envelopes and walked to a row of keys dangling from hooks on the wall. He removed a set and walked out the door.

We followed him outside, and walked across the back lawn of the building to a road. Across the road we went into another building and then down a set of stairs into the parking garage. At the back of the garage we passed through another door, and into a corridor and yet another set of stairs. At the bottom of the stairs was a door. The kid fumbled with the keys for a moment. Then the door opened. We were in a tiny room with two more doors. Again he went through the keys and finally popped open the first door.

We walked into a cold room, stacked floor to 20-foot ceiling with files and ledgers. On the files were the names of countries: Cambodia, Angola, Mozambique, Pakistan, Somalia. Jammed between the rows of towering steel shelves were cardboard boxes. I popped open one box and found more files.

Marco immediately became nervous. Suddenly his career became important to him. Maybe we shouldn't be here, he suggested. But I hadn't come all the way to Geneva to find the files and walk away. The kid left us alone in the raw, cold room and I began opening files. Everything was there: every memo and cable, cash disbursements for every shovel and pencil. I told Marco that I'd photocopy the documents I needed and return them to their files (not that I thought anyone would ever actually look at them again). Marco said no. He said he had to go back to work and asked me to promise not to remove anything from that room. I promised. He also asked me not to tell anyone that I knew him if I was caught.

For the next two days I sat on the cold cement floor reading aloud from UNHCR documents into my tape recorder. I never left the room, afraid that I wouldn't get back in. I found a drainpipe to pee in so I wouldn't have to go outside. And in the end, the documents I read told quite a story.

• • •

In one binder I found the CARE contracts. CARE's first-year budget for delivering food in Somalia totaled just over $7 million. This included salaries for fifteen international staff (i.e., Americans and Europeans) budgeted at $822,000, while fifteen local staff members (Somalis) were to be paid $128,000. Commodity monitoring, which was primarily salaries paid to an undisclosed number of Asians, consumed $525,000. CARE also received $432,000 for administration back at headquarters in New York. The following year the total budget went to nearly $9 million, with close to $1 million in expatriate salaries and $660,000 for CARE's administration back in New York.

Included with the budgets were evaluation reports. A report dated 9 April 1985 outlined the objectives of the CARE project as follows: "To continue assuring that adequate relief assistance is channeled to refugees in 36 camps in Somalia. The means for achieving a gradual withdrawal of foreign inputs shall be studied. This implies full financial support to the emergency logistics unit."

Later, the body of the report continued:

Throughout 1984 the refugees continued to be supplied with available relief supplies at camp level. Monitoring of the operation began with the clearance of goods at the port of entry to final distribution to the beneficiaries. Progress toward withdrawal of foreign inputs including expatriate staff were studied but agreed by all signatories of the project sub-agreement to be less of a priority in 1984. The same holds true for the proposed reduction in vehicle repair and fuel handling operations.

The project would continue and the expatriate staff would stay. The "all signatories" refers to UNHCR, Somalia's NRC, and CARE, three groups with a clear vested interest in keeping the money flowing and the project going—albeit for very different reasons. There is no further discussion in the long evaluation report about finding ways to send the refugees back to their normal lives, nor is there any discussion about why the signatories agreed that withdrawal of foreign inputs would be "less of a priority in 1984."

The report calls CARE the "most efficient agency in the Somalia refugee program" and notes that 1,800 national and international staff were employed by the end of 1984.

As it turns out, however, this "evaluation" of the CARE project was written by the CARE branch office in Mogadishu. It was the very people who were collecting that million dollars in salary who decided that phasing out their own jobs wasn't a priority. As I looked through UNHCR's files of evaluation reports, I realized that most of the reports proclaiming CARE's success were "self-evaluations" based on the "branch office's observation of the overall project implementation."

I had a vision of CARE, UNHCR, and NRC, alone in the desert with some Somali refugees and tens of millions of dollars.

There was no mention in any of the documents about repatriation, and of the hundreds of meetings logged that year, none was about ending the project. Everything was about delivering food more efficiently, nothing about ending it altogether. It was as if ELU/CARE was just another business planning for a bright and distant future. Whatever it was, CARE headquarters in New York gladly took its 7.5 percent administrative fee of at least $600,000 a year, on the way to building the largest NGO in the world.

There was all sorts of correspondence, but mostly there were cash requisitions: $10,000 for shovels, $4,000 for office supplies, $8,000 for tarps; money given from UNHCR to the National Refugee Commission adding up to millions and millions of dollars year after year after year. I thought about those refugee camps in Somalia, and I tried to imagine a UN auditor trekking through the huts with a translator who was working for the NSS, trying to ascertain whether all those tarps and blankets and buckets on the requisition forms had ended up in the hands of refugees.

And of course there were far fewer refugees than were actually budgeted for. After several failed attempts at counting the refugees, a number was agreed upon—750,000—although the Somali government and NGOs continued to use numbers from 1 to 2 million, depending on whom they were trying to impress.

Then, as I looked through the files, I found information about the final attempt to count the refugees. It was a letter from a Dr. Murray Watson, on the letterhead of his company, RMR (Resource Management and Research), written on December 20, 1990, a month before the government of Siyaad Barre collapsed. The letter was addressed to the recently appointed UN High Commissioner for Refugees.

> UNHCR has behaved incorrectly in its contractual relationships for political reasons and even now is hiding behind immunity to avoid facing its civil responsibilities to RMR.
>
> UNHCR under the same temptation has, it would seem, the same sort of wish to use the "numbers game" for its own interests as does the Somali gov-

ernment, Oxfam, and the world NGO community as a whole. For understanding why these bodies feel an exaggeration of the magnitude of impending famines etc. is justified, we cannot help but observe that so-called donor fatigue is more than just a reluctance to support the same emergency too frequently. It is also evidence of a growing public perception that there is a well-oiled begging industry which can create dramatic images of suffering and six-figure forecasts of death with considerable skill more or less regardless of the actual situation. Our company is very experienced in getting at the numbers behind the myth, be they elephants, Somali wild ass, or Ogaden refugees. We did indeed, despite continuous interference from the UNHCR branch office, develop an extremely usable methodology for refugee estimation.

Unfortunately no UNHCR personnel who came into contact with the work were able to understand the intricacies of the method, nor did they seem to understand why it was necessary for RMR to treat UNHCR and NRC evenhandedly, providing neither party with special explanations of the implications of the results.

Watson was claiming that he hadn't been paid. His attempt to enumerate the refugees was stopped.

Dr. Murray Watson is one of those big bwana figures who seem to wander into every African quagmire. A consultant based in London and Nairobi, Watson describes himself as an ecologist. He is also a pilot with his own aircraft. In 1978 he began using aerial surveillance to count cattle, elephants, and other large animals. He didn't figure that counting people would be all that different when UNHCR asked for tenders on a contract to "re-enumerate" the refugees. Watson had close connections with Somalia and the Somali government. Some Somalis claim that he informed on Somali dissidents in Nairobi who were later collected by Kenyans and handed over to the Somali NSS. Watson denies it.

The Somali government wanted Watson to get the enumeration contract. The UN wanted to hire I. M. Lewis, the Oxford-based dean of the Somali studies universe. Watson got the job. It was a small contract, $300,000, including money to hire the people and the Land Cruisers. He immediately embarked on a training program for his enumerators. Almost without exception, the people he hired criticized his methods. UNHCR also insisted on having an observer present while he was carrying out his operation. The UN observers agreed with the assessment and cut off his funds before the operation was completed.

Watson, who has been described as both a genius and a kook, rises to his own defense. "No one had the capacity to understand the process, my methodology," he says. According to Watson, his design had to be carried out in secrecy. UNHCR and the NRC were full of leaks. If word of the methodology got out or if their schedule for counting refugees got out, he wouldn't be able to do it. The Somalis, and even the NGOs, would do everything in their power to skew the count. Watson's claim is supported by some of the documents I found in Geneva.

Before Watson and his team started the count, they went to Beledweyne to do some training. The rumor spread that they were going to start counting for real.

Among the papers I found in Geneva was a February 1988 letter from the local UNHCR representative to the NRC commissioner Mohamed Abdi Tarrah:

Dear Mr. Tarrah,

Just a short note to inform you the re-enumeration team has started their two-month training program for interviewers on 11 February in Beledweyne. The following observations have been made:

—Many town refugees have gone back to the camps. It was observed that the main street in Beledweyne was indeed much less crowded, especially in the evening!

—Many refugees are coming back from Mogadishu!

—ELU/CARE ration trucks which usually have passengers on their return to Mogadishu are quite empty these days!

—New houses are being built in the camps!

—Refugee workers in town rush home immediately after working hours! ELU/CARE refugee employees do not come to English class in the evening anymore!

Though the team made it clear that they were here for training only, rumors have gotten around that counting has started. All the inhabitants in the camps have been alerted and those elsewhere have been alerted about the re-enumeration exercise.

The letter reconfirmed that many of the refugees were totally integrated into Somali society. The refugee camps were suburbs. People had jobs and businesses. The refugee supplies were subsidies, yet the NGOs and CARE continued to raise money to feed them.

Watson's method involved aerial photography combined with surprise raids on camps by his team of enumerators, who would take attendance in the refugee huts. Sometimes those raids were to take place at three or four in the morning. If a child was missing from a home at three in the after-noon, a mother could have any number of excuses. If that same child was also missing at three in the morning, the child either didn't live in the camp or didn't exist.

"You couldn't just look at refugees and accuse them of lying, but if the child was missing on both visits and they couldn't come up with a thesis, then I would know that they were lying."

Watson recalls that he had been warned by a UNHCR confidante in Geneva that he was "in for a rocky ride." UNHCR no longer wanted or needed this count by early 1988. Someone would have to pull the plug on the refugee programs no matter what kind of numbers Watson came up with. UNHCR was having its vehicles stolen at a regular rate—in the north, the SNM was stealing them to be made into technicals*; in the south, bandits and soldiers were looting them. UNHCR had begun to re-gard its personnel as hostages. Civil authority in the country was beginning to break down.

Watson also accuses ELU/CARE of getting in the way of a count. They refused to service UNHCR vehicles that he was using for the survey. "When the thing had broken down, they had actually refused to provide fuel," he said. In addition, the UN observers who accompanied Watson's teams criticized his methodology. "They wanted to sabotage any possibility I'd come up with the real numbers. They wanted to discredit the survey, degrading the role of objective science. These are things on which I cannot compromise."

Watson says that it was during the training exercise in Beledweyne that he realized things were not going to work out. "This is when I realized how dishonest and incompetent UNHCR was. They'd been working in Soma-lia in this crazy operation for a long time and were not objective. I was as-tonished by the lack of honor and their cynicism. They thought everything Somalis did was devious, sinister, and wrong."

"One UNHCR observer submitted a report on my method—which was not her job. It was her job to determine if procedures were being carried

---

*The use of the term "technical" for improvised battlewagons began in northern Somalia in the early 1980s. The Somali National Movement (SNM) had gotten their hands on some heavy ar-tillery but needed to make them mobile. Some engineers in the region had been trained by the Soviet arms manufacturer Tekniko, and they undertook the task of mounting the weapons on Land Cruisers. Early attempts failed, often leading to the destruction of the vehicles themselves. Once they'd worked out the engineering, the vehicles became known as Tekniko vehicles, which quickly became anglicized to "technicals."

out, to see if I was performing as a contractor, not a scientist. None of them was qualified to understand methodology."

Watson, for example, developed a language key so he could show the refugees pictures of a chicken, and, based on their pronunciation, determine where the refugee originated from. The UNHCR observer didn't approve. "This Japanese lady produced a report saying Dr. Watson was trying to find out where refugees are coming from. A better way would be to have a questionnaire about local names of commissioners and towns, et cetera. I responded: 'Do you know how much it would cost to produce that kind of database? And it would take all day to do that part of the survey. I have to develop something so we can interview a thousand refugees in an afternoon.' That was the sort of argument I was getting into."

Watson says that his initial data showed that the actual numbers were 40 to 50 percent of the number of refugees officially on the books. Of UNHCR he says, "They're the most unpleasant, dishonest people I ever met in my life. Dealing with them was worse than the money I lost on the project."

The real reason the UN ditched Watson may be found in this memo sent to Rome by Robert C. Chase, the UN World Food Program's operations director in Somalia, on January 12, 1989:

> Reenumeration . . . finally commenced, but the results are not expected until Spring this year. They are in any case not likely to be impartial since the north of the country has been affected by civil war and access to refugee camps has been impossible since June. In any case, UNHCR, who have been monitoring the progress of the survey, are not at all convinced that the methodology finally applied guarantees reliability of the final result. Doubts about the numbers will persist. . . .
>
> However, looking at events in 1988 . . . UNHCR feel the reenumeration will be less significant because there is no further reason for the refugees to remain in Somalia. WFP agrees with their views.
>
> There are many duplicate ration cards and there is reason to believe that the numbers of beneficiaries on the ration cards have been exaggerated. Judging by the extent to which sales of donated food took place, it was equally obvious that food was being received by beneficiaries in excess of their basic requirements. As a result, it was accepted that the most painless method of reduction of food supplies, and therefore passing across the message that international relief is coming to an end, would be to reduce the quantities of food supplied to the refugees.

That would be much easier said than done. In 1988, following the government assault on Hargeysa—one UN memo called it a genocide—the

UN knew the end was near. The programs would have to be ended before the government of Siyaad Barre was ended. The problem was how to get out of the refugee situation gracefully before the government collapsed, and how to get out without upsetting the armed refugees who were being fed. A blizzard of cable traffic followed between Somalia and UNHCR headquarters, as well as between Somalia and WFP headquarters in Rome. The UN wanted out but didn't have the courage to walk away.

According to Murray Watson, the NGOs agreed to shut down the refugee programs in the late 1980s for one reason: "The refugees ceased to attract funds. The event lost the power to pull in money. NGOs trade in the guilt industry. They could no longer sell hungry people."

On October 6, 1988, Jean Pierre Hocke, the UN High Commissioner for Refugees, sent the following trial balloon in the direction of Dr. Mohamed Ali Hamud, minister of state for foreign affairs of the Somalia Democratic Republic:

> The circumstances that caused the great majority of the refugees to flee no longer prevail. Their home areas are at peace and there have been other positive changes affecting their situation. For some time refugees have been returning to Ethiopia both spontaneously and in limited numbers with UNHCR's assistance. Thus, as a first stage in phasing out relief assistance, food supply in excess of the real individual needs must be eliminated. This is a precondition for durable solutions. For to make the phasing out of relief assistance conditional on attaining such solutions would be in effect to continue to offer the third option, open-ended relief assistance.
>
> With our colleagues in the world food program, we have been examining various ways of reducing the amount of food now supplied. As is to be expected after providing free food for so long, this will not be easy, but we believe that a progressive reduction in the maximum number of beneficiaries per ration card is the most viable approach.

On the same day, Hocke wrote a confidential memo to his staff in Mogadishu:

> It seems the erroneous belief that there is a third option is influencing many refugees. Their belief that international relief assistance can and will continue as it has in the past is unfortunate. As a matter of principle, the international community's responsibilities have changed with the refugees' changed circumstances. Furthermore, the international community's priorities for humanitarian relief assistance do not include the indefinite maintenance of dependent cases, as in the circumstances I have described above. It

is for these reasons that we plan to phase out relief assistance to Somalia by the middle of 1990.

A month later, Dr. Mohamed Ali Hamud replied to Hocke: "If UNHCR inexorably phases out relief assistance to Somali refugees by 1990, regardless of whether durable solutions are achieved or not, we will consider it as a clear violation of the mandate of the high commissioner's office. . . . The potential implications of such a hasty assistance pull-out, given the magnitude of the refugee case load, should not be underestimated."

Whatever those potential implications were, the UN interpreted this as more of a threat than a warning. The letter marked the beginning of a Somali government campaign to thwart any efforts to shut down the refugee programs and to keep the relief coming even as their government was collapsing under rebel assault. The United States and other Western donors had begun to drastically reduce economic and military aid to the Barre regime. The refugee inflows were more important than ever for the government as a source of revenue and, more immediately, as a slush fund so Siyaad could keep his army fed and his most loyal allies happy.

The UN was scared. Aid workers were stuck between the rebels and the government. On the one hand, the Somali government was slipping toward collapse. Siyaad felt abandoned by the international community, represented by the UN and the aid workers. He was also losing control of his troops, who began to attack the aid workers and to loot their homes and vehicles. At the same time, the rebels of the Isaaq-based SNM in the north and the Hawiye-based USC in the south were both aware that the aid projects had been supporting their enemies in the government. The aid community now wanted out. For the first time, there was a concerted effort from the UN and the NGOs to *solve* the refugee problem. They came up with a term for what it was they were now trying to achieve: Durable Solutions.

On the surface, they were trying to solve the problems of the refugees. In reality, the problem they were trying to solve was their own.

Around this time, NRC commissioner Tarrah wrote to UNHCR agreeing that "the time has come to tackle this problem head on." According to Tarrah, this would require an "increased resource allocation." More money—one last infusion of cash before the whole mess came tumbling down. Mohamed Abdi Tarrah, an Ogaadeen himself, had gotten rich from his eight years at the helm of the NRC. He was a realist, one of the few in Siyaad's inner circle who wasn't in denial about where the rebellion was leading. And he was one of the few who hadn't invested his wealth outside the country. Tarrah's money was in Somalia. If the country collapsed, he'd end up broke.

At the same time, Siyaad's emissaries in New York were busy trying to keep the gravy train on track. In January 1989, the head of Somalia's UN delegation, Ambassador Abdillahi Sayeed Osman, wrote UN Secretary General Javier Pérez de Cuéllar:

> Excellency, I am directed to write to you on a subject of paramount importance and concern to my government. It relates to the fate and destiny of more than a million refugees whose future happens to be in serious danger in view of the untimely plan of the UN High Commissioner for Refugees to terminate relief assistance to refugees by the year 1991.

Later, in February 1989, Somali Prime Minister Mohamed Ali Samatar would visit Pérez de Cuéllar in New York and plead on behalf of the poor refugees. Pérez de Cuéllar took notes at the meeting and reported, "The prime minister explained that while Somalia supported Durable Solutions through voluntary repatriation, he felt that in view of the large number of refugees involved, there was a need to ascertain their wishes." Samatar then presented the secretary general with the government's five-year plan for dealing with the refugees.

The cables that flew back and forth between UN agencies in Mogadishu and their headquarters in Europe are stark testimony to the failure of the Somali refugee circus. The memos acknowledged that the UN was going to have to bribe the remaining refugees to leave Somalia so they themselves could then leave with as little blood on their hands as possible. Arrangements were made to *purchase* ration cards from the refugees, but the operation had to be kept as confidential as a Wall Street leveraged buyout, and for the same reasons. If word leaked out that the UN was going to buy back ration cards, speculators would start buying them up. In fact, ration cards were traded and sold on the open market like stock options, their price rising and falling with perceived odds that the relief programs would continue.

At the end of 1988, the Mogadishu UNHCR office figured it was going to cost $93 million to buy off the refugees. The program would take two years. Yet another cable to Geneva reiterated the problems, as if they were just being discovered for the first time.

> There are many indications that many refugees have quietly returned to Ethiopia over the years to resume nomadic activity, while others have joined the military or moved to towns. At the same time, their family's rations are maintained by other members remaining behind in the camps.

There is no reason for the camp dwellers to decide to change the status quo as long as assistance continues in the camps. Many of the Ogaadeen who are nomadic and unlike some other refugee groups do not have a strong sense of home or place which we would count on to prompt repatriation whenever possible.

Many Somalis who have never lived on the Ethiopian side of the border have acquired ration cards over the years, and a kind of artificial economy has sprung up around the camps dependent on imported food and other assistance to refugees.

The people who read this memo from Mogadishu in 1988 must have had a sense of déjà vu. The problems had been noted over and over. This particular memo also anticipated a problem: "Staff in the [Mogadishu] office are convinced that the government will not cooperate with UNHCR and WFP's proposals without heavy pressure and support from the donors. (Not only to provide the funds but to spend them in the manner planned!) As shown in the draft, we believe that the [high commissioner] should consult the key donors . . . and ask donors to write letters to the government endorsing as specifically as possible the approach we intend to take." The tone of this and other memos on the same subject were filled with fear. As Murray Watson had said, UN staff were hostages in Somalia. For years aid workers came and played on the beaches, finished their contracts, and moved on. Now it was ending. It was getting increasingly dangerous—and no one wanted to be the last one out.

The countries of the Horn of Africa had a long-standing tradition of sheltering rebel groups trying to overthrow neighboring governments. In that spirit, Sudan helped out the Eritrean People's Liberation Front (EPLF) and the Tigrean People's Liberation Front (TPLF), which were trying to overthrow the Mengistu regime in Ethiopia. The Ethiopians returned the favor by supplying and sheltering the Sudan People's Liberation Army (SPLA) fighting the Sudanese government. The Ethiopians backed the Somali Salvation Democratic Front (SSDF) and later the Isaaq-based SNM trying to overthrow Siyaad Barre in Somalia, and Siyaad helped out the Oromo Liberation Front and the Western Somalia Liberation Front (WSLF) in their fights against Ethiopia. This is risky business for the liberation groups, as the SNM found when in April of 1988, Mengistu, whose government was on the verge of collapse, agreed with Siyaad Barre to stop backing rebel groups. The SNM was suddenly homeless, and as they were forced back into Somalia, they weren't about to give up their arms. They came home fighting. Suddenly the Ogaadeen refugees in Somalia, many of whom had assisted the government in its campaign against the Isaaq, figured it might be best to get out, go back to Ethiopia.

On January 16, 1989, the World Food Program representative in Somalia cabled his headquarters in Rome, apprising them of the situation:

> In the course of 1988, there were a number of important developments with regard to the future of Ethiopian refugees in Somalia. Indeed, long before the 3 April '88 agreement between Ethiopia and Somalia the refugees had shown by spontaneous return, whether temporary or permanent, and, since December 1986, by organized repatriation, that the causes of their original flight were for them no longer significant considerations. There is thus a real prospect for solution to this long-standing problem. To achieve this will require careful negotiation and, of course, cooperation of the parties directly concerned as well as the support of the international community . . .
>
> On 5 October 1988, the high commissioner wrote to the minister of foreign affairs addressing his grave concern over recent events in northwest Somalia as they affected refugees. This letter noted that Ethiopian refugees had been armed and become direct parties in the conflict, thereby ceasing to be refugees. Vehicles and supplies provided as UNHCR assistance had been used for other purposes. International monitoring of the use of assistance is no longer possible and there have been reports of military conscription in refugee camps elsewhere in the country. The high commissioner stated that in these circumstances UNHCR should only continue to assist those refugees who had taken no part in the conflict, and requested the minister's assistance in reestablishing the conditions necessary for the discharge of the UNHCR's responsibilities. No reply has been received to date.
>
> Meanwhile the limited information available from independent sources suggests that the situation has deteriorated further. Refugee camps that had been armed have been attacked by the other party to the conflict with loss of life. On 23 October 1988, the high commissioner addressed a second letter on the subject to the minister and a letter to the Somali Permanent Mission in Geneva on 28 December 1988. In the letter the commissioner stated that he agreed with executives of WFP that in present circumstances UNHCR and WFP were able to assist only those refugees who have not become party to the conflict and to whom access was possible.
>
> Please treat this cable with great discretion.

In the scramble to put things in perspective, the World Food Program also felt it necessary to get real about a number of issues, among them the

CARE food delivery system. The rosy reports of food delivery in the years preceding the chaos did not square with reality in Somalia. Food was everywhere. If CARE was actually delivering on their now $8 million contract, why was so much refugee food still turning up in markets, still in original bags, as far away as Addis Ababa, Ethiopia?* This was not food bartered by refugees. A WFP memo of June 12, 1990, coolly states that CARE was "routinely underestimating losses."

On June 12, 1990, the UNHCR representative, after reviewing some material, placed a hand-written note into the file:

> These documents indicate a very depressing state of affairs regarding receipt, transport, storage and delivery of food in Somalia. I'm most surprised by the losses and their size, which seems to be the responsibility of CARE. If indeed as WFP indicates this is a major reason for reduced rations for refugees in April, it is not an acceptable situation. I wonder why UNHCR has not expressed its concern to CARE about this as we pay for the people who would appear to be stealing. After all, ELU/CARE exists precisely to avoid losses and diversions. . . . Given all of this plus the sheer physical danger of working in Somalia, it would really not surprise me if WFP would not only wish to stop all operations in the northwest but in the south as well.

The note was attached to a casualty report indicating that during the period of April–July 1989, nine ELU/CARE local staff lost their lives and several others were wounded in Somalia. Yet CARE continued its operations, continued collecting its money to carry out a program that was clearly not benefiting anyone. Document after document said that the entire operation was a wasteful fraud. I'd sat on a cold cement floor for two days searching through thousands of papers, and not one of them was a positive independent report about people's lives being saved or of children being provided with a brighter future. Every document and confidential memo over a nine-year period concerned the politics of the relief operation, showing that everyone involved at every level knew it was a politically driven fiasco pushing Somalia to the edge of anarchy.

Yet through all of this, the UN agencies, CARE, and other NGOs stayed in Somalia. They stayed for the contracts. They stayed for the money. They were, in every sense of the word, mercenaries.

---

*The skills I had developed as a food monitor for USAID served me well in subsequent years as a journalist. I retained an eye for spotting U.S.-donated commodities in markets and the connections to trace the lot numbers on bags to find out for which programs the food had been intended.

8

SELLING THE CHILDREN

As communities often receive a small portion of the sponsor's contributed dollar, they are obviously going to ask questions about where the money goes. All the explaining in the world would not make this question go away or our own strategy look good in an investigative report.

—Charles MacCormack,
Save the Children
Confidential memo, 1993

Through the Freedom of Information Act, I was able to come up with several USAID evaluation reports of the Save the Children project in Qorioley. They didn't say much but generally indicated that an evaluation team dropped in on the project for an afternoon and then returned to Mogadishu the same day. The evaluations were completed, and the projects declared satisfactory, all in a few hours. There was no way the evaluators could have seen much of the project let alone studied its long-term impact on the people who were declared to be "beneficiaries."

As CARE evaluated its own projects, so too was Save the Children allowed to make its own reports on Qorioley. Across the board, NGOs make claims about how their activities are helping people where they are working, claims generally disseminated by the fund-raising department. But villages are not laboratories where factors can be isolated to determine how an organization has performed. NGOs tend to take credit for every positive development in a village where they happen to be working. Of course, they don't call anyone's attention to negative trends, or to places where things are deteriorating. And they don't broadcast internal complaints from people like Chris Cassidy.

Nothing that Chris Cassidy ever wrote or said about the project made it into any official report that I reviewed. It was as if he'd never set foot in Qorioley. But I knew Chris had complained loudly and sent letters back to headquarters. Did anyone ever care enough to read them?

When I returned from Somalia to New York 1995, I couldn't help wondering if there might be some correspondence buried in a file box up in Westport that would shed some more light on Chris's experiences.

I knew that Save the Children was under no obligation to show me anything, and that any organization that took such pains to construct its public image wouldn't let me rummage around in their file room. And I wasn't going to be as lucky as I had been in Geneva. But I started making calls, not through their official channels, but to former colleagues of mine who had worked for Save in the past. Through them I was able to locate several people within the organization who were willing to help.

What I got were files and documents predominantly covering Save's programs in the United States, but containing information about how the organization was run and how much time it spent covering up for its blunders. As I read through the papers, I felt guilty. When Cassidy had been relating his horror stories about working for Save I had reacted somewhat skeptically. Now, here in front of me were documents, evidence of massive internal dissent, that confirmed everything he had told me and more.

Most people know Save the Children from its recent print ads, which ask people to "help stop a different kind of child abuse," and from television advertisements that feature former *All in the Family* star Sally Struthers pleading on behalf of poor children who, she explains, are waiting for you to step forward and become a sponsor. Struthers's plaintive voice drifts over horrific images of fly-covered starving children. Then, with the lens tightly focused on one child, she informs the public that all it takes to redeem this child from a life of poverty is $20 a month, 65¢ a day. Your decision right now about whether or not to pick up the phone and take out your credit card will determine if this child lives or dies.

The ads seem to have been on the air for years, though Struthers has only worked for Save the Children since January 1994. Before that, for seventeen years, she delivered a nearly identical plea for Christian Children's Fund, another organization that raises funds through sponsorship. (It appears that much of the public thought Struthers was working for Save the Children all along.) A number of Save the Children staffers, especially those in fund-raising, thought the veteran pitchwoman was past her prime and doubted very much that her residual celebrity would translate to positive numbers on Save's bottom line. "She was delivered to us as a fait accompli," recalls Sally Franz, who used to work for Save as a fund-raiser.

But the move had the support of the senior staff at the organization, including Save's new president, Dr. Charles MacCormack. MacCormack had taken over a year earlier at a time when the organization desperately needed strong leadership, a new direction, and a calming influence.

During the 1980s, the organization had been shaken by the minor scandals about sponsorship that Cassidy had dealt with during his days in Somalia. David Guyer, who led Save through those storms, was a charismatic leader who ran the organization as a benevolent dictator. When Guyer was forced to resign because of AIDS-related illness—he died in 1988—he handed the reins over to James Bausch. Initially, Bausch was immensely popular, in part because he wasn't Guyer.

But Bausch was eventually hounded from office by a vicious staff rebellion waged with innuendo, personal attacks—including anonymous threatening letters to his wife—and leaks to the press about the ostentatious waste of sponsorship funds. Bausch was said to have been an embarrassment to the organization after it was revealed that his salary and benefits added up to more than $300,000 a year.* The leaks became so bad that Bausch came in one day and had all the fax machines disconnected. When Bausch finally left, he took with him a $225,000 severance package that itself became an issue of contention and led to the resignation of at least one board member, writer Michael Dorris, and a lot of bad feelings.†

MacCormack, who had been on Save's board, was brought in as a

---

*In fact, Bausch's salary was comparable to that paid to the heads of many NGOs. Bausch honestly, and perhaps foolishly, reported the total value of his salary and benefits package, while many charitable organizations keep actual salaries low for public-relations purposes, and compensate their top staff with cars, housing allowances, and bonuses that don't show up on public documents.

†Bausch is now the head of the National Charities Information Bureau, which monitors the fund-raising practices and expenditures of U.S. charities. He recuses himself when questions arise about Save the Children.

healer. And with their new leadership, higher visibility, and new celebrity spokeswoman, Save believed that the controversies were behind them, and they could move forward with the business of helping children.

Westport, Connecticut is among the wealthiest towns in America. Its shoreline, by Long Island Sound, is rimmed with multimillion-dollar mansions. Westport's Main Street runs along the Saugatuck River and is lined with upscale boutiques such as Laura Ashley, Brooks Brothers, and Barney's. Over the past fifteen years, it has been transformed from a quiet New England town to a less understated, more New York kind of suburb where, according to the complaints of one Westport native, the wives of big city executives drive the streets in expensive cars speaking on their cellular phones. Save the Children's headquarters sits just across the river from Main Street in a two-story former school building that once housed the Famous Writers' and Famous Artists' Schools. The building is actually three separate structures, awkwardly joined, each built in a different decade from the 1950s through the 1970s. Just beyond the reception area is Save the Children's gift shop, where a variety of Third World crafts are sold.

At first glance, one might think the trinkets are part of an income-generating project for villages where Save works. On closer inspection, however, it becomes obvious that the goods are fairly generic, nothing that can't be found in gift shops that line the boulevards in the tourist districts of any city. The charity's more distinctive products are tacked on a bulletin board outside the shop's entrance. Little red-and-white folders resembling greeting cards contain photos and thumbnail descriptions of children. Each bears the Save the Children corporate icon, a Gumby-like cutout of a child with its hands raised; employees refer to the symbol as Red Baby Jesus, or just RBJ. Below the folders a hastily hand-written sign reads: CHOOSE A CHILD. INQUIRE AT DESK.

This combination of generic Third Worldness, corporate imagery, and the sad faces of distant but real human beings sums up the charity's peculiar appeal. Its goals are satisfyingly broad—simply "the children"—yet achingly specific: Each sponsor receives, so to speak, a child. The sponsor can track the child's transformation with cards and letters from the child and through progress reports from Save the Children. The organization pioneered this fund-raising technique with Appalachian children in the 1930s. It has since been adopted by dozens of other charities around the world. (World Vision, Children Incorporated, Childreach, Plan International, and others also use sponsorship.) As a way to raise money, it is unparalleled. Sponsorship links the donor directly to a needy sad-eyed target of the charity's work, rather than to a faceless fund-raiser at the end of a solicitation letter. The charity's bureaucracy becomes invisible. The sponsor feels connected to an actual person and will believe that his or her money, or most of it, will be going to help that child.

But sponsorship is not always what it appears to be. In this case, the sponsor is seduced into believing the improbable because his or her judgment is clouded by the possibility of getting something valuable on the cheap. What sponsors are really buying is, as stated in Save's brochures, a sense of well-being and "deep satisfaction." That's a real bargain at $20 a month, but it doesn't leave much for the children. The pitch, so appealing to donors, seems absurd when one is in the field confronting the challenges of economic development. And it puts Save in a bind: If they ignore some of the sponsored children, they can do more effective work for the others. If they try to do something for everyone, they run the risk of accomplishing nothing at all. Its commitment to sponsors clashes with its promise to save the children.

Despite the string of controversies that have dogged it, Save the Children enjoys one of the best reputations in the charity business. As it announces in its own advertising, "Today, Save the Children is one of the most respected relief and development organizations in the world." That is certainly true. *Money* magazine, in its annual ranking of charities, recently rated it third among relief and development charities and noted that 82.1 percent of its expenditures were used for "program services." According to Save's tax forms for the 1994 fiscal year, that number is up to 82.9 percent. The newer numbers show nearly $80.5 million going to "programs," from total revenues of over $97 million collected from more than 100,000 sponsors.

Every year, Save prints a pie chart divided into three slices. The two little slices always represent fund-raising and management, the big slice, always more than 80 percent, is "Program Services." The pie chart is packed into all of Save's promotional mailings and proudly displayed in all the pamphlets hanging from the bulletin board.

Charlie MacCormack is proud of that pie chart and of the sponsorship program, which he regards as the real strength of Save the Children. Sponsors are not driven, he said, by the "crisis *du jour.*" Instead, they become interested in the child. "If they're supporting a child in activity in Bangladesh, they're gonna stay for ten, twelve, fourteen years whether Bangladesh is in the newspapers or not." This solves one of the biggest problems relief and development organizations face: If they start raising money for a calamity in Rwanda or Somalia, by the time the funds are gathered and dispersed, the worst of the emergency has usually passed and the organization is sitting with millions of dollars earmarked for one place while a new crisis is forming somewhere else. Sponsorship is a steady and predictable source of operational funds.

MacCormack's office is located on the second floor beside what Save employees call the fishbowl, a conference room with large windows opening up to the river, and a glass inside wall that allows sunlight reflected from the water to fill the wide corridor lined with Save's executive offices. From his sparsely furnished office, MacCormack can see the back side of shops along Westport's main street and watch the water rise and fall with the tide.

MacCormack is in his mid-fifties with gray hair and mustache, rosy cheeks, and a round face. He speaks clearly and quietly in calm tones. When he talks about the children, a thin smile breaks across his face and his voice radiates warmth. "The goal of Save the Children," MacCormack began, "is making better lives for children." What followed was a well-rehearsed recitation of good works and lofty aspirations, but nothing much more specific or quantitative than "making better lives for children."

When pressed for more concrete details, MacCormack's relaxed confidence wavered somewhat and then became completely shaken when I began to ask questions about Save the Children's financing, questions about the pie chart. It is the deception inherent in the pie chart that provides the key to unraveling the deception that is Save the Children.

The pie chart is misleading in two ways: First, it tracks the proportion of all *expenditures* that go to programs, not the proportion of all *donations*. The distinction is probably lost on potential sponsors, who might naturally assume that the pie chart is a representation of how their donations are being spent. But most of Save's funding comes not from individual sponsors but from U.S. government and United Nations project grants. Expenditures are nearly three times donations, so even if Save spent none of the sponsors' money on programs, they could still find a way to claim that 75 percent of the money they spend is going to program services. The pie chart really says nothing about how sponsors' money is spent.

The second misleading thing is that neither the pie chart nor the pamphlet explains exactly what "program services" are. The reason Save the Children and *Money* emphasize the program services statistic is, presumably, that it is seen as a rough approximation for money that actually helps people, as opposed to funds spent on overhead and fund-raising expenses. Program services, one would assume, is what should go to the children in the folders. Why else trot out the statistic to use for rankings and as pie charts in promotional literature?

But Save's idea of programs is probably broader than that of its sponsors. In fiscal 1994, it included nearly $4.5 million for travel, $3.5 million for supplies, $15.5 million for salaries, and $2.2 million for rents. Save's non-public financial statements show that film, holiday cards for sponsors, the gift shop, and the craft catalog were also charged to program expenses. The total of the sponsors' dollars that actually went in grants to field programs was $45.1 million, less than 50 percent. In turn, just over half of that money was given in grants to other organizations to actually implement projects. Those organizations presumably have their own salaries and administrative expenses to pay as well. None of that is reflected in Save's official representations.

Over the last few years, the pie chart has been more than an illustration used in Save the Children's advertising. It has been a contentious issue within the organization. In 1994, Save's general counsel convinced the organization to remove it from print ads because it put them in violation of solicitation laws. Beyond that, a number of Save staffers and employees have begun to suspect that the organization is more concerned with keeping the proportions of the pie chart intact than with actually helping children.

I asked MacCormack how he thought sponsors might interpret the organization's statements about the amounts of money going to programs. "When they see that on average 82 percent goes to programming, well, they think that's great," he said. "They think that's what it ought to be."

"Do you think they understand that the program includes rents and salaries?"

"Well, first, I mean, 82 percent is going to the program, on average, of all . . . of the hundred million that comes in here . . . 82 million goes to the program . . . but then if you look at everything that goes in and everything that goes out, 82.7 million goes to . . . to the program. So that is, that's correct." MacCormack seemed to have expected the question, while at the same time he acted as if he were puzzled by it. This was the reaction of all the Save executives I spoke with that day: It was as if no one had ever been thickheaded enough to raise that issue before.

But that specific question had come up frequently, from people within and outside the organization. And MacCormack himself had been concerned enough about the deception to raise it in a letter to Save the Children's board of directors. In fact, there are hundreds of pages of reports and memos from within Save the Children revealing that its top executives have long been aware that the organization is not delivering on its promises.

A year before I'd met with MacCormack, an internal report by a Save the Children consultant had specifically examined the question of how sponsors' money was being spent. The consultant, Shelby Miller, is a recognized authority in the field of early childhood development, and someone with much more than an outsider's view of Save the Children. For six years she had been a program officer for the Ford Foundation, supervising grants made to Save. When we met early one morning at a Manhattan diner, she prefaced our discussion by telling me that she'd only agreed to talk because Save had done nothing to address the problems she'd found a year earlier despite the fact that she made a series of detailed recommendations for improving Save's programs.

Her criticisms fell into two broad and related categories, developmental and operational.

Discussing Save the Children's operations, Miller's report says the actual amount and proportion of each sponsorship dollar that reached the children is "woefully inadequate." While sponsorship is an effective tool for raising money, it requires a tremendous amount of administration to track all the individual children, which Miller pointed out in her report: "Typically, there is little or no relationship between those arranging sponsorship and those administering services. However, a huge amount of staff and volunteer time is devoted to the maintenance of sponsorship." In our conversation, Miller described this as a chasm between what sponsorship means to donors and what it means to the children and their communities. "The chasm has a big price tag. On the sponsor side, you're sold the concept that for $20 a month or whatever it costs, we're going to transform this kid's life through all these kinds of strategies—or whatever it is they put in the ads. On the sponsored family side, it's sold as whatever it takes to sign them up; but it's a much more minimalist promise."

On the developmental side, she said that Save lacked "a commonly accepted and understood theoretical perspective" on which to carry on and evaluate its own work. It's not enough to just say you're helping children. Childhood development is a science, Miller explained. There's no room for a sentimental, *noblesse oblige*, pity-the-poor approach to the work. "Programs must be carried out over long periods with demonstrations and models and constant analysis to find out what works. Then the programs must be focused. Few of Save's projects fit these criteria. It's because of a lack of commitment. Save has no detailed objectives, no strategy. It's a freeing experience if you can commit to a strategy. If you know what to do, you don't waste time and money. Then you can commit 80 to 90 percent of your time on what you want to achieve." The bottom line is this: Save the Children's projects don't work.

Miller's anger with the organization is not over the duping of sponsors but from two kinds of damage she sees the organization doing in the field of childhood development. First, at a time when funds are in short supply, Save is spending money to create the illusion that it's helping. And second, Save is spreading the idea that it's easy and cheap to change the lives of children. "We know how to help kids," Miller said. "We do. The models and methods are there. The fact is that it costs four to five thousand dollars a year for a preschool intervention. The research has been done. With very few exceptions, Save isn't delivering. Their approach to development work is totally scattershot. The problem with Save is that they're wasting resources and goodwill, and they're doing it in the name of children." Miller's annoyance grew as she spoke.

She concluded our first conversation with the suggestion that maybe Save the Children should just liquidate all its assets and make a block grant to another agency that is doing some good somewhere.

When I raised Miller's report in my meeting with MacCormack, he briefly stared out the window. His face grew red and then he said, "I haven't read it, so I can't say there but certainly, the sort of the arguments are, that you can't get enough out into the communities . . . I don't know whether she makes this argument or not, but you can't get the development results, you know . . . And if that's what's said, then that I wouldn't agree with."

Whether or not he had actually read a report that his organization had spent $15,000 to produce, MacCormack did know what I was talking about. It was an issue that had been repeatedly brought to his attention by Save the Children's in-house attorney and at least once by the organization's outside auditor.

And MacCormack himself, in the spring of 1993, was extremely worried about the amount of money that the organization was able to deliver to projects. At that time he visited Christian Children's Fund at their headquarters in Richmond, Virginia. MacCormack was in familiar company there because CCF now employs a group of former Save the Children staffers, including at that time its president, Paul McCleary. The purpose of the trip was to do some fact-finding and compare notes. When Mac-

Cormack returned to Westport, he wrote a concerned memo to the board of directors.

It began with the usual self-congratulations: "Save the Children takes justifiable pride in the fact that between 80–85 percent of our income goes to program services." Then the tone quickly shifts as it focuses on the central problem that has long haunted the organization: "However, this is an average figure. It masks the fact that some of our income streams go 100% to program. . . . For example, our food aid is 100% program and our public funding from the U.S. government and the United Nations probably averages 90% to program. This means that, on average, a much smaller percent of our private revenues are allocated to programs," he wrote. In other words, 80 percent of a sponsor's contribution does not go to program expenses, even under the organization's broad definition of what program services are.

As the memo continues, MacCormack eases his own concerns by invoking the magic word *leverage*: "In general, we use these private funds to leverage other sources of funding, thus achieving a multiplier effect on terms of our private donations." This concept of leverage was raised in every conversation I had at Save the Children. What it means is that Save receives grants, mostly from the U.S. government, that it must use in very specific ways on specific projects. These are restricted funds. Even though a sponsor donates money to Save the Children with a specific child in mind, sponsorship funds are really the only unrestricted assets Save has. Save has no obligation to spend the money on the sponsor's child, in that child's village, or on projects at all. Save, in fact, uses those funds to pay for administering the restricted money it gets from the government. That's leverage.

The relative calm that MacCormack conveyed to the board was missing from a memo written a day earlier to the files: "Our Save the Children 'alumni' at CCF consider our situation 'a disaster waiting to happen,'" he wrote. "As communities often receive a small portion of the sponsor's contributed dollar, they are obviously going to ask questions about where the money goes. All the explaining in the world would not make this question go away or our own strategy look good in an investigative report."

If MacCormack had any concerns about the small amounts of sponsorship money getting to the field, a year later he hadn't done much about it. Shelby Miller produced her damning report in April 1994. On May 6, 1994, Pamela R. Winnick, Save the Children's in-house counsel, returned from a tour of the organization's projects and wrote a memo to the board of directors, revealing:

1. In some of our programs, *no* sponsored children are receiving benefits.
2. Even in our best programs (e.g. Kentucky), only 60% of the sponsored children appear to receive any benefits.

In this memo, Winnick is clearly in MacCormack's camp, worried about Save the Children's public image. She wrote that she was anxious to put Save in a "defensible position in the event of an investigation by a government agency and/or media." But over the next months she would visit more projects and discover that Save the Children's only concern was their image. A series of memos and letters document her growing disillusionment and frustration with Save the Children.

Winnick first sought confidential outside legal advice from Daniel L. Kurtz, an attorney in private practice who had once served as assistant attorney general in the Charities Bureau of the New York State Attorney General's office. Kurtz reviewed Save's fund-raising materials and compared them with the reality of the organization's projects. He sent his opinion to Save: "We believe that the situation at present is likely to constitute a substantial violation of state solicitation laws." Kurtz warned of serious problems for the board and recommended that Save change its advertising, which would solve the problem in the short run, until it could change its programs to more closely approximate the claims being made for how funds were spent.

Winnick apparently tried to coax the organization toward revising those claims. A month later, on June 15, she wrote a memo advising that callers to Save's 800 number be told that "83% of SC's overall expenditures goes to program services," as opposed to 83 percent of *donations*. But if callers insist on knowing more, they should be forwarded to Westport. "Under no circumstances can we make the direct representation that 83% of the sponsorship dollar goes to programs."

In the summer of 1994, Save's outside law firm, Day, Berry & Howard of Hartford, Connecticut, addressed Winnick's concerns. Their assessment was much more measured and diplomatic, but echoed Winnick's opinions.

Thomas J. Groark, Jr., of Day, Berry & Howard also checked with KPMG Peat Marwick, Save's outside auditors. Edward J. Molloy, a partner in the accounting firm, wrote to Groark on June 30, 1994, saying that he had been in contact with Najeeb Halaby, the chairman of Save's board of directors. "I indicated to Mr. Halaby that there was increasing pressure on all non-profit organizations to provide donors with accountability for their donations and in this regard, I saw even more pressure on SC. . . . I expressed my concern on the frequency with which problems kept surfacing.

It was obvious that in many programs a gap existed between what was said and what was done.

"In my mind, the sponsorship program is a very difficult and expensive program to administer and can go wrong very quickly . . ."

Molloy mentions several times in his letter that senior management is aware of the problems and is in the process of correcting them.

On July 7, 1994, Winnick wrote back to the board members: "While I commend Day, Berry & Howard and senior management for concluding that there exist problems with sponsorship, I must, with all due respect, take issue with the implicit conclusion that the problems are being resolved in any significant manner."

She restated the problem: "Even our best U.S. field office, Appalachia, using volunteers and community workers, spends 30% of sponsorship money on actual programs. It does not appear that we will ever exceed that amount in the U.S. In Senior Management Team meetings, the figure of $60–70 per sponsored child (25–30% of the sponsorship dollar) seems to have evolved as the optimal amount.

"According to the analysis prepared by Program Operations, *actual* program delivery in Bridgeport will be $22.82 per sponsored child in FY '94, under 10% of the sponsorship dollars attributable to that site. Further, in that location, a significant proportion of sponsored children will *not* be served by that office."

Winnick writes of the Waltersville Elementary School in Bridgeport, Connecticut, with 400 sponsored children, which should have generated $96,000 in sponsorship donations in that year. "I visited that school on June 8, 1994, and learned that for over two years, no benefits whatsoever have gone to this school. In July 1994 a check in the amount of $10,800 (barely 10% of the aggregate amount attributable to the four hundred children) will be given to the school for an 'academic Olympics,' a writing contest for all 840 children who attend that school. In a city such as Bridgeport, is this an appropriate use of sponsorship money, both qualitatively and quantitatively?"

Winnick continues: "In light of examples such as Bridgeport, our presentation of sponsorship is highly misleading. The Sponsorship Guide, our communication with sponsors, states that '[Y]our sponsored child begins benefiting from your support right away—perhaps through nutritious food and clean drinking water . . . education . . . basic health care . . .' and '[Y]our continued presence in this young life can mean the difference between sickness and health, illiteracy and education,' and that '[o]ver 84 cents of every dollar we raise goes directly to benefit needy girls and boys.'

Television ads featuring Sally Struthers promise that 65 cents a day will bring 'lasting benefits' to communities and 'help rescue one girl or boy.' How does a writing competition 'rescue' a little girl or boy?"

In the same memo, Winnick reminds the board members: "The rules of the Better Business Bureau clearly state that 'at least 50%' of public contributions be spent on the programs and activities described in solicitation, in accordance with donor expectations."

In the fall of 1994, Winnick left Save the Children for "ethical reasons," as she explained in a statement issued through her attorney. "During my tenure, I became concerned, both legally and morally, about their fundraising practices and undertook my own investigation. I presented my findings to Dr. MacCormack and then to the Board of Directors."

Delores Tootsie and Phyllis Wittsel were trying to remember what it was like when they were sponsored children on the Hopi reservation in the 1960s. The sisters didn't recall much. Those were the check-to-child days when Save sent a portion of the sponsor's donation directly to the children. Check-to-child was phased out in the late 1970s and early 1980s. They remember getting $10 every three months or so that they would use to buy a new pair of shoes or some school supplies. Then Phyllis suddenly recalled getting a record of the soundtrack from the movie *Help* from her sponsor, a Beatles fan club, but she can't remember where they were from.

In the spring of 1995, we were having lunch at the tribe-owned restaurant, on the northern Arizona reservation just outside the town of Kykotsmovi, which everyone calls K-Town. The town is a collection of ramshackle buildings and mobile homes on a gentle rise emerging from the Arizona desert. It's just off the main road, not a place where the tourists stop. Road signs direct them past the town to the Hopi cultural center, restaurant, bookstore, and museum. In the middle of the morning, the town was completely silent. The most modern building in town is the two-story tribal council headquarters where Delores works in the personnel department.

The patrons of the restaurant were evenly divided between Hopis and tourists. As it was the only restaurant for miles, the dining room was hectic and loud. Many of the Hopis there seemed to know each other and many worked for the tribe, the only real employer around. The sisters were in their forties, soft-spoken, and well-dressed. Dee was more talkative but more cautious about what she said.

I asked them if sponsorship had changed their lives in any way. They both laughed. But, Dee explained, families whose kids are being sponsored now would rather go back to the check-to-child days. "At least that way they know where the money is going," she said.

Both sisters have worked with Save the Children recently. Dee was a community development coordinator for Save from 1988 until the end of 1992. And although Phyllis doesn't work for Save, her job on her village development committee puts her in charge of Save's project there.

"Westport was never really satisfied," Dee said. "People here wanted funding for cultural type programs. They wanted to hire Hopi people to come and teach about Hopi things. Save wanted more visible projects. They were more interested in Christmas parties and Easter egg hunts. The parties were to serve as enrollment drives as well or as vehicles to gather already sponsored children to update their status for sponsor reports."

Tootsie figures that, on average, Save's project grants were in the area of $1,800 for a year. That would be in a village of some fifty or sixty sponsored children, averaging $35 or less per child per year. (Those same sponsored kids would have generated more than $10,000 a year for Save the Children's administrative costs.) From here the gap between "program expenditures" was very real. While Save the Children might consider its executives' salary to be legitimate program costs, only the sum cash available for projects made much difference here.

Each year the local committees would have to produce a project proposal that Save would choose to either fund or return for changes. Year to year, the projects were unconnected. One year a playground might be built, the next year a summer program might be funded, but then there would be no money to maintain the playground.

"They would start projects that were never completed," Tootsie said. "A greenhouse project was started one year. The greenhouse was built, but there were no funds available to keep it going. It's sitting there unused. There is playground equipment still stored. In my village, there is a foundation for a warehouse that's been there for years."

It was a complaint I'd heard at two other Arizona sites I visited. The Save grants were so small that they would be used for little treats for the kids, not for serious developmental purposes. At the Gila River reservation outside of Phoenix, for example, Jeff Williams, who works for the council there, told me that Save's funds one year covered a couple of weekend trips to a swimming pool in the summer for fifty-six sponsored children.

Williams's Sacaton community was due to be phased out not long after I spoke with him in 1995, but he seemed unconcerned. I asked him if losing Save the Children would hurt the community? Williams shook his head.

"Has Save changed the lives of anyone here?"

"No, nothing has changed."

"Did they ever provide medical care?"

"No."

"Education?"

"No. It's fluff. We're not losing much."

Williams told me I should talk with Christine Thomas, who used to work in Save the Children's Phoenix office as a donor services coordinator, the liaison between sponsors and children. Thomas lives on the Gila River reservation, just past where the air-conditioned shopping mall culture of Phoenix stops and the rural emptiness of the reservation begins. One of her jobs at Save was to open all the mail that passed between sponsors and children, mostly for the protection of the child, but also to prevent kids from asking sponsors for horses and cars and things that might alienate them. She would often send letters back to be rewritten. She also spent a lot of her time driving around delivering packages that sponsors would send to the kids. Shelby Miller referred to this as the Pony Express problem. Because of the vast distances between projects, people from the branch offices could spend ten hours driving just to drop off a small package of clothes.

"We're not benefiting all sponsored children," she said right from the start. "We're not. We never have been." Thomas said that when she went into the field, she found some sponsored kids were nineteen or twenty years old and were raising families of their own. "Some of them—quite a few—don't realize they're being sponsored. And a lot of the children aren't needy. The pressure is on from headquarters: We're given a month to sign up so many children or our budgets will be cut. So we signed up anyone who came through the door. As long as the sponsor doesn't ask, then there's really no problem according to Save the Children." This was also a reaction that Delores Tootsie got when she first went into the communities. Thomas confirmed how little money was actually getting out to the villages. "Save doesn't like the communities asking where the money goes. I know several cases—like Blackwater—where we phased out because communities asked too many questions."

And then some of what little money they had was spent on what many regarded as frivolous activity. According to Thomas and others, communities were told to use some of the available money to celebrate Save the Children's Founder's Day every May. The parties were designed as recruiting tools. "We were told it was mandatory," she said.

Thomas lost her job at the end of March 1995 when the Phoenix office was closed down as a cost-cutting measure. According to Thomas, sponsor notification letters went out on March 24. "We had known since October, but we were instructed not to tell anyone." When communities phoned the Phoenix office to ask questions, they got a recording saying the number had been disconnected. Even as they were making plans to close the office, Save was still recruiting children and was distributing a flyer around Gila River, which read:

SPONSORSHIP

BRINGS

$$$

INTO YOUR COMMUNITY

No one familiar with Save the Children found it surprising that they would still be looking for children while phasing out their programs. Recipients long ago seem to have accepted the fact that there is no connection between program and sponsorship. "What you've got is a system built on the backs of low-income communities," Shelby Miller said. In fact, Save seems to be less of a development agency than a professional fund-raising operation, but with one big difference. No professional fund-raiser could get away with keeping 80 percent of the gross.

Save's rationale for spending most of the money in Westport, for charging executive salaries against "program," is that people in Westport do "programming." But there was little evidence of Save's hand in any of the development projects I saw in Arizona or anywhere else. In Brooklyn's Bedford-Stuyvesant neighborhood, for example, Save was a relatively minor contributor to the Tabernacle Elementary school. The small private school supplied 325 children to Save's sponsors, and Save returned $16,000 a year, about 20 percent of the $78,000 it would have collected. The money was a tiny part of Tabernacle's budget, but it did help to slightly reduce the tuition costs for students' families. Save never did any programming, but they did hang a Red Baby Jesus outside the school, and would often show the school off as an example of its inner city projects. They were, in essence, trading photographs and biographies of their children for a small annual cash allotment.

In all the years that Save has worked on the Hopi reservation, Dee Tootsie can recall much activity aimed at signing up kids but can name only one or two projects that ever did any good. She doesn't remember ever getting any guidance or programmatic assistance from Save the Children, only pressure to sign up more children and keep the reports coming. One of the final insults came in 1992 when the organization turned down projects in eight villages, and the committees failed to come up with any proposals acceptable to Save. According to the rules, if a community can't spend the allocation by the end of the fiscal year, the funds are lost. They can't, for example, wait two years and do a larger project. As time was running out, Save came up with a solution, and in 1992, several hundred children in villages received gift certificates to Wal-Mart for denominations of between $10 and $25. The store was located in Gallup, New Mexico, some ninety miles away. Dee Tootsie typed up the gift certificates and delivered them herself. Then she resigned.

Based on her sister's experience, Phyllis Wittsel wasn't eager to get involved with Save, but thirty-five sponsored children and an ongoing project fell into her lap. In June 1994, they submitted a proposal for a summer program for the kids, designed to keep them away from drugs and other problems that are common on reservations. The community wanted recreation equipment, arts and crafts supplies, and electronic learning games. Because the proposal was submitted late, the Save office in Gallup said it would take a few days to cut the check, but the money never came. The village ran the program anyway, ending it in late July. Two weeks after the program ended, they were contacted by Save, which told them that the money had been converted into a $1,700 credit at that same Wal-Mart in Gallup. They had two days to spend the money or lose the funds. "We couldn't find anything we needed," Wittsel says. "So we called Save and asked if we could spend the money somewhere else and were told no. Get a VCR or a TV, they told us. Save only cared that the money was spent."

Arizona is unquestionably the worst Save the Children has to offer. Its internal documents show that only $21.54 per child reached the field in 1993 out of the $240 donated. But, according to the same document, other regions didn't fare that much better.

Appalachia	$67.22
Bridgeport	25.18
New Mexico	38.59
Southeast	26.05
Southwestern	24.36
Mississippi Delta	44.07

On average, that comes out to $35.29 per child across the United States. (The Appalachian program, which Save considers to be its best, is also its oldest. One of the reasons the numbers look better is that half of the 6,000 sponsored children have two sponsors.)

"Get this," Wittsel said as we were finishing lunch. "A couple of months ago, Save the Children sent us a plaque in a Save the Children tote bag. The plaque read, 'In Appreciation of Excellence,' or something like that. I don't know what it was for. Maybe they thought it was necessary to do *something.*"

Similar stories emerged from Save the Children's overseas programs. One former country director in the Middle East described how, upon starting his new job, he learned that most of the sponsored children in his program were receiving nothing more than Save the Children T-shirts, hats, and invitations to parties. When he eliminated the toys and games, fewer than half the children enrolled in sponsorship programs were receiving anything at all.

"Sponsorship pays for sponsorship," a former director in the West African country of Cameroon said. "In Cameroon, this included two women in Yaounde [the capital] to run the MIS software to track these kids down and keep track of them. Then there was a similar infrastructure in [the city of] Doukoula, where the best trained and most expensive personnel were involved in finding new kids, and tracking down old ones. None of our sponsorship money ever got used for development."

When this particular officer complained to Westport, he was told: It is a $24 million industry! You got a better idea?

"The fact that it was a $24 million industry that paid for itself—and itself only—never seemed to bother anyone, except those of us in the field."

The information for Cameroon was sent to me after I'd published some of my initial findings about Save the Children. It was one of many messages I received beginning with phrases like, "you don't know the half of it." Of all the letters, however, the most detailed and moving came from a Bolivian:

I am a resident of Provincia Inquisivi, Bolivia where Save the Children has wasted money for about seven years.

When Save the Children inaugurated their program there in 1987 or 1988 [there] were some fairly large parties. I was invited to two of them. Community leaders served meals and cocktails. The U.S. Ambassador, his wife and child came to the inauguration in Quime and gave some blankets to the hospital. In turn, the people gave them locally produced gifts.

Save the Children signed up the next door neighbor kid, Maritza. She has six people in her family. Maritza lives in a falling down one-room adobe hut with a grass roof. There is no potable water, electricity or outhouse near her family's hut. Her grandfather recently died of tuberculosis, and I often hear convulsive coughing coming from their house. Maritza's older sister, a teenager, practically died from postpartum fever last year. Like Maritza, many of my neighbor's children signed up for sponsorships with Save the Children. Peace Corps volunteers were used to sign the children up, and take their pictures. In 1993, Maritza wrote a letter to her sponsor, copying it from a worn out practically unusable blackboard at the school. Most, if not all, of the Quime school children replied using the same formula. It's easier to translate 300 letters that all say the same thing.

More than three hundred children signed up in the Quime area. Quime children brought an estimated $72,000 of benefits into Save the Children's coffers per year. That amounts to about $576,000 of benefits over an eight year period. In comparison, the annual budget of city of Quime during those same years was about $5–7000. I estimate that, minus salaries and office expenses, Save the Children spent less than $10,000 of the $576,000 in Quime. A half million dollars in a town of four thousand could have gone a long way to solving the real, primary problems of hunger, disease, shelter and education. What happened to Maritza's sponsorship money?

An addition to the elementary school was added, but I understand from conversations with town leaders, Eriko Herguero and David Argollo, that very little of the financial support came from Save the Children. Save the Children does have a sign painted on it, the local joke is that the only thing they paid for was the sign. The elementary school, at present, has broken windows shuttered against the wind, a few bare electric lights in some of the classrooms, stucco and paint falling onto the cold cement floor, three children to a single desk, not a single poster to liven up the walls, one outdoor unisex bathroom without a water supply for six hundred children, and exceedingly dangerous three-story staircases and balconies. I know because my daughter goes to school there. Nothing at all was done with the 6–12th grade school: steel railings hang loosely over the edge of balconies, the stairs could give way at any moment and the same general conditions as the elementary school apply. Save the Children has relatively elaborate signs painted all over the Province, but if they really wanted to help children they could have used some of the $576,000 to provide materials and hire local people to make the schools in Quime a suitable place to learn.

The pesticide death of three children by a mother using Save the Children–supplied undiluted pesticide to rid her children of head lice is widely believed locally. Early in their program, Save the Children supplied and pushed pesticides. They created a loan program so that farmers could buy imported potato seed, chemical fertilizer and pesticides. For two years afterwards, a blight killed most of the potato crop in the villages near Quime. I can't prove that the blight was brought in with the imported seeds, or if it was a result of fertilizers, pesticides, or an act of God. Many peasants believe the blight came in with the imported seed. Supplying chemical fertilizer made it more difficult to obtain traditional fertilizers from sheep herders in the highlands.

At first, the people in Quime were very hopeful that Save the Children would do something to really help their children. Representatives combed the town and the hillside villages. Remembering the dolls and small checks from the previous program, parents were happy to sign their children up. They were quickly disillusioned. Practically nothing happened to help the children of Quime. Many of the villagers realize this and complain, but I don't think that anyone realizes how badly they've been ripped off, or how utterly paternalistic the philosophy of the organization is.

Knowing firsthand the grinding poverty in rural Bolivia and some good programs exist, I cry in frustration that Save the Children came to our province. As far as I am concerned I would like to sue Save the Children in the name of Provincia Inquisivi children.

Sincerely,
Marko Lewis

When I spoke with Charles MacCormack again, he didn't dispute any of the facts I had, but he insisted that I wasn't telling the whole story. Westport, he said, delivers much more than sponsorship dollars. He offered two examples.

"We are looking at a kind of emergency response, early childhood center kits to jump-start early childhood programs after floods and earthquakes and other natural disasters. And we have learned that what children most need at that time is a reestablishment of continuity, of normalcy. They need to kind of get back into their regular lives. And so we've put a trunk together that has coloring books, crayons, disinfectant, plastic sheets, toys, etc."

At the time MacCormack was talking, the kits didn't exist yet. And when they were put together, most children weren't able to benefit from them anyway. But, beyond that, the emergency kits are exactly the kinds of programs that Save needs for the pie chart. The materials are donated by companies that are able to write off the full wholesale value of the materials. That value then becomes a donation to Save the Children, which can register it as a donation that goes 100 percent to "program" to counterbalance sponsorship funds used for administration.

MacCormack's other "major example," was the "Eyes on the Future" program, which provided eyeglasses on Indian reservations. On the phone, MacCormack told me that sponsorship paid for the program, but later his office sent me a fact sheet that contradicted that claim, noting that eyeglass frames were donated by the ClearVision Optical Company, and tools and materials came from the American Optometry Association and Hilsinger Corporation. The total value put on the in-kind contributions was $500,000. Again, that's 100 percent in and 100 percent out, to beef up the pie chart.

"The Eyes on the Future program was dreadful," said Connie DiLego, who worked for Save the Children as a full-time volunteer on the Navajo reservation in Tuba City, Arizona. "It was just awful. This was a one-time deal, not a commitment to eye care."

DiLego had moved to Tuba City from Massachusetts to do volunteer work with the Navajo. At first she thought Save the Children was the perfect vehicle, but she soon soured on the organization. For her, Eyes on the Future was typical of Save's programs: "We were informed there was going to be an eye exam plus free eyeglasses. They were also supposed to examine the elderly, which I thought was wonderful. When the day came, hundreds of people showed up. I think they were a bit overwhelmed. People were supposed to get glasses within a month or two. We waited well over a year in some cases, and then some glasses came with the wrong prescriptions. They wouldn't mail them to the people directly, so we had to go to Gallup to pick them up."

So many people began calling the Tuba City office that DiLego started handing out the 800 number in Gallup. "You've got a seventy- or eighty-year-old couple calling Gallup, and they're told they have to drive four hours to pick up their glasses. Many of these people don't have cars or can't afford the gas if they do. Then Save said they were going to start charging for the glasses. It seemed that they were making up the rules as they were going along."

DiLego also pointed out that many children had grown or their prescriptions had changed while waiting for their glasses to arrive. And since it wasn't a long-term commitment from Save the Children, there was no telling where the kids were going to get glasses the next year. Children who broke their glasses or outgrew them couldn't count on getting a new pair either.

"It seemed to me that the child didn't matter," DiLego said. "The children were a means to their end. And the end was their pie chart. It didn't matter if Jeffrey Yazzie had shoes or not." In response to a question, DiLego said, "I'm trying to think if there is one kid whose life was changed, who's going to have a better future because of what Save the Children did. No, I honestly can't. I can't name any one person about whom I can say his or her life was changed."

It is "lasting, positive change in the lives of children worldwide" that Save the Children sells to sponsors in ads placed in newspapers and magazines across the country. Those ads always feature photographs of emaciated or disfigured children in the most extreme conditions, not the children that Save usually works with. Almost everyone I spoke with on the reservations felt stigmatized by the ads. "In earlier times, sponsored families in the United States were not that likely to see Save's advertising, because of the absence of television and magazines," Shelby Miller wrote. "Now they do, and some are offended."

Many of the people who have worked with Save, as well as others in the charities community, have been offended as well. Sally Franz, who formerly did fund-raising for Save, was sitting in her office one day in early 1994 when a colleague rushed in to show her the new Save the Children ad from their new advertising agency. The headline read, HELP STOP A DIFFER-ENT KIND OF CHILD ABUSE. It was printed across the bottom of a photograph of a dying and abandoned Sudanese child being observed by a patient and healthy-looking vulture. The ad copy continued: "This abuse is merciless. It preys on innocent, fragile lives and brutalizes them with utter poverty . . . with constant hunger . . . with relentless diseases . . . with no hope for even a basic education." Franz looked at the ad and was horrified, not at the photograph but at Save the Children for using it to raise money. To her and other people in the organization, the irony wasn't very subtle; it was Save the Children that was merciless, preying on inno-cent, fragile lives.

Franz recalls that one of her African colleagues was particularly upset by it, both agreeing, "The message of all our advertising at Save was that Africans are too stupid and ignorant to take care of themselves. And if we don't do it, their parents and their government aren't responsible enough to do it."

In addition, Save wasn't even working in Sudan, where the photograph was shot. And even if they had been working in Sudan, they wouldn't have been providing famine relief. This was a famine caused by war, nothing that a small Save the Children community development project was going to address in the least. No amount of money donated to Save was going to help that child or the thousands of others in the region.

As word spread around the organization, Franz recalls, most of the staffers had the same overwhelmingly negative reaction. MacCormack and the executives, however, were proud of it. "They were very proud of it because they said it was gonna get a great response and it was hard hitting," Franz says.

The ad also managed to annoy the community of relief organizations at large, not exactly known, themselves, for their sensitive portrayal of Africans and other dark-skinned people. Jerry Michaud, the executive director of the End Hunger Network, wrote to MacCormack, calling the ad a "cheap shot," and described it as "hunger porn." "At first I thought it was a Feed the Children ad," Michaud wrote, referring to the Oklahoma City–based organization that is universally despised for their lack of ethics in the charity world.

Michaud wrote that he was reminded of an angry African delegate to a conference who said, "The more desperate our conditions are portrayed in the U.S. media, the more money you American organizations seem to raise for your own overhead and projects." The delegate could have continued and said that the more desperate Africa seems, the less likely it is to get investment and the assistance it really needs to develop.

Michaud also wrote a letter to InterAction, the NGO consortium complaining that the ad violated the "minimum standards for fundraising solicitations."

Soon after the first Save the Children ads appeared, the photographer Kevin Carter was awarded a Pulitzer Prize for his photograph. Save's executives felt exonerated. They called a staff meeting to gloat. "They just thought that was so sharp of them that they picked out this Pulitzer Prize–winning photo," Franz recalls.

One of the executives stood up and said, "Just goes to show ya, you just have to go ahead even when you have criticism." They also announced that there had been a 10 percent increase in phone calls to Save's 800 number since the ad had run. "Nobody talked about the fact that a 10 percent increase in calls didn't mean they were all positive calls. And nobody ever showed me figures that those calls equaled money," Franz said. (Four months after he won the Pulitzer, photographer Kevin Carter committed suicide. Save continues to use his photograph in its ads.)

The impression still lingers that "your" child is receiving your gifts. Shelby Miller pointed this out in her report: "There continues to be some lack of understanding among sponsored children and their families that the funds raised through sponsorship are pooled for community programs. This has been confounded by the following facts: that there have been no activities in some communities, that some sponsors send checks and gifts directly to the child, and that the information given to both sponsors and sponsored children's families is not entirely clear. The sponsor is still 'sold' the concept on the basis of an individual child."

In 1992, as the staff uprising against president James Bausch went into full swing, the *Washington Post* began an investigation of Save the Children, sparked in part by leaks about Bausch's salary, but Bausch and board chairman Dana Ackerly resigned before the article was published. The story was killed as the new chairman, Najeeb Halaby, former director of the FAA and president of PanAm, ascended to the chairmanship.

The possibility of a negative article sent the organization into a panic, leading many Save staff members to conclude that the organization devotes more energy to repairing its image in the press than it does addressing the concerns that have been raised. One of those most bewildered by the organization's strategy was former board member Michael Dorris. On July 22, as the organization was expecting the *Post* article to appear, he wrote to board chairman Dana Ackerly, "We should take responsibility for 'news' about Save the Children, especially if it is potentially damaging, thereby defusing any impression of our being reluctantly 'exposed'. . . . If we've made mistakes, let us admit them and go forward." Dorris was also miffed because he had been asked by Save the Children to talk with the *Post* reporter, writer to writer, to see about getting the story killed.

Three days later, Dorris wrote to the board, protesting the confidential severance package that had been approved for James Bausch. The $225,000 settlement had been approved because Save wanted to avoid the publicity of a potential lawsuit from Bausch, who had grounds to sue for breach of contract. "Having recently seen first-hand the situation in Zimbabwe," Dorris wrote, "I cannot in good faith agree that it's better to avoid embarrassment or the threats of litigation than to pay for the digging of 9000 new wells in a country on the verge of fatal thirst." He said that Save "must be scrupulously honest and forthcoming with financial information; to that end, I urge that a full disclosure of any settlement terms be made public."

Dorris's advice was not taken, and on August 13 he resigned from the board, citing "the non-acknowledgment of past errors of judgment, to a general wariness toward legitimate outside, objective scrutiny of our operation." Dorris also wrote that he was disturbed by "the fact that my mailings from Westport have contained far more information about procedures (i.e., who one may or may not talk to) than the content of our programs."

After ignoring Dorris's advice, Save the Children called James Lukaszewski, a corporate public relations commando hired by companies expecting bad publicity over chemical spills, hazardous-substance exposure, faulty and dangerous products, or nasty labor problems. Lukaszewski, whose high-priced consulting firm is based in White Plains, New York, met with Save the Children executives on September 2, 1992, to discuss the *Washington Post* investigation. Among the materials Lukaszewski was given were the three letters from Dorris.

It was through this maelstrom that Charles MacCormack ascended to Save's presidency in 1992 with the clear intention of making changes. His visits to Christian Children's Fund and other organizations were meant to chart a program for the future, and to learn from the "best practices" of other organizations.

CCF, MacCormack noted in his March 15, 1993, memo to the files, was a much more efficient organization than Save. "They have very lean headquarters staffing. Their entire fundraising staff, producing over $100 million in private funding, is seven. This compares with 36 fundraising and public relations employees at Save the Children (58 if one counts the sponsor servers and sponsor fulfillment employees)."*

MacCormack concluded: "It seems clear that our own sponsorship strategy is flawed from beginning to end. We have to make sure that sponsored children, families and communities have a real stake in the success of our program. As a quid pro quo, we have to make sure that these groups take on much more of the responsibility for administering the sponsorship program at the field level. As a result of this, we can reduce our field office staffing. Finally, we must invest in the systems and the customer service people to make sure that our sponsors know that we are meeting their needs."

MacCormack's conclusion is probably the only one the administrator of a sponsorship agency could reach. Given a choice of how to spend limited resources, the needs of the sponsors must come before the needs of the children. The survival of the organization depends on it. Fewer staff will work in the field. More staff will be in Westport to keep the sponsors happy. Save will become a much more efficient fund-raising machine. But one, as Shelby Miller said, built on the backs of children.

---

*One of the reasons CCF is so efficient is that they don't put a lot of effort into designing development projects. They are, in effect, purely a fund-raising operation that takes a fixed cut for their own overhead. CCF has had its own ethics problems and been the subject of several critical investigations.

MacCormack's memo about Christian Children's Fund reflected the fear that Save the Children was in danger of being left behind in the fast-changing world of development charities, where organizations were becoming more professional, businesslike, and streamlined: "Paul McCleary, the CEO of Christian Children's Fund, envisages that, in the next century, there will be a handful of major worldwide relief and development organizations. These organizations will be looked to by government and international organizations because of their professionalism and their worldwide outreach. He considers CARE, Catholic Relief Services and World Vision to have already reached their critical mass. He intends that Christian Children's Fund will be in this key group."

The pressure is on NGOs to build bigger bureaucracies and improve the proportions on their pie charts, but not necessarily to do better relief and development work; the people working for Save the Children and other organizations in the field feel it. Like Chris Cassidy, they go to the farthest reaches of the globe believing that the organization exists to serve them in their work. They often learn that the opposite is true: They are in the field to fuel the fund-raising machine, to send back the images and information that become the public image of the charity. Their presence in certain places is required to keep the machine working. And oftentimes it appears not to matter that their work is pointless or counterproductive or that their lives are in danger.

9

CREATING DEPENDENCY

[I]f you are really looking for a way for people to lean on you and to be dependent upon you, in terms of their cooperation with you, it seems to me that food dependence would be terrific.

—Senator Hubert H. Humphrey, 1957

In early March of 1991, just over a month after Siyaad Barre and the remains of his army fled Mogadishu, some 700 Somalis of the Daarood clan crammed into a 60-foot wooden dhow in Kismaayo and set out on a 250-mile journey toward what they thought was safety in Kenya. Some of the refugees had paid as much as $500, an entire life's savings, to board the broken-down boat. Among them were low-level government officials and professionals with their families, men not near enough to power to have stolen large amounts of money, yet too close to escape the vengeance of the surging armies of the revolution. There was one passenger on board who didn't fit this description, Yusuf Abdi Shirdon.

Shirdon had been involved in Somalia's refugee program at the highest levels. Without much effort, he could have taken the food-aid route to riches and a smooth escape from Somalia. By March, most of his former colleagues, and many of his subordinates, were living in luxury hotels in Nairobi and staking out tables at the city's best restaurants. But Shirdon never took any money. As a result, he was forced to scramble for space on a crowded boat headed for disaster off the Kenyan coast. When the dhow hit a sandbar and began to sink near the town of Malindi, the refugees panicked.

A report by Jane Perlez of the *New York Times* described what happened: "Antonio Carbone, a diving instructor at a beachfront hotel [in Malindi] who was the first to reach the dhow, described a scene of bedlam as people . . . screamed for help in the darkness. He said he feared his small outboard boat would be overcome with refugees jumping onto it if he got too close. Instead, he threw a rope, rescuing 8 and then 28 people on two trips. He screamed at people, urging them to try to swim 60 yards to a sandbar, from which they could walk to shore."

Nearly 200 people died in the panic, mostly women and children, who were drowned as men flailed past them toward the shore. People who knew Shirdon guessed that he would have stayed to help as many of the women and children as possible. Shirdon was one of the few men among the dead buried in a mass grave in Kenya.

Between 1993 and 1995, I traveled between Kenya and Somalia looking for people who could tell me something about the abuses of aid in Somalia during the 1980s. Shirdon was the person with whom I most would have wanted to speak. He knew everything about the refugee programs and, most important, he wasn't afraid to talk about it, even when Barre and his secret police ruled Somalia. I looked for other people who had worked with refugees in the hope that with the Barre era over, the people involved in his government would be willing to speak honestly about what they had seen and done.

Early in the process, and quite by chance, I met up with Mohamed Abdi Tarrah, former head of the National Refugee Commission. Tarrah frequented one Nairobi café where former government officials of the Daarood clan met every afternoon for tea and pastry and to exchange news about the anarchy in Somalia. They nodded knowingly at each other as reports about battles among the factions of the rival Hawiye clan arrived every day. The continuing chaos gave them a sense of superiority and buoyed them as they fantasized aloud about returning to power—and most did believe that they would someday rule again in Mogadishu. For that reason, I suspect, they were reluctant to come clean.

The first time I entered the café I recognized Tarrah from several meetings we'd had when I was with USAID a dozen years earlier. He hadn't changed much; he was gray, bearded, and bald on top and carried himself with slow, confident, and regal air. But now it was all an act. Tarrah was a defeated man. He'd once been rich—among the richest men in Somalia—but he'd also invested most of his aid loot in Mogadishu real estate, villas to rent back to the aid agencies and NGOs. His holdings were in the hands of the *mooryaan,* Aydiid's fighters, who weren't inclined to have any sympathy for him. We chatted amicably until I told him what it was I really wanted to talk about. He paused and suddenly told me he was late for an appointment. We arranged another meeting at the café for the following day. He never showed up. Whenever I was in downtown Nairobi at that time of day, I'd stop by his hangout. If he wasn't there, I'd talk to his friends, and when he was there, he was always rushing away for something or other while inviting me to stop by tomorrow.

This went on sporadically for nearly a year. Tarrah was a man with a great deal to hide. One day I finally did corner him. He was alone with his coffee, and I sat myself at his table. He pled ignorance of any kind of corruption in Somalia. He knew nothing, he said. When I asked him about his wealth, he gathered himself into a forlorn look and informed me that he was living on a stipend sent from Italy by his brother. It was strange, this man who once ruled the refugees, asking for sympathy. I paid for the coffee and stopped bothering him.

Back in Mogadishu, I met Abdirahman Osman Raghe. Raghe had spent his life as a public servant, and, for a while, he had worked under Shirdon, administering food aid at the Ministry of the Interior.

Raghe, I figured, was in as good a position as anyone to tell me what effects foreign aid had had in Somalia. He'd seen a lot and had nothing to hide. Before he started telling me about how the system worked, he wanted me to know about Shirdon. He wanted to be sure I understood there were Somalis who stood up to the massive aid abuses. There were Somalis who protested the use of the refugees as political pawns. There were honest men in Siyaad's government, men who were willing to pay the price for their principles.

Raghe told me his story slowly and passionately. There was a look of perpetual sadness in his eyes. At forty-seven years old, his hair was flecked with gray and the vertical lines in his face conveyed the unique sadness of a man who has been helpless to prevent the ruin of his people.

Shirdon was born in Aden and had come to Somalia, where he spent ten years as a member of Parliament. Later he became general manager of the National Refugee Commission. "He had a different attitude than everyone else there," Raghe said. "He saw the NRC as an agency to help refugees, not as a vehicle to support the goals of the military government." Shirdon, Raghe told me, had spent much of his career trying to close down the refugee programs. He spoke to anyone who would listen, at NGOs, foreign embassies and within the Somali government. His concern, he said, was for the lives of the refugees and the soul of Somalia. Day after day, Shirdon refused the graft that had made his bosses and underlings wealthy men. His superiors even begged him to take a chunk of the loot.

Shirdon firmly refused. At the same time, he refused to moralize about those who give in to the temptations of instant wealth. Day after day, these Somali civil servants, earning the equivalent of $50 or $80 a month came into contact with foreign officers earning $60,000 a year, or with foreign "volunteers" earning $1,000 a month. He blamed the aid for the distortions in Somali society, not the Somalis who responded to the distortions.

"Shirdon had a way of reaching people," Raghe said. "Intellectuals from different clans respected him even though he wasn't rich. Everyone else at NRC was rich. There was no other official like him. That's why we admired him. After a time, I established a friendship with him.

"We'd sit and have some tea and meet at a lot of different locations because it was dangerous to be seen together too often. If an international agency would have some sort of party, if there was a ceremony or something, we would meet and talk quietly. We used to talk very secretly and criticize together. Sometimes he spoke openly in the Parliament of a need for change.

"He was against military recruitment from among the refugees. He was critical of foreign aid. He would complain that foreign aid was coming in like hell and there was no monitoring by the donors. In front of the donors, aid was being divided among officials and the sons and daughters of bosses, and nothing was being done. They were pouring the aid in without any conditions; aid must have some sort of conditions. The donors didn't care if it was all going to the politicians, and they accepted none of the blame.

"We would talk about how food aid destroyed our systems. For many years we weren't dependent on food aid. We had droughts before, but in the past there was a credit system; the nomads were coming to the urban areas and taking loans that they would pay back when times were good. There was a system among the nomads of sharing resources. People worked together."

It wasn't only the food, Raghe said. "Look into drug donations and how they destroyed our developing health system," he told me. "We once had so many pharmacies here. Pharmacists knew their jobs. Now there are people handing out drugs who are not trained, because of the donated drugs from the international community that are so cheap. Any kind of drug is in the market from all countries."

I asked Raghe if Shirdon had written down any of his observations. "We were afraid of writing. To keep a diary was dangerous. We had to be very careful about keeping documents around. The intelligence forces could just enter your house and take things. But it doesn't matter. The truth is the truth whether there are documents or not. Everyone knows what happened."

In 1984, Raghe joined the Department of Food Aid at the Ministry of the Interior, and in 1989 he was appointed director general of the Ministry, just about the time his northern relatives fell under a relentless bombing attack from the very government that employed him. His clan was being run out of their homes by the refugees he was working to feed. Raghe eventually couldn't take the contradiction and soon found a job with the United Nations Development Program (UNDP).

After Shirdon's death, Raghe followed the path of his role model and started his own organization in the bloody ruins of Mogadishu. He formed an NGO called AfriAction with the hope that he could contribute to the reconstruction of his country.

Then he learned it wasn't that simple. The UN intervention in Somalia had once again brought hundreds of foreign NGOs. The foreign NGOs got money and resources from their governments and the UN. Then the UN invited Somali NGOs to register and apply for grant money. Suddenly more than 1,000 Somali NGOs appeared from the rubble of the city. Local businessmen began calling themselves NGOs in order to compete for UN contracts or subgrants from foreign NGOs. Driving along Mogadishu's bullet-scarred streets, one saw the signs: The Somali Society for the Protection of Children, Somali Children's Aid, Action for Children. It was endless. Some were cynical attempts to make money. Others were a practical result of the fact that in Somalia (as in much of Africa), relief and development are the most dynamic growth industries. An African entrepreneur doing a rational analysis of his economic opportunities would likely conclude that the future was in relief and development work.

And while the NGOs and UN helped create this atmosphere, they held in contempt many of the Somalis who tried to cash in on the relief and development explosion. At the UN's humanitarian affairs office in Mogadishu where the so-called local NGOs had to register, one expatriate officer waved a fat pile of registration forms he had received in the previous days. Who do these people think they're trying to con, he wanted to know.

No matter what Raghe did, he was seen by foreigners as another Somali profiteer jumping on the aid bandwagon to make a buck. He was still struggling to build his organization when I began to quiz him about the aid abuses of the past.

Raghe explained some of how it all worked: "Institutional feeding was going to hospitals and schools and orphanages. Each agency was collecting its allocation from the food-aid department. We would get it from the Ministry of the Interior, which got it from the Ministry of Planning, which got it from the World Food Program. Everybody wanted to have some. We thought the Ministry of the Interior should have control, but it was very sensitive. The Ministry of Planning had legal contacts with the UN agencies and was responsible directly to the president. And then we had to involve the Department of International Economic Cooperation, which was part of the Ministry of Planning but was then moved to the Ministry of Foreign Affairs, which was controlled by the president's half-brother, who wanted it there because he wanted to sign all agreements. He took the whole department and put it under his command."

Raghe went on describing the maze of ministries involved in the food procurement and, ultimately, diversion. The Ministry of Health was involved with food for hospitals, and the Ministry of Education got their hands on food that was sent to schools. The systems were ad hoc and changeable day to day. The sole purpose of the exercise was to get as many loyal hands as possible into the grain bin. The government kept changing the rules. The donors grumbled among themselves but kept the food flowing.

"This was a formal misappropriation by the authorities," Raghe said. "It was systematic, not some small employee stealing food for his family. The worst was the Commodity Import Program [CIP] from USAID because of the amount of food involved. It usually arrived when people were harvesting late in September. Many rich people in Somalia are rich as a result of that program."

Although the most visible American food in Africa is relief food donated in "Gift of the People of the United States of America" bags, that is actually the smallest part of the American food-aid program. The vast bulk of food aid comes under other auspices.

All U.S. food arrives under the authority of Public Law-480. The law has three mechanisms for delivering food to poor countries. The food we see on television being fed to starving children is Title II, which is emergency food. Title II food is also used regularly for food-for-work projects and nutrition programs such as school feeding and mother-child health. Most of these are administered by NGOs.

Much food also arrives in poor countries under Title III, which is "food for development." These are commodities that are sold in developing countries and the money used for development projects such as the Save the Children project at Qorioley. In all, some 300 development projects in Somalia were funded with the proceeds from American food.

The largest part of PL-480 is Title I, foods which are simply sold to merchants at bargain-basement prices, rates so low that they often don't even cover the cost of freight. This part of the program is administered by the U.S. Department of Agriculture. If Somalia had had some semblance of a free market, auctioning U.S. food would still have undermined farmers' attempts to get a fair price for their agricultural produce. But an additional injurious factor often intrudes when this food is sold in Africa. Almost all governments require that merchants have permission or otherwise be licensed to purchase foreign commodities. The buyer pool is entirely controlled by the man at the top. Permission to benefit from the foreign aid flow is bestowed as a favor upon close kin and loyal political allies. In Somalia, Siyaad's authorization to buy Title I food was a license to print money.

Indeed, when it came to buying up the U.S. subsidized food in Somalia, it was the president's inner circle who grabbed all the grain. "This CIP food was meant to be monetized as budget and development support," Raghe explained. "This is where the government's friends put their hand in. A normal man can't get an allocation from that. A minister sends his brother or cousin. So farmers are reduced to beggars."

As Raghe continued assembling the pieces of the system for me, I realized for the first time the extent of the malfeasance involved. The minister of agriculture was one of the people profiting from selling imported food, he told me. He paused to let this sink in. Did I understand what this meant, he wanted to know. The very people whose job it was to promote agriculture and increase production were instead making money selling imported food they were, in essence, given for free. Their personal economic interests fell into direct conflict with their jobs.

"The minister was a farmer, trader, landlord, everything," Raghe said. "We were developing the beginning of feudal systems. The inputs to small farmers were diverted to large estates owned by government officials. Every officer in the Ministry of Agriculture had a big farm in the Shebelle region.

And when the minister wakes up in the morning, the first thing he thinks about is his own business."

The minister, who was supposed to help farmers produce food, was now working to keep production low and prices high. And since many of the farmers were from the despised and powerless Rahanwiin clan, there was little fallout from suppressing food production. And not only did donors undercut farmers, they undercut legitimate Somali importers. An entire segment of the business community vanished as high-quality American and European cereals were sold at 50 to 60 percent less than they could have been purchased for. Food aid, Raghe emphasized again, had turned Somalia from a self-sufficient exporter of food to an aid-dependent "kleptocracy."

But the corruption didn't stop there. The government elite reaped additional benefits from the destruction of Somalia's agricultural self-sufficiency. Most of the country's agricultural land along the rivers was ideally suited for growing bananas, melons, and other fruits that could be exported for hard currency and huge profit. A joint venture with Italy, Somalfruit, was the country's single largest export firm and was largely controlled on the Somali side by Siyaad's family and friends. With cheap food imports replacing homegrown grains, more land was free for planting lucrative export crops.

Ironically, the United States was promoting free markets and privatization at that time in Somalia. Siyaad Barre's socialist policies were being officially blamed for the country's food problems. So the large state-run farms were broken up by the Ministry of Agriculture. Abdi Aden Ali, aka Abdi Dheere (tall Abdi), had been a regional director for the Ministry of Agriculture in lower Juba. He considered himself a scientist, a technician concerned with pest control, irrigation, and other matters. One morning in the mid 1980s, he got a letter from the Ministry in Mogadishu ordering him to transfer a state farm to a wealthy individual in Kismaayo. The letter also instructed him to use the government's resources to help revitalize the farm. Abdi Dheere wasn't sure what to do, so he stalled for time by writing a letter back to the minister asking for instructions on the procedure for transferring public property to private hands. He was summoned to Mogadishu and told that he had no right to pose that kind of question. He apologized.

It was then that the young technician realized for the first time what his real job was. As an officer of the Ministry of Agriculture, Abdi Dheere was expected to help the friends of Siyaad. For years it had been illegal to sell or transfer land. Now it was happening quickly, outside of any new laws or procedures. Government ministers were buying the land and planting it or reselling parts of it for huge profits.

"One thing is very clear to everyone," Abdi Dheere said. "The government cared only about the production of bananas. Siyaad gave as much as possible to any group that wanted to produce bananas. But these groups were his own people. In all the time I worked there, I never heard a thing about encouraging the production of basic agriculture. Ninety-nine percent of letters and circulars were about banana production."

Some of the policies he was asked to execute were actually detrimental to food production. For example, he was told to implement flood-prevention procedures to protect the bananas. In the same areas, small-scale farmers relied on floods to irrigate their land. "In lower Juba we have land depressions where water gathers during rains. Eighty percent of the farmers planted behind the receding water. If you wanted to help small farmers you shouldn't be protecting the land against floods. We really needed to be helping people capture the water before it receded back to the river. But the regime was never interested in helping people become self-sufficient."

It wasn't just the former state-owned farms that were being snapped up by Siyaad's inner circle. Traditional farmers were forced out of business by low prices and were either driven off their land or forced to sell it cheaply. In essence, the West's surplus grains were subsidizing the production of bananas and other crops that did not compete with Western agricultural interests. And Somalia's elite were making millions of dollars at both ends of the system. All this was made possible by food aid—and as more farmers were forced off their land, food aid became more necessary. The cycle of food-aid dependence was self-sustaining.

And what about the donors? Did they care what their aid was doing? A World Bank study charged that donors were concerned only with their own domestic agricultural situation. "[D]onors' food aid budgets are primarily influenced by prospects for commercial exports of their food surpluses rather than being determined in accordance with the needs and objectives of recipient countries to reduce their food import dependency. Accordingly, donors usually reduce their food aid budgets when prospects for commercial exports of surpluses are good and increase than when those prospects are poor. As a result, significant price fluctuations are likely to occur in the domestic food market, particularly when the former decision of donors happens to coincide with a poor harvest in the recipient country and the latter with a good one."

The World Bank released this study in the form of a "discussion paper" entitled *Food Import Dependence in Somalia: Magnitude, Causes, and Policy Options,* by Y. Hossein Farzin in 1988, when Somalia was well past the point of no return. The introduction to the paper points out that this is not a full-fledged study but *merely* a discussion paper: "preliminary and unpolished results of country analysis or research that is circulated to encourage discussion and comment; citation and the use of such a paper should take account of its provisional character." In reality, the "discussion paper" format is a technique used to release controversial data. It gives the Bank the option of distancing itself from the conclusions while at the same time covering its ass when, down the line, someone asks them how they could not have known what was going on. By 1988, when it had long been apparent that food aid had methodically undermined Somalia's civil society, such a study was required. The Bank released it just in time to relieve itself of responsibility when the government collapsed.

The paper concluded: "Somalia has become, alarmingly, and more than any other country in Sub-Saharan Africa, dependent on imported food. This is particularly striking when one notes that the Somali economy has been predominantly agricultural/pastoral and that, up until the early seventies, it used to be self-sufficient in food grains." Farzin examined Somalia's food imports, excluding emergency food for war and drought, and concluded that food imports had grown at an annual rate of more than 21 percent.

"[T]he share of food import in total volume of food consumption rose from less than 33 percent on average for the 1970–79 period to over 63 percent during the 1980–84 period." This later period coincides with Western involvement in the Somalia economy and the beginning of U.S. and EEC food-aid programs to Somalia. It should also be noted that this was a period without a significant drought or food emergency in Somalia, nor was there any increase in Somali exports: Food-aid imports were replacing production, putting farmers out of business.

The discussion paper determined that the growth of food aid in Somalia was fourteen times higher than the growth of food consumption. Food was dumped into Somalia as fast as donors could get it there. The discussion paper then said what everyone knew, and what most avoided saying: "[B]y increasing the supply (or sometimes oversupplying the market), food aid often acts to dampen domestic food prices or, at least, prevent them from rising, thereby reducing incentives to domestic producers of food crops and exacerbating the national food deficit. This disincentive effect had been strong in the case of Somalia because food aid (a) substantially augmented total food imports rather than just replacing commercial imports, and (b) has been sold in the domestic market at prices significantly below import parity levels evaluated as a realistic market exchange rate."

Farzin identified another problem with food aid: "Food aid, when provided for an extended period of time, can change the food habits of consumers (particularly that of urban groups) in the recipient country through replacing traditional food grains by imported substitutes. This has certainly been the case in Somalia, where there has been a notable shift in consumption out of sorghum and maize to rice and wheat products." This, of course, is the primary goal of food aid in the first place as articulated in congressional testimony and in the language of the Food for Peace Act. Get them hooked so they'll buy our food.

Despite all this evidence, NGOs and advocates of food aid continue to hoist up pictures of starving children and claim that food aid has brought significant improvements to the developing world. USAID continues to claim that its programs improve "food security" in countries where they operate. However, in July 1993, the U.S. General Accounting Office had this to say about the food programs: "AID has no strategy for assessing the impact of its programs on enhancing the food security of people in recipient countries, nor has it determined whether food aid is an efficient means for accomplishing this goal."* This might have been an interesting comment when food aid began back in the 1950s, but coming as it did in 1993, after more than thirty-five years of food-aid programs, it points to gross negligence or perhaps malfeasance on the part of USAID, the Department of Agriculture, and NGOs involved in food aid.

Here are other comments from that same report:

AID has not developed guidance on how food aid programs should be developed to enhance food security. . . . AID has not systematically collected relevant data or developed methodologies to assess the impact of [food aid] on the food security or recipient countries.

. . . AID has not maintained staff expertise in food aid; it no longer recruits food aid specialists from outside the agency.

For the most part, AID determines the success of Title II programs with short-term quantitative measures. For example, Catholic Relief Services' evaluations of school feeding programs in Burkina Faso are based on the quantity of food delivered and number of children served, rather than on how the food distribution program has improved the children's food security.

---

*GAO Report #GAO/NSIAD-93-168, *Food Aid: Management Improvements Are Needed to Achieve Program Objectives.*

This is what I had noted when I worked for Catholic Relief Services fourteen years before the GAO report was published. The organization's definition of success was based solely on the number of people fed. Neither CRS nor USAID had the expertise or the inclination to seriously study what all that food was doing to the individuals or the societies where it was being dumped.

A separate but related problem in Somalia was caused by the currency generated by the sales of food. First, sales of Title III commodities were supposed to be used in development projects. But donors turned a blind eye as those "counterpart funds" were pocketed by officials all along the food chain. Farzin's study found that "the donors of food aid have rarely requested the government to use the counterpart funds (local currency) generated from the sales of food aid to provide incentives to domestic food grain producers. Where there had been any conditionality on the use of such funds, it has often been limited to payment to donors' project contractors and personnel to cover their local costs." In other words, as long as the donors had their expenses covered, they let the government do as it pleased with the rest of the money.

A separate U.S. study also criticized the use of these counterpart funds: "Control of these funds was sloppy at best. Despite donors' efforts to monitor use of counterpart currency, ministries used development projects for personal gain through sweetheart contracts, overinvoicing, and false documents."

The author of the U.S. study, David Rawson, is too kind to the donors. The truth is they didn't want to monitor the use of funds. It was a no-win proposition for them. The government was going to steal the money whether the donors could account for it or not. Siyaad Barre was not afraid of aid bureaucrats and foreign diplomats. The only way donors could control the funds would be to cut them off—stop the food—and they weren't going to do that. Siyaad and his cronies knew it. The donors would keep dumping food; the regime could keep the cash flowing.

The donors used the food aid to save themselves money. It never mattered that the Somali economy was being destroyed, that corrupt Somali officials were getting rich. The elite of Mogadishu society, donors and government big-wigs, were fat from aid. And when they met at diplomatic cocktail parties they could slap each other on the back and congratulate themselves on a job well done, while servants offered hors d'oeuvres and Indian Ocean breezes filled their seaside villas.

In 1991 and 1992, the U.S. Department of State's Center for the Study of Foreign Affairs, noting that a number of African states were drifting, or had drifted, into anarchy, decided to look into aid programs to those countries. Rawson's report was the result of that concern. It had not escaped the attention of the policymakers in the State Department that the three largest recipient states in Africa—Somalia, Zaire, and Liberia—had drifted over the edge and experienced a total governmental meltdown. *The Somali State and Foreign Aid* is a fascinating study that concisely summarizes what all the diplomats in Somalia had known for a long time: Rawson's findings corroborate what many of my Somali sources told me. As Raghe explained, few documents confirm what was going on in Somalia. Or, as Rawson writes, "The Somali government, already the least literate of bureaucracies, has lost such government documents as existed in the chaos of civil war."

Rawson doesn't issue indictments, but he asks the right questions: "Were donors aware of Somalia's intractable problems? Or had they unintentionally contributed to those problems?" From the report, the answer to the first question is, clearly, yes.

In 1987, donor assistance to Somalia was at an all-time high. Even as Siyaad increased repression, Germany, the United States, and Italy kept pouring money into the country to support what it perceived as its transition to a free-market economy. But, as Rawson notes, "Cooperation with donor guidelines was ad hoc and arbitrary at best. By September 1987, Somalia had fallen off the stabilization/structural adjustment wagon and attempted a return to fixed currencies and state controls.* When that happened, the state discovered that the production of Somali shillings to provide counterpart currencies for donor inputs in commodities and foreign exchange had so pumped up the economy that inflation went through the roof. The demand for goods fueled by intakes from false invoicing, inflated contracts, and outright appropriation of donor funds sent the Somali economy into a deep trade and payments imbalance."

Instead of converting hard currency to Somali shillings to pay for development work, the foreign organizations were importing food. The Somali government printed the currency to pay for it—but the new bank notes weren't backed by new reserves of foreign exchange. The more develop-

---

*With the guidance of the World Bank, Somalia was supposedly embarking upon what is called a stabilization/structural adjustment program. Under the terms of the agreement, the country received massive loans in exchange for dropping government controls over exchange rates, and for undertaking other measures to decontrol the economy. Somalia took the loans but quickly dispensed with the reforms.

ment projects NGOs did, the more money the government printed. The result was massive inflation.

Rawson writes about a World Bank $33 million structural adjustment loan given to Somalia in June 1989: "In retrospect, nothing about Somali economic behavior inspired optimism, particularly the kind of optimism that would advance a $33 million loan on the basis of Somali 'commitments' to reform." The misleading part of this statement is the opening "in retrospect." It was clear at the time, but aid organizations tend to fulfill their own mandates; they give aid, regardless of circumstances. All this happened while a civil war in the north was spinning out of control. The writing was on the wall; Siyaad would fall. But the IMF (International Monetary Fund) and the World Bank were plotting their next moves to finance Somalia's economic transformation.

And these so-called development agencies kept right on financing the destruction of a country. Their actions were eroding Somalia's economy, making people poor, and, in a bizarre way, creating a need for more and more aid, more and more NGOs. It was a cycle that eventually would consume itself.

At Raghe's urging, I traveled to the northern city of Hargeysa—capital of what, since 1991, has been the self-declared independent republic of Somaliland—and met with Abdi Aden Nur, who had once worked for the NRC and now held the title of Director of Food Aid and Relief Services. Abdi Aden was one of those whom most people regarded as honest. Like Shirdon, he had done his best to make things work from the inside. I had also dealt with him when I worked in Somalia, reporting back to him on occasion about the corruption I found at the NRC. A small, wiry man in his late seventies, with bright eyes and a quick step, he spoke freely about his days at NRC.

He talked a bit about his former boss, Tarrah, and repeated some of what I'd already heard about the corrupting influences of aid, how it stopped trade and led to corruption. Yes, Tarrah became rich, he told me, but that was nothing compared to the former finance minister, Mohamed Sheikh Osman. "Siyaad Barre wanted all the money from food handed to Mohamed Sheikh. One year we were instructed to place all the money from monetizing food into a special account controlled by Mohamed Sheikh. There was about $195 million in there at one point. Then suddenly the account was closed. The money disappeared."

"I was very much disgusted by everything that went on," Abdi Aden said. "If they start food aid here in Somaliland it will be the same thing."

• • •

In Mogadishu again, I tracked down Mohammed Sheikh Osman. He had started out as a policeman in Mogadishu and ended up with the minister's portfolio in 1971, after testifying against enemies of Siyaad Barre's regime. His testimony led to the execution of several "traitors," the first of Barre's long reign of terror. Ultimately it led Mohamed Sheikh to a real estate empire of more than 100 buildings in Mogadishu, and other holdings in Dubai. Those buildings include numerous homes and offices rented by NGOs and the UN Operation in Somalia, from which the total rent is said to exceed $500,000 a month. That explained why this man of massive wealth chose to remain in a war-torn dangerous city. (Mohammed Sheikh was from the Hawiye clan, which made his presence more palatable to the warlords and their fighters.) There was something boldly poetic about the way he and others stole from the UN and NGOs, used the money to build houses, and then rented those same houses back to the UN and NGOs.

Mohamed Sheikh's own home was a virtual fortress. I was frisked by his young guards at the gate. When I entered, there were another half dozen armed men in his front yard. Flowers bloomed everywhere. The gardens were delicately manicured. Ten people sat on his front porch, apparently waiting for an audience with the former minister.

A young man led me to a large, plush velvet couch in a spacious living room, and as soon as I sat, Osman entered the room. An energetic man in his sixties, he was wearing one of those tropical leisure suits in a style popular among members of the former government. Sensing he might be pressed for time, I got right to the point: I wanted to know how much aid was stolen over the years and exactly how the thievery took place.

Osman seemed surprised. Then he yelled for a servant to bring some grapefruit juice. He told me blankly that there was no corruption he knew about in the Siyaad Barre government. I changed the subject to American politics.

As our conversation wound down toward silence, Osman sat upright and looked at me. "It is delicate," he said softly, thoughtfully. "Some of the people involved are alive and active in Somali politics, and sometimes it is not easy to tell the truth. You become a target. You may be killed." His eyes softened, and he made himself comfortable in his chair again. "I was thinking of writing a book about my twenty years in government. But what I know I cannot say. This looting today, a few lorries and the relief food, is nothing compared to what happened here before. This is not looting. I know about looting.

"Myself, I've been in politics thirty years. I can't say why certain things happen. No one can teach these things. I stay here because I was born in Mogadishu. I'm sixty years old and surrounded by family and the people I love. They are here. And I fear. Three or four guys can come and they can kill you. I have an office in Dubai, but most of the time I'm here. I lost a son in the war. He was a doctor, an M.D., shot in Afgooye while he was saving a life. My first son. So this is the situation in Somalia. The country is destroyed morally, economically, and physically. There are half a million to a million Somalis living outside. When they come back, there will be another civil war."

Raghe is not a man given to bitterness. He gamely maintained his optimism through three years of anarchy in Mogadishu that were preceded by three years of terror from Siyaad Barre's troops against his Isaaq clan. His solution was to keep working, keep talking it through. I spoke to him periodically during the time of the U.S. and UN intervention in Somalia. Sometimes I couldn't get to his house in the Medina neighborhood of Mogadishu because militia fighting made it too dangerous to drive through the narrow streets or because someone or another had decided to throw up a roadblock and prevent people from moving. But when I did get through, he was always willing to talk, always prefacing his comments about corruption with some bit of optimistic news.

Raghe watched as new foreign NGOs with fresh young foreign faces came into Somalia and received grant money to work. AfriAction never collected a cent. The foreigners lurched from place to place, from project to project, retreating when things became dangerous and returning to start all over again when it was safe and more money was available. His years of experience were not in demand.

At the end of 1995, Raghe gave up and emigrated to Canada.

10

WITHDRAWAL SYMPTOMS

[E]very decrease in power is an open invitation to violence.
—Hanna Arendt, *On Violence*

In 1986, as the deluge of aid into Somalia reached new heights, the country began its slow descent toward anarchy. The foreigners at the beach clubs didn't feel it at first. They watched the waves and delighted in the warmth of the safest city in Africa. Their futures there seemed secured by the seemingly insoluble refugee crisis. The Cold War would never end. The money and the jobs would never leave. Somalia would always be a land of great opportunity.

That was the year Siyaad Barre was nearly killed in a car crash. The rebels noted that the dictator was vulnerable, and they were emboldened. In 1987, the rebel Somali National Movement attacked the Hargeysa prison. Bombs went off in Mogadishu. Aid agencies that had tolerated political repression and executions of dissidents for years paused to wonder for the first time how safe it really was in Somalia.

In May 1988, the SNM attacked the town of Burao in northern Somalia and boldly took on government troops, who exhibited something less than soldierly valor.* A few days later they attacked the city of Hargeysa. They also went after refugee camps and Somali refugees from Ethiopia who had been taking over businesses in Hargeysa.

The government responded by bombing Hargeysa to the ground. (Estimates of the death toll ranged as high as 50,000—probably an exaggeration. Nonetheless, tens of thousands died at the hands of the government. The SNM rebels were also responsible for some civilian casualties.) Refugees from the Isaaq clan fled across the border into Ethiopia. When the international community remained mute over the killing, the government stepped up its repression, killing civilians and others suspected of backing various rebel movements.

A 1989 State Department report concluded that the Somali army murdered at least 5,000 civilians over an eleven-month period.† That year, the United States cut off all military and economic aid to Somalia (while retaining the use of air and naval facilities in Somalia's northern port of Berbera).

In early 1990, several aid agencies withdrew foreign staff from Beledweyne after Hawiye soldiers in the town defected from the army, which then retaliated by attacking civilians. Soldiers rounded up local men, burned houses, killed villagers, and executed a number of refugees.

With the Cold War a nonissue, Siyaad had lost his leverage with the Americans. So he attempted to position himself as a foe to a new perceived danger, Islamic fundamentalism. On July 9, 1990, the bishop of Mogadishu, Salvatore Colombo, was murdered at the Mogadishu cathedral. Despite a huge reward offered by the government, the lone gunman escaped. Siyaad said it was the work of Muslim extremists, but even his most ardent foreign backers saw the murder for the despicable ploy it was. Although the killing resulted in an uproar in Italy, Italian Foreign Minister Gianni De Michelis a few weeks later rejected calls by Parliament for the suspension of economic aid to Somalia. Rome did withdraw fifty-three Italian air force and army personnel helping to train men for the Somali armed forces. But the

---

*The army by then was predominantly Ogaadeen, but the Ogaadeen were suddenly betrayed by Siyaad. In order to flush out Ethiopia-based rebel groups, Siyaad made an agreement with Ethiopia's dictator, Mengistu Haile Mariam, renouncing Somalia's claims on the Ogaden. Ironically, this agreement forced the SNM into an offensive position at the same time it made the Somali army less willing to fight. The Ogaadeen then formed several liberation groups and joined the fight against Siyaad's government.

†*Why Somalis Flee* by Robert Gersony, State Department report, August 1989.

foreign minister said that cutting off economic and development aid "would not mean the end of Siyaad Barre but the end of Somalia."

The U.S. ambassador, T. Frank Crigler, agreed. While acknowledging Siyaad Barre's "appalling human rights record," Crigler argued that by pulling out all aid at this point, the U.S. and Western donors were losing the possibility of engaging Siyaad. Somalia had become so addicted to aid, its political system so accustomed to ingesting large amounts of foreign cash, that, like any redundant junkie, it had reached a point where withdrawing the aid would do more damage to the system than keeping it flowing. But political pressure from home prevailed, and as Western countries pulled back, Siyaad began to lose control of his troops and his underlings. He also lost any sense of indebtedness to world opinion. Aid workers who administered the drug now became the enemy, targets of the regime's malevolence. Siyaad's minions, fearing the aid was about to end, set out to milk the last drops before it was withdrawn.

Western aid agencies began scaling down much of their work in Somalia because of security threats to staff in many parts of the country, particularly in the north. Several times, aid workers were withdrawn and then returned when it was decided that stability had been restored to Somalia.

Now that the refugee relief operation was untenable, UN agencies officially started to complain about such things as the inflation of refugee numbers. Now that it was unprofitable, they had become idealistic. For the first time, UNHCR became concerned with the arming of refugees and the use of aid to fight the war, and a rift developed between the American approach to Somalia and that of the UN and its aid-giving institutions.

The following January 1989 memo from the head of the UNHCR Branch Office in Mogadishu to headquarters in Geneva outlines the disagreement between the UN and the United States. It was among the documents I found in Geneva. Some excerpts:

> Following donor Liaison Committee meeting on 15 January the BO [Branch Office] requested a meeting with the U.S. ambassador Crigler in an effort to explain and clarify UNHCR's position on the closing of six eastern camps in the north.
>
> Ambassador Crigler addressed the meeting at length speaking with enthusiasm of recent concessions made by the president after recommendations from the council of ministers . . .
>
> He repeatedly referred to HCR's concerns as "an annoyance" and a "sideshow," which he felt were the primary issues, i.e. the government's dealings with the rebels . . .

It is the BO's opinion, however, that the ambassador's optimism is misplaced. All Somalis are aware of the gravity of the situation throughout the country and the need for major changes. The recommendation of senior officials to the president indicate, if nothing else, a government out of control and without real leadership. (The ambassador himself referred to the minister of defense being essentially beyond even the president's control. This is the government on which the ambassador is placing all his hopes.)

The BO tried to explain that fundamental UNHCR principles are at stake as a result of the wanton arming of the Daarood refugees and that to ignore these was tantamount to undermining the integrity and the mandate of the organization. The ambassador minimized this saying that UNHCR's assistance was insignificant. He did, however, reiterate his support for UNHCR's general plan for phasing out in 1990.

The BO's impression was one where the U.S. government, with its back to the wall as a result of congressionally imposed limits on aid to Somalia, is prepared to sacrifice UNHCR principles in an effort to establish itself as a power broker, whose clout is coming under continued question. It is encouraging that other donors are considerably more supportive of UNHCR/WFP's position. The BO seriously fears it will be compromised by the U.S., which has its own agenda.

I shared the memo with Crigler, who had never seen it before, for his reaction:

"At the moment described in the memo, the refugee issue was NOT important; it *was* a sideshow," Crigler wrote to me. "I had placed all my emphasis on 'national reconciliation'—a chimera, of course, but there was no other option that would have reconciled our prime policy objective—maintaining a strategic foothold at Berbera—with the realities of the country's slide into chaos. What did it matter whether the government was (or maybe was not—we weren't sure at the time) arming the Ogaadeen refugees to fight the Isaaq? In my view, it was one of those things you could pretty well expect, like crooks siphoning off food from the refugee feeding centers and selling it in the markets. UNHCR, though, was absolutely consumed by these "violations" of its sacred principles, which as far as I was concerned didn't matter a hill of beans.

"As long as our marching orders were what they were—'Keep that strategic foothold, but don't ask for any more military aid money'—we were doing the right thing to downplay UNHCR's sacred principles. The important thing, and we sadly failed to pull it off, was to bring about some kind of accommodation between Siyaad Barre and the SNM/Isaaq.

"Siyaad's was, after all, the only government we had to work with! Our only alternative would have been to fold our tents and (figuratively) leave, like the Brits did, tossing away any chance of moderating the course of events. We chose to stay the course, keep our eye on the main chance, and ignore the whines and whimpers from the incredibly pedestrian, narrow-minded UNHCR bureaucrats."

Crigler felt that aid should have continued so the United States could have leverage with Siyaad. Human rights violations only got worse when the aid was being phased out. Siyaad had nothing more to lose except his own power, and he was now prepared to do anything to hold onto it.

Later I questioned Crigler: "Then aid to Somalia, as you saw it, had nothing to do with development?"

"Shit, no. Aid is not development; it doesn't do diddley-squat."

Matthew Bryden, on leave from the Canadian military, went to Africa as a tourist in 1987 and ended up working for CARE, repatriating refugees for $50 a day. He started out in Nairobi without knowing where it was or what he was going to do there. He spent three months traveling around Kenya, Uganda, Rwanda, and Tanzania. In Uganda he met up with an Italian journalist whom he accompanied to the northern part of the country, where he witnessed the rebellion of the Holy Spirit movement, led by a woman named Alice Lakwena. She was the one who told her followers that bullets would pass through them like water. Thousands of them died.

"I saw orphaned kids and I saw displaced kids, I saw all the trash and the decadence of war without seeing the fighting. We saw villages that had been smashed and burned, and this made a really strong impression on me. I asked the local Red Cross office if they needed any help, that I could stay and work, and they said, 'No, you can't do it like that. You've got to go back and go through the head office.'

"I traveled a bit and while I was traveling I reflected on it and I thought: No, what I really want to do is come back and rather than be a soldier, what I'd like to do is be on the other side of the divide. I don't want to be the one who creates this sort of destruction and violence; I'd like to be helping pick up the pieces, helping people recover from violence and destruction."

So he went back to Nairobi and spent three months hunting for a job. Nairobi was full of aid workers and would-be aid workers. Itinerant world travelers who'd gotten a taste of the Third World life and found it to their liking, slapped together résumés and went looking for jobs. Some of them found jobs, and a few even found careers.

Then Bryden heard about the job with CARE in southwestern Somalia. CARE needed bodies to fill in registration forms. It was January 1988. Bryden was told that Mogadishu was still safe, though the countryside could be dangerous. But not long after he arrived, Mogadishu was shaken when an ammunition dump just outside town was blown up.

In the refugee camps, he was part of what UNHCR called its "Durable Solution" to the refugee problem. Durable Solution offered three choices: repatriation to Ethiopia, integration into Somalia, or resettlement in a third country such as Canada or Sweden. The third choice wasn't really an option for most refugees, and the first two choices weren't very attractive. Somalia was on the verge of a civil war, and the refugees weren't exactly popular with the forces that would likely take over. Conditions in Ethiopia weren't much better, and much worse than they would have been a few years earlier. Still, CARE and UNHCR acted as if conditions were finally right for solving the refugee crisis. In reality, the refugees weren't useful to anyone any more: Siyaad had other problems, and the Ogaadeen people had formed their own rebel group, the Somali Patriotic Movement (SPM), to challenge the government. And with the Cold War over, there was no more money available for the UN and NGOs who wanted to take care of the refugees.

The problem had to be dispensed with, and itinerants like Bryden could do the job as well as anyone. Bryden didn't stay ignorant very long. He developed an instant attachment to Somalia and quickly began to learn the Somali language and to grasp the nuances of the country. "I became aware pretty quickly that this was a buyout, that UNHCR was essentially bribing the refugees to go away, to avoid embarrassing the UN. CARE wanted it finished. They knew that there was going to be an outrageous inflation of figures. They thought, 'We'll buy every ration card we've ever handed out. We'll pay, and then it will be over.' So they didn't give a damn that the figures were inflated. In the camps, we didn't care when we saw kids registering in two different families. We'd see the same family register in two different, three different camps. We knew there were families with fifty, a hundred ration cards. There were token attempts to stop it, but we all understood by then that the whole system was so corrupt and so flawed that the only possible solution now was to get out.

"The only limit was that the damage couldn't exceed a certain dollar value. So they were ready to pay just to call an end to this twelve-year scam."

When his CARE contract ended later that year, with the job far from completed, Bryden found work with the United Nations Development

Program (UNDP) in the northwest, in the coastal town of Berbera, the main port in the region and the site of the still-unused American airbase. On one of his trips to the northwest, he was accompanied by Abdirahman Osman Raghe. "I went to the north with Raghe to distribute plastic sheeting to some new arrivals displaced from the fighting around Boroma. It was during [the Muslim holy month of] Ramadan, and I had an enormous fight with Raghe because we couldn't get the workers at the airport to move the stuff. They all wanted to go home early. I still had my fresh ideals about aid and how there were people suffering and we had to get them this plastic sheeting before the rains. And Raghe said, 'Look, you can't make these people work. It's dangerous. They don't care. They're not interested in the end result of all this.' And I got on my high horse and said, 'Okay, fine if *you* don't care. But I care enough that we gotta get this stuff moving.' And Raghe blew up and told me that I was coming into this as an arrogant, young *gaal* who thought that aid work was the only thing people cared about. We were having this big fight at the airport. It would have continued but we got distracted because some soldiers started shooting at us for fun. And that was my introduction to Berbera."

Bryden was learning lessons that all aid workers learn, eventually. He was just absorbing them faster in the context of the frenetic collapse of the Somali state. On Bryden's second day in Berbera, someone tried to kill the head of UNDP in the town. An administrative screw-up meant that people weren't getting paid on time. One of the workers returned with a gun and fired on the man. He missed, but the officer broke his hip diving out of the way. He was sent back to Mogadishu, and Bryden, twenty-four years old, was left in charge.

"The only help I had was the driver in the office, who was made a field assistant because he was the only one who spoke English and knew the system. His name was Mohamed Abdi Mohamed. An old man. Very gentle. He was from the Isaaq clan and was stuck in Berbera. Because the government troops in Berbera were Ogaadeen and Hawiye, and other clans from other areas, they spent the nights basically taking a turn in the town looting, pillaging, and raping in one of the blocks in town where there were Isaaqs. And the Isaaqs were powerless. Little by little, Mohamed tried to explain to me what was going on, when we were alone in the car on the road. He'd try to explain to me what the SNM was, what the fighting was about."

Bryden was on six-month contracts and at the end of the first one, he took leave to attend a wedding in Canada. Mohamed Abdi drove him to the airfield. He took all his belongings with him. As he looked across the flat, hot coastal plain to the mountains in the distance, he turned to Mohamed and said, "I'm not finished with Berbera yet. I'm coming back."

After three weeks, Bryden was back in Nairobi at the UNDP office to collect his ticket back to Somalia. The man at the UNDP travel agency looked at him and asked, "Are you coming or going?" Bryden replied, "I'm going. I'm going back to Mogadishu. I'm going back to Berbera." The man said, "Oh, you haven't heard, but there was a massacre in Berbera. Twenty-one people were shot. Four from the Red Cross and one from UNDP." The army had gone around, taken people who were identified as being Isaaq—twenty-one of them—took them behind the UNDP office and machine-gunned them. Bryden knew the one from UNDP was Mohamed Abdi.

"I remember that I used to kid myself thinking if I hadn't left, they wouldn't have dared," Bryden said. "Not when I was there. But I took my leave, I came back, and he's dead.

"I think I was protected in the sense that I represented a lot of aid, and even the generals in the army didn't want this aid to stop. That was my protection. I didn't realize that. I thought the UN was my protection. I thought I had some kind of diplomatic immunity."

Bryden nevertheless returned to Berbera. There were new refugees and new problems, and the World Food Program and the NGOs were back in the business of sending food. As usual, most of the food was being stolen by the local military commander who, in the absence of any real government authority, was acting as a warlord. He was the one who had executed the Isaaqs in town, and now he was getting rich and feeding his troops on relief food. Bryden thought someone would care. He was still too new to Somalia to know any differently. "When I reported this back to a heads of agencies meeting in Mogadishu, people just didn't want to hear it."

At one meeting in 1990, when I was complaining about diversion of relief food, I remember the head of WFP saying, 'Yes, that's all very interesting, but we need to maintain a presence. It's important that the UN have a presence in the northwest.'"

That presence was costly. Soon after, a Red Cross representative, Peter Altwegg, was killed near Hargeysa by the SNM, and two other Red Cross workers were kidnapped. "The Red Cross delegation in Berbera was fairly traumatized by all of this," Bryden said. "It was dramatic; when Peter's body came back to Berbera, I was pretty traumatized. I went down to Mogadishu at that time as well to say, 'Hey, I'm not working.' At that time I was doing no work, essentially. I'd do administration for UNDP in the morning and by noon I'd run out of things to do. I taught English for an hour every day at the Red Cross Hospital for the Somali staff. I had a class of sometimes fifty people who I'd teach for an hour. After that I'd usually give a hand in the operating theater in the wards because there was a lot of work to do and I wanted to learn.

"And I'd travel back to Mogadishu to say that to me there was an imbalance—we were taking risks, we were doing no really effective work, and yet things like Peter's murder were becoming more common. There was more shooting in Berbera toward the end of 1990. People were beginning to get killed in Mogadishu as well. By then I think there had been a German killed; his girlfriend had been raped. There had been an American marine from the embassy shot through the back three times, badly injured—though he was okay. Violence was becoming part of the atmosphere and I was worried and upset, and the response that I remember getting from UNDP again was, 'Yeah, but we need a presence in the northwest.' And privately, I thought, I don't want to be just a presence. Not that I didn't want to risk my life—that went without saying—but also I didn't want to have to watch other people get killed. I had to stand by and watch this and suffer the loss of friends and colleagues for nothing—because the UN wanted a 'presence.'"

The hit song in Mogadishu in those days was by a woman named Saado Ali Warsame. It was called "Land Cruiser."

> It's a bad idea and wrong way of thinking
> to buy a Land Cruiser while you beg for maize.

> The house is dark
> with no water flowing in the taps,
> and the babies have no food to eat.
> While seeing the shining car
> and hearing the sound of its powerful engine
> you think you're powerful in the Horn of Africa.

> Dear relatives, do you all agree with
> the lack of food in our homes
> without raising any objection about the luxury cars
> and the buying of Land Cruisers.

> It's a bad idea and wrong way of thinking
> to buy a Land Cruiser while you beg for maize.

Bryden remembers driving around Mogadishu with Somali friends blasting the song out the window. The symbol of wealth, power and the NGOs had become the anthem of the revolution.

• • •

By August of 1990, the Americans started to play it safe. Dependents and nonofficial Americans were asked to leave. In November, the UN started to evacuate all its nonessential staff. Bryden was sent to Nairobi against his wishes. After a few weeks there, he felt a hunger to go back. He'd seen so much violence and tension building up. He'd seen a government stagger- ing under the weight of a rebel assault. Now the rebels were marching to- ward Mogadishu, and he didn't want to read about it in the Nairobi papers. Under strict orders not to return, and banned from official UN flights, Bry- den bought a ticket on the last commercial Somali Airlines flight from Nairobi to Mogadishu. He arrived on December 30, 1990.

"On the flight I met an American diplomat. We had three or four beers together on the flight. Got a little bit tanked. And when we set down in Mogadishu, they opened the door of the aircraft. Then we heard it. Heavy machine gun fire and explosions and mortars. There were a lot of people trying to get on that flight out. And I asked one of the guys, a Somali I saw as I got off the airplane, I said, 'Who is it? Is it the USC?* What's going on?' And he said, 'It's the Hawiye.' And that's all he said. And it was true, because what happened in Mogadishu that day was not the arrival of the USC. It was just the uprising, in mainly Hawiye neighborhoods, where kids started putting up barricades, taking out their guns, and started shooting at soldiers, started arming themselves, forming militia units."

Bryden drove through the streets and saw a city panicked. Refugees were on the move. Looters had begun to empty houses of everything that was left behind. It was surreal and cinematic, too strange to feel really dan- gerous.

On New Year's Eve, the American presence was down to thirty-seven people. They gathered at the K-7 compound for a party. Bryden showed up, joining American security officer John Fox and several others.

Bryden recalls that around midnight, the UN got on the walkie-talkie net and started passing around ridiculous New Year's goodwill messages. Bryden remembers it going something like this: "First, the UN special co- ordinator, the UNDP resident representative, the UN special coordinator for emergency relief operations, would like to thank the members of the UN community for their hard work and blah-blah-blah throughout the year and to wish them the very best in the new year, blah-blah-blah. And then the representative of WHO would like to thank the UNDP resident

---

*The USC (United Somali Congress), under the leadership of General Mohamed Farah Aydiid, were advancing toward Mogadishu.

representative for his good wishes and for his support during blah-blah-blah and to wish all of the staff of the UN family and community in Somalia the very best for the coming year. And then the director of WFP would like to thank the . . ."

Then Joe Borge, the deputy chief of the mission, led the party in singing of "Amazing Grace." John Fox recalls: "We hadn't finished the chorus when all hell broke loose, close to the compound, and then we heard quite heavy fighting going on in the distance."

Naturally, everyone ran up to the roof, one of the highest points in the city. From there they watched the first rounds being fired into Villa Somalia. Suddenly, shooting broke out in the street, just beside the building. And then bullets came right over the top of the building. "We all hit the ground," Bryden recalls, "and I noticed that most people had managed to land without spilling their drinks. I remember that distinctly."

Fox described a rainbow arc of fire going into the airport where Barre's bunker was located. No one slept much, and they had breakfast by the swimming pool in the morning.

Fox peered out from the compound and saw "streams of refugees carrying nothing at all. Then we saw looters from our own houses, our own staff going by, our furniture on trucks. We could see individual houses being broken into from the top of K-7. Typewriters and computers were carried down the streets."

The Siyaad Barre regime lasted until the end of January 1991, when the rebel forces actually arrived in town. This time the Americans evacuated for real. Operation Eastern Exit might have gotten some press, and the marines involved might have been considered heroes except that the Gulf War had just started, and the fireworks there were much more dramatic.

The Americans airlifted most of the expatriates out of the city, including the Russians. Somali staff who had worked for the U.S. and other embassies were left behind to their fate. As the last helicopters lifted off from the new U.S. Embassy compound, looters poured over the walls and grabbed everything that was left. And from above, the former Cold War adversaries safely observed what twenty years of the superpower competition had brought to Somalia.

11

PIGS AT A TROUGH

Our national generosity seems to have been perverted.

—Senator Patrick Leahy

In October of 1993, U.S. Representative Tim Penny of Minnesota proposed an amendment to the Maritime Security and Competitiveness Act of 1993. The amendment restricted American ships carrying food aid overseas from charging the U.S. government rates in excess of "twice the level of competitive world market rates." The amendment was opposed by representatives from maritime states and supported by representatives from farm states, who figured they could export more food if the freight costs were reduced.

This fight concerned a little-known government regulation known as cargo preference, which requires that 75 percent of certain foreign food aid be shipped on privately owned U.S.-flag vessels. According to the General Accounting Office, cargo preference laws increased shipping bills to taxpayers by an estimated total of $578 million per year from 1989 through 1993. For the same years, USDA and AID report that the additional transportation costs of the preference cargo they shipped on U.S.-flag vessels averaged about $200 million and $23 million per year, respectively. Most of their preference cargo is foreign aid. From 1988 through 1992, USDA and

189

AID shipped 36 million metric tons of food aid. Of the total amount, 27.5 million tons (approximately 77 percent) was shipped on U.S.-flag vessels.

Cargo preference is just one of the hidden ways that U.S. companies get their hands on foreign aid money.

In support of the amendment, Representative Pat Roberts from the farming state of Kansas said,

> When it came time to pay for the freight—listen to this—when the USDA asked for bids from U.S.-flag carriers, one of the early bids came in at $138 per ton, more than five times the going world rate of $20 to $30 per ton. The Secretary of Agriculture wisely refused to accept a freight bid that was fully one-third higher than the value of the grain to be shipped. But as later bids came in, the USDA was forced to accept rates upward of $90 per ton, three times more than the world rate.

These funds, spent entirely to support American private companies and retain American jobs in the shipping industry, are called foreign aid. Predictably, Representative Jack Fields of Texas, a state from which much grain is shipped, spoke in opposition to the amendment. "How does the cost of cargo preference compare to agricultural subsidies?" he asked.

> Agricultural subsidies dwarf cargo preference. If we are going to be talking about subsidies, we ought to talk about agricultural subsidies. The U.S. government spends 8 of every 10 of its export financing dollars to promote the export of agricultural commodities, which account for only one-tenth of all American exports. The U.S. Government spent about $12.2 billion in domestic and export subsidies for agricultural products in 1992, about 15 times the total amount spent to promote the whole maritime industry and 90 times the amount spent on cargo preference.

And so the real battles over foreign aid are fought not in terms of helping the hungry but in this arena of battling subsidies. The companies and industries that line up at the subsidy trough—the agricultural industry, the shipping industry, the big private food exporters, and the NGOs—speak about food security, jobs, humanitarianism. The words they use to get their piece of the action are determined by their audience. The rationale can be hard-nosed utilitarian or weepy humanitarian or a mixture of the two. But at the tail end of the debate, there is always the same result: public money destined for private hands. The massive amounts of this money dwarf the few million here and there ripped off by corrupt Third World dictators. The prizes on this side of the ocean are much bigger, and entirely divorced from what actually happens to the food once it leaves these shores.

What was interesting about the debate on the Penny amendment was that it pitched two titanic interest groups against each other. The ensuing battle tore gaping holes in the wall of silence that often rises across both sides of the congressional aisle when talk turns to government pork. These are regional and individual economic issues, beyond the control of the party whips and others who would normally suppress a discussion.

In addition to highlighting the issue of agricultural subsidies, the Penny amendment debate led to the following statement from Representative Charles G. Rose III of North Carolina.

My 21 years with the House Committee on Agriculture have taught me that this debate is less about cost savings to the U.S. government and more about increasing the profit margins of multinational grain merchants, many of which have financial investments in foreign-flagged ships.

I attended the hearing that we had several months ago, June 1993, of the House Subcommittee on Foreign Agriculture and Hunger. And I asked a question of the president, Steve McCoy, of the North American Export Grain Association as to how many of his members owned or had interest in foreign-flag ships. He did not send me a straight answer to what I asked him in committee, but I have a list of the members of the North American Export Grain Association, and I think Members would probably all be interested to know that A.C. Toepfer International of Minneapolis, Continental Grain of Chicago, Interstate Grain of Corpus Christi, Cargill of Minneapolis, Ferruzzi Trading of New York, Matsui of New York, Richo Grain Limited of Stamford, CT, Archer Daniels Midland, Louis Dreyfus, and Mitsubishi, all who are members of the North American Export Grain Association, all who support the Penny-Grandy amendment, all have large interests in foreign-flag vessels.

I would ask Members to carefully look at who actually takes the risk in the sale of grain overseas. There is no risk on the grain exporters. The U.S. taxpayer pays about $1.25 a bushel on top of what the farmer gets of about $2 a bushel. The grain company gets—for $2 a bushel—the grain, and then can deal with it in foreign markets. But the American taxpayer pays a subsidy to the corn farmers in the districts of some of my friends of at least $1.25 a bushel.

Now, I want to see American farmers growing corn on the high plains of America, but I want to see American bottoms carrying American grain in American bottom ships on the high seas of the world. Why is that too much to ask for?

Richo Grain Co., one of the members of the North American Export Grain Association that opposes this amendment, is owned by a Swiss company owned by Marc Rich. He is in Switzerland. He is wanted for tax evasion, racketeering, and trading with the Ayatollah Khomeini. Among Rich's operations is an oil company and a fleet of 7 foreign-flag tankers.

Can Members wonder why he supports the Penny amendment?

Rose's statement seemed the stuff of high scandal. Nothing of what he said ever got far beyond the House chamber.

This time the Penny-Grandy amendment was defeated. But it was only one battle in a forty-year-old war that has been waged since the beginning of U.S. food-aid programs. It is a battle that has been waged out of the public's view as if it was the private affair of a few members of Congress, the way it has always worked, ever since an idealistic senator from Minnesota got the idea to change the name of the Agricultural Assistance Act to Food for Peace.

At the close of the Second World War, the United States was exporting food to a devastated Europe. The Marshall Plan's food component was a boon to American agriculture. But it was a short-term program. Europe rebuilt quickly and its agriculture was back on line by the early 1950s. Meanwhile, American farmers were still producing far beyond the demands of the domestic market.

In a normal world, the rising surpluses would lower prices—and profits—driving people out of the grain market until supply and demand would settle into some sort of harmony. That wasn't about to happen in the United States because, since the 1890s, a system of price supports has been in place. In order to take up the slack in demand and to ensure a floor price for commodities, the government's Commodity Credit Corporation would buy up any surplus.

The problem farmers had was that they had very few places to sell their grain. There were millions of farmers and a handful of grain companies who could easily and quietly fix prices. In addition, the farmers had another disadvantage: Since most harvests were ready for market at the same time in the fall, supply was highest and price was lowest just as farmers were ready to sell. To protect the farmers, the federal government, through the CCC, set up a mechanism that worked like this: Congress would determine a floor price for a commodity such as wheat, say $1 a bushel. The government promised farmers that if the big grain buyers bid the price below that level, if they only offered 90¢ a bushel, the farmer could go to the CCC and borrow $1 a bushel for the amount of wheat he had. When the grain companies finally needed the grain and bid the price back up, the farmers would sell it and repay the loan with interest.

If no buyers were in the market, however, the government would serve as the buyer of last resort. In order to protect itself, several years later, the government instituted a ceiling price for grains. If prices went above a certain level, the government released onto the market enough grains from its surplus stock to drive prices back down into the accepted range. But as farmers kept producing surpluses, the government ended up with too much stock. The only option was to destroy it. Soon it became easier and cheaper to pay the farmers *not* to grow food. That way no one had to worry about trucking, storing, and dumping it. It was much neater just to send a check to the farmer.

This worked as long as there were restrictions on imports. If grain companies such as Bunge and Cargill and Archer Daniels Midland were allowed to buy wheat from Argentina or Canada at 75¢ a bushel (or sugar from Haiti or peanuts from Senegal), the system would collapse. It required tariffs and quotas to keep foreign commodities out.

By the 1950s, technology was adding to America's surpluses, food stores were bulging, and the country was buried in its own abundance. The cost of storing the grain began to outstrip the value of the grain being stored. The storage cost was $6.5 million a month in 1952, increasing to almost $29 million monthly in 1957. Beyond that, there was a problem of deterioration, shrinkage, and spoilage, which in 1953 cost the government an estimated $20 million. The price was going to keep climbing.

The farm sector began to demand that the government take action to prop up prices, dispose of surplus, and bring back export markets. Having created a massive and wildly expanding supply, the federal government now had to create demand. With Europe's markets satisfied by their own domestic production, there was only one place to go: U.S. grain would have to be sent to the Third World—to Latin America, Asia, the Middle East, and Africa—where new states were emerging from colonialism.

The only problem was that these countries were broke. They had very little foreign exchange, only their own soft currencies, which American grain-trading companies had no use for. In the eyes of the grain exporters, the Third World needed a benefactor, someone to buy the food for them, or at least accept their rupees, cidis, and shillings while paying the exporters in dollars. The answer was obvious: The U.S. government would have to be the middleman and absorb the foreign currencies.

The mechanism that Congress finally adopted was Public Law-480, the

Agricultural Trade Development and Assistance Act of 1954, signed into law by President Dwight D. Eisenhower on July 10. The language in PL-480 clearly explained its purpose:

> to make maximum efficient use of surplus agricultural commodities in furtherance of the foreign policy of the United States, and to stimulate and facilitate the expansion of foreign trade in agricultural commodities produced in the United States by providing a means whereby surplus agricultural commodities in excess of the usual marketing of such commodities may be sold through private trade channels, and foreign currencies accepted in payment therefor.

The prime sponsor of this bill was the senator from the agricultural state of Minnesota, Hubert Horatio Humphrey. The bill seemed the perfect liberal panacea: On the surface, at least, it looked after the needs of the American farmer while spreading the benefits of American abundance to the impoverished masses of the Third World.

An early food aid prototype program was instituted in Vietnam during the 1950s. Testifying before Congress about that program, Eileen Egan from the American Council of Voluntary Agencies for Foreign Service testified to the success of the program there: "So here we have the use of American surplus to bring stability to people, and to give them a chance to produce for themselves. The area of South Vietnam was one of the least stable in Asia. It was torn by strife, and was the victim of an 8-year war; there were brigands roving the countryside. At this point, partly because of the use of American surplus foods, it is one of the most stable areas in Asia."

Ms. Egan's optimistic assessment of the stabilizing effects of food aid in Vietnam would be echoed again and again by other food-aid advocates in the coming decades. In the same hearing, Richard Reuter, executive director of CARE, boasted that his agency was feeding 7 million people worldwide and was planning to up that to 11 million people shortly. Reuter mentioned that CARE was supplying dairy products and added, "I think one of the school feeding programs is going to develop a market for milk, cheese, and some of the other items on an on-going basis."

"Mr. Chairman," one senator chimed in, "I might add that the use of powdered milk in these programs goes a long way toward stabilizing the dairy industry in this country."

Yes, Humphrey agreed. "You also develop eating habits which are very good for long-term American agriculture. Cheddar cheese, for instance, was not the most desirable product in some parts of the world, but now they are beginning to like it."

Responsibility for administering the program was spread over two congressional committees and nine federal government agencies. Among them was the Interagency Committee on Agricultural Surplus Disposal chaired by Charles Francis, chairman of General Foods. Despite the bureaucratic morass, the program was a huge success. In 1956, PL-480 accounted for 32 percent of total agricultural exports. Income to farmers increased by over $600 million in the first three years of the program as prices for food rose. And then there were the intangible benefits of the program as outlined by Senator Humphrey in his 1958 report entitled *Food and Fiber as a Force for Freedom.*

> A child in India could put his finger into the butter oil and taste it and say with a very loving sound in his voice—America. That is how they know America.
>
> Housewives in West Germany have been exposed to the idea that turkey is a good food at any time and not just during the Christmas season. The German government recently agreed to additional imports of turkey for United States dollars.
>
> A new brand of cigarettes containing a larger proportion of United States leaf has been put on the market in Japan. Estimated consumption of United States leaf last year increased by 1.6 million pounds above 1955.
>
> Schoolchildren in Yugoslavia have grown to like the taste of powdered milk so well they prefer it to the taste of fresh milk.

Still, it wasn't enough. Food surpluses continued to grow as farmers were paid for producing more food than the markets demanded. Swimming in waves of grain that threatened to wash away their profit margins, agricultural marketers prescribed their surpluses as a cure for all the world's ills.

The report began, "America's abundance of food and fiber is a tremendous asset in the world's struggle for peace and freedom—an asset still awaiting to be fully utilized with greater boldness and compassion."

In 1957, the Soviet Union had launched Sputnik I and the United States began gearing up for a crash program to launch itself ahead of the Soviet space program. The communists were ahead in the conquest of space and seemingly gaining in the conquest of the earth. To a rattled nation, Humphrey's report delivered these comforting words:

> In areas of Africa and Asia, as well as in other parts of the world, food means far more to vast millions of people today than any space satellite in the sky. Bread, not guns, may well decide mankind's future destiny. Thanks to our farm people, the United States is in a far better position than Russia to lead

the world toward the conquest of hunger and want. At a time when we are trying to catch up with the Soviet Union in other areas of competition, agriculture is one segment of our economy already geared to meet any emergency challenge, already offering us fully productive resources to meet any Soviet threat of economic warfare throughout the world. No crash program is needed in food and fiber production.

Humphrey had masterfully couched his argument in terms of the contemporary American obsession. He created the food race and made it seem as important as the arms race and the space race. "Khrushchev has served notice publicly that he intends to make Russia the world's leading supplier of food." Humphrey threw down his own challenge. "While it has proven a valuable and successful adjunct to national farm policy, the Public Law-480 program has far outgrown the narrow concept of serving primarily for the disposal of farm surpluses. It has become, as it should be, an important tool in foreign economic policy."

Fixation on the Soviet Union and patronizing attitudes about Africa and the Third World were such in the 1950s, that there was no taboo against proclaiming that America's bounty should be used to achieve political ends. No thought was given to the idea that recipient countries might be insulted by the food-for-loyalty exchange. "There needs to be greater recognition and acceptance of Public Law-480 as a government-wide instrument of international economic policy in support of our foreign policy objectives, rather than the narrower concept of it being merely an agricultural surplus disposal program," Humphrey wrote.

In 1959, Humphrey introduced the International Food for Peace Act as a response to his own study. While essentially similar in mechanics to the existing legislation, Humphrey's bill shifted the rhetorical emphasis away from commodity disposal and emphasized, instead, humanitarian and foreign policy objectives. There were some objections, most colorfully from Harold Cooley, Democrat from South Carolina and chairman of the Agriculture and Forestry Committee: "We are primarily interested in getting rid of these surpluses and we don't care how you do it and under what authority. We have told you we want the commodities sold for dollars first and then for foreign currencies, or then donate them."*

---

*Quoted in Vernon W. Ruttan, "The Politics of U.S. Food Aid Policy," in *Why Food Aid?* ed. Vernon W. Ruttan (Baltimore: Johns Hopkins University Press, 1993).

After some revisions and compromises, Humphrey's bill passed, the cosmetic changes were in place, and Food for Peace was institutionalized as part of America's foreign assistance program. John F. Kennedy's second act after his inauguration was to establish the Office of Food for Peace. At the head of the new office was a former congressman from South Dakota, George S. McGovern. When McGovern resigned to run for the Senate in 1962, he was replaced by CARE executive director, Richard Reuter, and the link between NGOs and Food for Peace was set.

Under Kennedy, food poured into Vietnam, where it was sold for local currency, which was used to pay for the growing American military presence there. The irony of using Food for Peace to wage a war wasn't lost on anyone, particularly not on Humphrey and McGovern, who were still championing the "Peace." Lyndon Johnson's response was to shift the Food for Peace office to USAID, where it continued to be a battleground of competing interests.

Food for Peace would be all things to all people, its image fluid and dependent on those to whom its virtues were being promoted. Advertised outside of America and by NGOs as humanitarian sacrifice, Food for Peace was always sold domestically as a program to aid American farmers.

In reality, however, it was neither.

The real beneficiaries of the aid program were, and are, the American equivalent of Siyaad Barre's inner circle. They are a small group of men with connections and money and influence. They are America's merchants of grain.

While Hubert Humphrey was touting the benefits of PL-480 in the 1950s, he breezed over one significant fact: Although total income was up, and the price per commodity was up, farm income actually fell, and the total number of farms in America was beginning to drop by 1 or 2 percent per year. The extra profits were being made by a group of middlemen, the very same grain-buying middlemen the original farm legislation was designed to circumvent.

America's largest grain-trading companies have something important in common with the grain merchants of Somalia: their franchise rests largely on the pleasure of the government in power. In Somalia corrupt officials gained control of the country's grain trade by cozying up to the government; in America they do it with massive political contributions. In the 1996 election year, as in every year since the beginning of the U.S. food-aid program, the list of the biggest campaign contributors to both political parties includes America's largest grain-trading companies. And at the very top of that list is the master of grain, Dwayne Andreas, CEO of the Archer Daniels Midland Company, the world's largest grain-trading company.

As Humphrey traveled the globe promoting American exports and American aid, he took with him an entourage of agribusiness giants, among them his close friend and regular travel companion Dwayne Andreas, who at that time was a vice president at Cargill, the massive, privately held grain-trading company based in Minneapolis. Andreas credits himself with educating his good friend Humphrey about the world. (His friendship with Humphrey never stopped him from contributing to Richard Nixon's presidential campaigns.) In a fawning authorized biography, Andreas recalls: "When Hubert was new to the Senate I would take him to places like Switzerland and Germany and London, and educate him about things like foreign exchange and the interlocking relationships of currencies. But then he became a *senior* senator, and afterward *he* took *me*."*

In 1977, ADM invested $80 million in plant and equipment to produce fructose, an artificial sweetener that would be profitable only if it could be sold more cheaply than sugar. Shortly thereafter, Senator Humphrey pushed through legislation that maintained an artificially high price for domestically produced sugar.

But it wasn't all that blatant. Under Humphrey's guidance, agribusiness interests became allied with the liberal agenda, government intervention, and food stamps. Giving food away suited the needs of the grain traders and could be easily camouflaged under the cloak of fighting poverty. Agribusiness became one of the leading advocates of the War on Poverty. What they wanted was simple: move the food without giving it away. The answer was food stamps. If you gave cash to poor people, they could do what they wished with it. They could buy alcohol, or they could invest it in a business. Food stamps ensured that the money would make its way back into the agribusiness food chain. In essence, the corporations got the government to buy their food.

In the 1980s, Humphrey was replaced by Senator Bob Dole as ADM's main man in Congress. And Dole became the most forceful advocate of what was one of the largest corporate subsidies in history: Archer Daniels Midland's ethanol project.

By adopting the popular causes of environmentalism and American fuel

---

*Quoted in *Supermarketer to the World*, by E. J. Kahn Jr. (New York: Warner Books, 1991). The book turns the now-embattled CEO into a legendary crusader for justice and capitalism.

self-sufficiency, Andreas and ADM were able to get taxpayers to fund a risky, and self-serving project to produce ethanol, a gasoline additive. No senator from Kansas was willing to raise the obvious questions about a program that resulted in $1.2 billion in annual net income for corn growers, even if it cost taxpayers more than $700 million a year.

But ethanol is a government boondoggle, a business venture that can not succeed without public support. And the only beneficiaries of the project are the corporations receiving the tax breaks.

It costs almost twice as much to produce ethanol as gasoline and, according to estimates from the Department of Energy, it sometimes takes more energy to make ethanol than it actually contains. There is no way to make it profitable.

Environmental claims for the product haven't panned out, either. While ethanol can reduce carbon dioxide emissions, it evaporates more quickly than gasoline, increasing emissions of volatile organic compounds and nitrous dioxide.

Trying to make good on pledges to reduce government waste, the House Ways and Means Committee voted in September 1995 to terminate ethanol's 17-year-old tax break. House Speaker Newt Gingrich, after a call from Dole, had the measure killed.

Andreas gives money to both Republicans and Democrats. He has donated $230,000 to Dole and allowed him to use the ADM corporate jet during the past two decades. And he gave Dole and wife Elizabeth a bargain price on their condominium in Bal Harbour, Florida. (The Andreases also have a condo in the same complex, and the two couples often keep each other company there.) The Andreas Foundation and other interests controlled by Andreas also donated $3 million to the American Red Cross after Elizabeth Dole became president of the charity in 1991.

The Andreas Foundation gave nothing to the Red Cross in the five previous years, but contributed $500,000 in 1991 and another $500,000 in 1992, after Andreas's wife, Inez, was named to the Red Cross board. The balance of Andreas's donation to the Red Cross were contributions in-kind: $2 million worth of ADM-produced vegetable burgers to feed the people in Haiti, all tax deductible, of course.

When Bob Dole resigned from the Senate to pursue the presidency in the spring of 1996, the ethanol industry braced for the worst.

"This is definitely not good news for the ethanol industry," said Doug Durante, executive director of the Clean Fuels Development Coalition [an industry group]. "I doubt that it will have much impact between now and the

November election, but the longer-term picture is much more uncertain for ethanol with Bob Dole in a leadership position."*

Andreas has also given more than $250,000 to the Democratic party since 1994. He co-chaired a 1992 dinner that raised money for President Clinton, and another one in 1994 that brought $2.5 million into democratic coffers. A week later the Environmental Protection Agency ruled that 10 percent of all gasoline must contain ethanol. Clinton has continued to support tax breaks for ethanol that will cost taxpayers an estimated $3.4 billion by the turn of the century.

And it isn't likely that much will come from a current criminal investigation against ADM for price fixing and fraud. Andreas has beaten the rap before. He was acquitted of federal charges of having arranged an illegal corporate contribution of $100,000 to Humphrey's unsuccessful 1968 presidential campaign. And later, ADM pleaded no-contest to charges of price fixing in its sales to the Food for Peace program and paid $200,000 in criminal penalties.

Rather than pointing out who really makes money from foreign aid, members of Congress have tended to blame lazy Third World recipients for the vast sums of wasted aid money. The leader of this charge is Senator Jesse Helms of North Carolina—himself the king of tobacco subsidies—who has spoken repeatedly about U.S. taxpayers' money going down "foreign rat holes."

"We have a Congress full of a lot of people who don't want to even hear the words 'foreign assistance,'" Jay Byrne, a spokesman for the U.S. Agency for International Development told the *Los Angeles Times* in October 1995. "When they say foreign aid is money going down a rat hole, the fact is that that 'rat hole' could be their district."

And most likely it is.

In fact, USAID doles out close to 80 percent of its contracts and grants to U.S. firms—which in turn provide food, supplies, or assistance to recipient nations overseas.

Organizations that lobby on behalf of aid understand that. They know the way to sell aid in Congress is to emphasize what we get from it. Yet these organizations, NGOs mostly, are put in a position to lobby on behalf of multibillion-dollar corporations so they can do their little piece of work and get their relatively tiny slice of the pie.

---

*Quoted in *Oxy-Fuel News*, May 20, 1996.

The grain-trading companies dominate the world of food, and in this scheme of things, the NGOs and charities serve two very important functions. First, they are the primary lobbyists for sending food to the Third World. Sally Struthers and Mother Teresa make better pitchmen than Dwayne Andreas on this account. Second, they are the agents, the contractors who move the food.

Yet even NGOs know that they have to pitch food aid for its domestic benefits. Ken Hackett, director of Catholic Relief Services, selling the idea of food aid to Congress said, "Each food aid dollar has at least a double impact. First, the funds are spent primarily in the United States on U.S. commodities, processing, bagging, fortification, and transportation. This enhances economic activity and increases the tax receipts to the U.S.government. Second, the food is provided to people and countries which cannot afford to import adequate amounts of food on a commercial basis. Finally, when PVOs are involved, we leverage funds and services and gain broad public participation."

The modern role of the NGO developed in the years following the creation of the Food for Peace program, and much of that early activity took place in Vietnam. The U.S. government found PL-480 to be a handy way to get around agreements limiting the amount of aid funds that could be sent to Vietnam. NGOs were under tremendous pressure to cooperate. As Professor Vernon Ruttan noted, "While cooperating with the government, the PVOs voiced their dissatisfaction with the increasing politicization of their programs. In spite of their reservations they allowed themselves to be used, because they were dependent on government money and supplies; most were willing to do whatever was necessary—including distributing food in situations that were at best questionable and at worst harmful to recipients."

That was in the early 1960s, and little has changed. CARE, the largest American NGO, has a budget that approaches half a billion dollars annually. More than half of that is in the form of commodities and funds they receive to administer the distribution of commodities.

According to the General Accounting Office in fiscal year 1993, NGOs distributed almost 1.2 million metric tons of U.S.-donated food aid, not including emergency aid, to fifty-eight countries. PVOs sold about 13 percent of the Title II commodities in 1993 to generate currency to pay costs associated with direct feeding projects and to conduct nonfood projects. The GAO has noted that NGOs tend to distribute food first, and examine the consequences later:

AID and PVOs have generally evaluated food aid projects based on commodity management and outputs, such as numbers of children fed or miles of road constructed, but have not assessed the impact of their projects on long-term food security. AID has stated that it and the PVOs are fully committed to doing a better job at evaluating the impact of food aid development projects on long-term food security and are making progress in developing and applying methodologies.

Humanitarian organizations have become comfortable in bed with the grain companies. Their survival and growth depend on it, but they must realize how the humanitarian instinct has become perverted by its partnership with domestic special interests. Humanitarians speak eloquently about the need for relief of hunger in the Third World. Yet most of the food aid they hand out—about 90 percent—is not emergency aid for starving people. (In fact, by law at least 76 percent of the commodities provided under Title II must be used for nonemergency development activities.) When food aid is criticized, their response is, "Do you suggest we let people starve?" It seems they've learned much from their partners in agribusiness, who see starving people as little more than another market for their products.

Hubert Humphrey's response to such accusations was: "So what's wrong with this?" Perhaps Somalia would have given Humphrey an adequate answer to the question. That, of course, might not bother some of the more cynical advocates of food aid. Crippled societies are just another marketing opportunity for those looking to get rid of free food. As long as there are aid workers willing to risk their lives to move the commodities, or the world is willing to send troops to move the food, anarchic societies are not an obstacle.

12

FEEDING THE FAMINE

At 3 p.m. the first relief flight appeared over the newly-liberated airport. It was a UN World Food Programme flight: the first for weeks to arrive at Mogadishu international airport. It circled for over half an hour to give Mitchell, the WFP man on the ground, time to ensure that all the television cameras were trained on the aircraft's WFP insignia. It landed. It slowly edged its way along the tarmac. It taxied for 20 minutes. It usually takes five minutes to maneuver from the runway to the airport apron but the UN had to get its publicity just like everybody else. Mr. Mitchell was heard saying with elation how he had secured more live television broadcasts for WFP than his "rival" UN agency, UNICEF.

Mark Huband reporting for *The Guardian*

Late in the evening, after the last American troops had left Somalia in March 1994, I sat with a group of Western journalists in a room at the Sahafi Hotel conducting a postmortem on our own performance. There was a sense among us that though the battle for Somalia was far from over, our role as reporters would be very much diminished from then on. No Americans meant no interest in this story from America. Without American papers buying stories from Somalia, the reporters would move on. The economics of journalism would prohibit the kind of day-to-day coverage that had been conducted for the previous sixteen months.

On that last night, one of the reporters in the room raised a question: Did we, the press, do the right thing bringing the troops in here? Among the assembled journalists, all experienced Somalia hands, not one raised an eyebrow about the pertinence of the query. The discussion that followed indicated that these journalists, though perhaps deluded about the extent of their power, understood quite well that they had raised the level of horror high enough to provoke an international military response.

To say that journalists in Somalia conspired in some organized way to do this would be wrong. Rather, reporters got caught up in the gathering momentum of their own stories. By the time U.S. Marines hit Mogadishu's beaches, Somalia, a journalistic backwater even by African standards, was the world's biggest story.

In the weeks preceding the arrival of U.S. forces, when every local TV news anchor in every American city was struggling to pronounce the names of towns like Jalalaqsi and Baidoa, conditions within Somalia actually were improving. Remarkably, the problem that supposedly required military intervention was becoming less of one every day. But the journalists in Somalia—or their editors at home—proved incapable of altering the terms of the story they had often simplistically shaped, a tale in which the United States had to do, as *New York Times* columnist Anna Quindlen put it, "the moral thing," i.e., send in the troops. Seen for what it was, Somalia was as much a story about the media as it was about the famine in that country. Specifically, it was a story about how journalists helped feed a famine and create a crisis demanding international attention.

Famines and wars differ from natural disasters in that it's usually easy to see them coming. For editors and reporters, a decision has to be made about when to report the story. "Famine on the Horizon" is a nonstarter. Even in times of relative peace and prosperity, people in Somalia, and all over the continent, die of diseases related to malnutrition. But like "Famine on the Horizon," the Somalia story is filled with economic and political intricacies that can't be photographed or quickly explained by a TV news correspondent reporting in front of dying people.

Occasionally, pieces are written that delve into the root causes of famine. Michael Hiltzik of the *Los Angeles Times* wrote on September 24, 1992, that famine is a "man-made" phenomenon that "can be created by misguided government policies that restrict the movement of food or disturb traditional practices." But for the most part, reasoned reportage such as this is buried amid the more marketable emotional story.

The Somali famine was no exception. Like most of the African continent's famines, it had its roots not in poor harvests or drought but in colossal malevolence on the part of the country's civil authorities. Food and food aid became highly contested economic and political tools, just as they had in famines in Biafra, Mozambique, the Sudan, and Ethiopia. The images of nefarious warlords and drug-crazed looters only added a touch of evil and spice to this all-too-common story of African starvation. And, as in all of these cases, press coverage—or the lack thereof—figured heavily in the events that unfolded.

The Somali famine of 1992 differed from other famines primarily in terms of the magnitude of the international response it received. American press coverage of starvation often reaches the point where it helps attract thousands of dollars and hundreds of aid workers from around the world. In Somalia, however, the coverage helped attract millions of dollars and thousands of aid workers, and, in the end, thousands of foreign soldiers.

Coverage of Somalia followed a progression of five steps that have become a template for famine reporting. These steps can be taken gradually or quickly—sometimes even two at once. Somalia in 1992 and Ethiopia in 1984–85 completed the five-step cycle. For various reasons, other famines, such as the ongoing one in the Sudan, never move beyond the first step or two. What is important to understand is that as press coverage of a particular famine reaches Step Three and beyond, it typically has gathered such momentum as to be impervious to facts that do not fit the popular story line.

Here are the five steps:

Step One takes the form of what might be called the early predictor story, which usually appears as a wire service piece from Rome (headquarters of the UN's World Food Program) or Geneva. Such stories warn of huge populations in danger of famine if something is not done, and say more donations are needed to avert disaster. Sometimes there are follow-ups to this story, but unless photographs of the famine materialize—which is to say, unless the next step is reached—the early predictor story remains just a news brief.

Step Two occurs as the few relief organizations working in an area persuade some members of the news media—especially those who work in television—that the press is ignoring a famine story. A few news organizations show up, usually at the invitation and with the assistance of the relief organizations, and produce stories that do have pictures. These stories are about not just the hunger but how it has been ignored. Having "discovered" the famine, the correspondents vigorously publicize it.

Step Three is taken as more news organizations show up and, with the story now thoroughly simplified, "expose" the famine, commenting on "forgotten people" in remote and dangerous places. The suffering of people is a morality tale starring the news media. News accounts imply that neglect by the West is partly responsible for the mass starvation. Readers and viewers are supposed to be concerned, even feel guilty: The West must act now. News reports are saturated with graphic descriptions of hunger and misery. Numbers of people dead and in danger are offered as TV coverage dominates.

Step Four occurs as the numbers of starving and dying people grow. This is the key moment in the evolution of famine coverage. How many people have to die before the famine fires its booster rockets and becomes a major media event? There doesn't appear to be a set number. But one can be sure of a turning point when words like "holocaust" or "hell" or "famine of the century" are found regularly in media accounts.

Step Five is reached when more journalists arrive from smaller papers and local television stations. Now the crisis has become a cause. An international public has been mobilized. Donations flow to relief organizations. Newspaper articles include lists of relief agencies accepting donations, and during newscasts, television networks provide the toll-free numbers of the agencies.

In reality, parts of Africa are always at Step One, though often the predicted famines fail to materialize either because the people predicting the famine are wrong or because governments find other ways around food shortages. For example, in undramatic fashion and without the aid of CARE or the UN, governments purchase food on international markets to shore up reserves.

In Somalia's case, articles about an impending famine were published as early as February 1991, just after the fall of dictator Siyaad Barre. "Twenty-seven million people in Africa are threatened with starvation in a disaster that aid agencies fear could be far worse than the 1984–85 Ethiopian famine," *Newsday* reported on February 21, 1991, on the basis of wire service accounts. This early predictor story listed Somalia along with Ethiopia and the Sudan as crisis spots. For the next two months, UN agencies flogged the 27-million-in-danger story, which ran in most U.S. papers. It bears noting that a famine "far worse" than the 1984–85 Ethiopian famine never materialized—not in the Sudan, Ethiopia, or Somalia. Similar stories ran at various times in 1994 and 1995, claiming that upwards of 30 million people were in danger of starving. Neither famine materialized.

Step Two coverage generally follows immediately from Step One. If a follow-up story is going to be written about a predicted African famine, it is usually about how nothing is being done. This reflects the agenda of the aid agencies, who are the main source of the story—and who are trying to raise money to mobilize.

Steps Two and Three occurred over the next year. The ouster of Siyaad Barre didn't get much press coverage because it coincided with the beginning of the Gulf War. But the war soon became more than just the reason Somalia was ignored. It was seen as the moral antithesis to feeding the hungry. News reports started quoting aid officials who blamed the United States for pouring all its attention and resources into the war while Africa was facing starvation. On February 18, 1991, Julian M. Isherwood of United Press International wrote: "The Gulf War, potentially one of the most devastating wars in history because of its use of advanced technology of destruction, has stolen the headlines from these other wars and catastrophes around the world, as well as the diplomatic momentum to solve long-standing armed quarrels and help those in need."

On March 10, 1991, the St. Louis Post–Dispatch reported from London, "Aid organizations believe the Persian Gulf War is largely to blame for the huge shortfall in government donations, diverting attention from the African drought." The challenge to America was apparent: You are willing to use your money and might to kill, but not to help starving Africans.

By the summer of 1992, months of lobbying by aid agencies resulted in a jump in press coverage about starvation in Somalia.

By this time, too, the morality of U.S. policy in Africa had particular resonance; the presidential race was moving into high gear. The Bush policy regarding Haitian refugees had been attacked as "immoral and racist." At the same time, there was an expectation that the United States soon would militarily intervene in the Balkans and that Somalia would be ignored. In July, UN Secretary General Boutros Boutros-Ghali chastised the Security Council for ignoring the fate of Africans and focusing too much on "a rich man's war" in former Yugoslavia. Boutros-Ghali borrowed this slogan from anti–Gulf War protesters who had chanted: "Why should the poor fight a rich man's war?" With the Gulf War a distant memory, Somalia was now held up against Bosnia as a morality test for President Bush's foreign policy. The press corps duly assisted this effort.

On August 12, the Washington Post headlined an article by Nairobi correspondent Keith Richburg, "Somalia's Overshadowed Tragedy: World Anxious About Balkan Turmoil, Aloof to That in Africa," in which Richburg wrote: "If tragedy were measured simply in numbers of human lives destroyed, the one in Somalia would, by many accounts, be judged greater than that in Croatia and Bosnia. Here, civil war has been compounded by a famine that is starving entire villages. But unlike the Balkans, the Somali crisis has attracted little international attention or aid, and only faint, distant calls for Western military involvement."

Richburg quoted Sanford J. Ungar, a former *Post* correspondent stationed in Africa who is now dean of American University's communications school. Speaking of what he called "a Eurocentric bias," Ungar told the *Post*, "It's part of the old myths and assumptions that the most important things happening in the world at any given time are the things happening in Europe."

The same day, Anna Quindlen in her *New York Times* column sounded the interventionist war cry, blaming United States inaction on Eurocentrism: "But the truth is that we are a deeply Eurocentric nation. . . . Bosnia, with all its horrors, is at the center of public and political dialogue and Somalia, with all its horrors, is a peripheral discussion." She quoted Jack Healey, executive director of Amnesty International to explain why: "It's racism." That tons of relief food and supplies were flowing into Somalia, with more on the way, did not impress Quindlen. "The United Nations has agreed to airlift food into the interior," she wrote, "but that is neither an adequate nor a long-term solution. Senator Nancy Kassebaum, who sits on the Senate Subcommittee on African Affairs, supports the use of an international force of soldiers to make sure food shipments get to the people."

Quindlen then played the Gulf War card: "Just a year ago some of us, unpersuaded by the high moral principles involved in giving our all for cheap oil, were saying that America could no longer afford to police the world. With the President's Gulf War bluster about liberation, we lost sight of the best reason to involve ourselves in foreign affairs—because it is sometimes obviously the moral thing to do." Her conclusion: "Surely our empathy can transcend race."

This was a perfect foreign policy cudgel to use on President Bush—no one expected him to send the marines to Somalia. Once he did, however, those who were so quick to point out the immorality of inaction seemed utterly unprepared to deal with the entirely new set of moral quandaries that accompanied the use of overwhelming military force in the service of humanitarian goals.

Although most Americans know about Operation Restore Hope, the military intervention in Somalia, few know about Operation Provide Relief, the massive airlift of food that began in the summer of 1992 and was financed primarily by the United States. As a result of this effort, food was reaching those in need, and death rates were beginning to fall. But the possibility of an invasion already had been raised, and this began to shape the famine coverage in the papers and on TV.

Indeed, it was this possibility of U.S. intervention—and far less the hungry people of Somalia—that led to the surge of media attention in the fall of 1992. Journalists who had never been to Africa were horrified at what they found and filed gruesome stories. Though no one really knew how many had died, press accounts were filled with numbers of dead and dying. Coverage of the famine in Somalia had moved to Step Four—the growth in the number of deaths.

On September 15, the Associated Press quoted CARE president Philip Johnston: "'From 2,000 to 5,000 Somalis are dying each day,' he said." Johnston, described in the article as a "private relief expert," was in the United States raising money for CARE.

On October 2, the *Washington Post*'s Richburg found an honest source to comment on the death rates in Somalia: "'I don't think anyone has a clue how many people have died,' said Roy Williams of the International Rescue Committee."

On October 4, Associated Press correspondent Mort Rosenblum wrote: "Even now, the relief officials said, efforts lag far behind the need. An estimated 1.5 million Somalis are in danger of starving to death and already are dying at a rate of 2,000 a day."

On October 8, the AP reported: "Up to two million Somalis are said to be at imminent risk of starving to death. Estimates of the number who have died vary widely, but experts agree it far exceeds 100,000."

That figure appeared in thousands of newspaper articles until October 12, when Boutros-Ghali's special envoy to Somalia, Mohamed Sahnoun, told a fund-raising conference in Geneva that 300,000 people might have died from war and famine while the United Nations did nothing and Somalia "descended into hell." The 300,000 figure was then cited as the UN estimate, while the Red Cross and CARE continued to tell reporters the death figure was around 100,000. But the higher number prevailed in news accounts.

Reports conflicted on the severity of conditions in Somalia. A careful reader would have noticed that the situation in Baidoa was improving, while the situation in Bardera was getting worse. These details, and the questions they might have raised about the localized impact of the famine, were lost in the overall impression that the entire country was starving. Television cameras continued to seek out and broadcast the worst cases, while print coverage took a backseat to the pictures. On October 11, Reuters reported that the international relief efforts had turned the tide of death in Baidoa, a symbol of Somalia's agony. "The known daily death rate has dropped from 400 to around 100 in recent weeks, [the Red Cross] says."

Jane Perlez, then covering Africa for the *New York Times*, was one of the few correspondents who tried to be more specific. On October 22, she reported that 65 people in Baidoa had died that night. (In fact, 65 deaths per day was about average for the month of October according to official Red Cross documents examined later.)

At the same time that conditions in Baidoa were improving without international military intervention, news accounts conveyed that 1,000 people were dying every day in Somalia. Most echoed this October 29 report from the United Nations as found in the *Washington Post:* "The new UN plan comes amid growing concern that unless international relief efforts intensify, an estimated 250,000 Somalis could die by the end of the year and an additional 4.5 million could face starvation."

In fact, 4.5 million represented the vast majority of the total population of Somalia, and it would have been clear to anyone traveling beyond the immediate famine zone that the vast majority was, to the contrary, not in any danger at all. (Some sources place the entire population of Somalia at 4.5 to 5.5 million.) The entire population of the famine-affected areas of the country was actually only 2.5 to 3 million.

The point of such UN reports is clearly to generate big numbers in the hope of provoking a response. What does it mean to face starvation? Nomads, I suppose, "face" starvation all the time, which is all the report was saying, since there were fewer than 4.5 million people in the entire affected area of southern Somalia. The media uncritically passed along all of the UN's propaganda as if it were blasphemous to demand details and hard facts during an emergency.

Nor did anyone in the press point out that earlier dire predictions had not materialized. Typical of summertime newspaper stories was this AP dispatch: "The United Nations estimates 1.5 million people are in imminent danger of starving to death in Somalia while another 4.5 million are nearing a food crisis."

Though aid agencies often generate baseless numbers on their own initiative, reporters also play a large role. I've been to hundreds of news conferences in the midst of crises where journalists relentlessly demanded figures from reluctant spokespersons. Numbers make journalists sound authoritative—and editors back home demand them.

In the Somali context, and during most crises, this is idiocy. Numbers are usually baseless fabrications. As an example of how difficult it is to come up with numbers, Murray Watson wrote the following in an unpublished critique of aid agencies in Somalia.

> Between 1978 and 1989 the World Bank, USAID and other donors invested about $600 million in development projects, many of which were concerned with generating a knowledge base about how rural Somalis were using natural resources in generating food and cash for survival and socio-economic advancement. At some periods there were almost fifty expatriate professionals with degrees in statistics, agronomy, sociology, livestock science, ecology, nutrition, public health, demography, fisheries, economics, agriculture, meteorology, pedology, hydrology, etc. working in Somalia. Most of these professionals had long experience working in Africa . . . Many of these were either based for long periods in the rural areas, or making frequent visits to them. At that time it was possible to drive and spend the night ANYWHERE in Somalia. And even then no professionals knew enough to say that "x" percent of the population were malnourished, or that "y" thousand tons of food would be needed to keep them alive, although droughts and famines did from time to time occur or were claimed to occur.

Reporters used manufactured statistics to back up their own very real observations, yet few put their observations in context. Most were reporting from the so-called triangle of death that encompassed the towns of Bardera and Baidoa. The reporters were brought there, housed, and fed by relief agencies working in those towns. They drove along the very roads that four armies had passed as Mohamed Farah Aydiid battled first with the forces of Siyaad Barre and later with soldiers loyal to Barre's son-in-law, Mohamed Hersi Morgan. Bardera experienced a large jump in deaths in mid-October after Aydiid's forces pulled out and Morgan's fought their way in. This temporary surge in the death rate coincided with a huge increase in media attention that made all of Somalia seem like Bardera. In addition, relief camps were set up in major towns, and victims flocked to those towns, presenting to visiting reporters a concentration of misery that was indeed shocking.

There was very little reporting that let people know that most of Somalia was fine.

• • •

Aid workers who weren't in the relief business at the time had a very different perspective. Willie Huber had flown with Murray Watson over the Baidoa area to try to get some firsthand perspective on what they'd been getting from the media. "We kept hearing that this is the biggest catastrophe in the world and that millions of people were at risk and thousands of people dying every day, and so on. We really wanted to know a little bit more. From the plane we saw all the areas of the country which were not accessible by jeeps and by cars. There were people down there who probably at that time did not even know that a civil war had hit their country. They were going on about their life as if nothing had happened.

"Baidoa became really a focus. And as soon as the food was being distributed from there, a big rush of people arrived from other parts. I also believe people who have not been that much affected by the drought had been going toward Baidoa for this food in search of relief. But just 10 kilometers from Baidoa you start finding a completely normal life."

On November 25, 1992, President Bush offered to send American troops to Somalia. Even though the food situation had improved dramatically, the country now was in full-blown Step-Five famine coverage. CBS's Dan Rather and ABC's Ted Koppel were en route, ahead of the American soldiers. Reporters from dozens of local television stations were arriving. Many would have been shocked at Somali living conditions, even during the best of times. None of these reporters questioned why troops were needed, although they themselves could move safely throughout Somalia.

Yet when the troops landed in Mogadishu in full combat gear and met reporters wearing Levi's Dockers and T-shirts, everyone should have known something was wrong.

Months later, having returned to New York, I was watching the action on television as the U.S. networks joined CNN in starting to lay on the video coverage. Newscasts faded into ads for Save the Children. At first I thought, How tricky of Save the Children to make their ads look like news. Then I realized that it was the other way around. The news was looking like Save the Children ads. The massive concentration of images of death was moving, but this was not the Somalia I had seen.

In Somalia I had seen the day-trippers—the camera crews that bounded off relief planes and asked the nearest relief worker to take them to the sickest children before the plane took off again in thirty minutes. The relief workers usually obliged. For television, the worst, most despairing picture was the best. Famine and horror became a commodity. The worse it looked the better it sold. At the same time, the possibility of American intervention increased the value of that commodity. This was the first Africa story ever that had a solid hometown America angle to it: For the first time, the sons and daughters of middle America were in Africa.

Returning to Nairobi, I went to the Reuters television archives and began poring through hours of raw video footage of the famine. The scenes were gruesome, but before the editing, certain things were clear. The sound track was filled with voices of people going about their lives, children playing and shouting in Somali at the cameraman. One kid screamed, "Hey, infidel, stick that camera in your butt."

As cameras panned away from the sullen faces of the sick, they passed across the faces of the curious—children and young men who had come to watch the news media. Though the scenes of death were horrifying, the raw footage held none of the helplessness and hopelessness that was conveyed by the edited news footage.

The morning after the American troops left Somalia, most of the press followed. The story was over. The predictable tale of famine, upon running its course, had become an American story, a military odyssey, a failed but exciting hunt for a fugitive warlord, and then an American tragedy. A noble gesture by one president had become a foreign policy debacle for his successor. A cartoon by Oliphant seemed to sum it up for most Americans. In frame one, a soldier is feeding a hungry Somali child. In frame two the child shoots the soldier. Copies of that cartoon hung in the offices and barracks of the American military.

The journalists sitting around that hotel room their last night in Mogadishu seemed to know this, acknowledging their own contribution to the endgame. And the reporter who had raised the question about the press corps' role in the U.S. intervention answered it. "We were wrong."

The effect was that 30,000 American troops poured into an improving situation. If the press reports had emphasized that things were getting better, there would not likely have been much support for the intervention. And journalists sent 9,000 miles to the Horn of Africa by their hometown papers weren't about to report that things had gotten better. First, they couldn't have known. And second, no editor wants to shell out all that cash only to learn that his reporter missed the worst of the situation. Reporters, especially TV reporters, like to put on their flak jackets and khakis and do their stand-ups in front of the worst devastation possible. Reporters, after all, want to be noticed. That's why they become reporters.

They want to put themselves into dramatic situations. That's how they become famous reporters.

So how many people did die? How many lives were saved? NGOs are in need of a number so they can attempt to quantify the effects of their efforts as well as brag about it. A total number of lives saved becomes a kind of community property. Everyone who was near Somalia or raised money for Somalia or spoke about Somalia can speak proudly about the numbers of lives that were saved there.

One unbiased attempt to quantify things was made by the Refugee Policy Group, an independent NGO based in Washington. Their November 1994 report, *Lives Lost, Lives Saved: Excess Mortality and the Impact of Health Interventions in the Somalia Emergency*, offers some numbers, despite the candid admission that the process of arriving at figures is "so fraught with methodological problems that it is rarely attempted."

The report states: "By the time the first feeding programs had been established, excess mortality had already peaked. By the time the media had visited Baidoa and relief flights were ongoing, the peak of the mortality had already passed."

The RPG study concludes that some 202,000 to 238,000 people died from famine in Somalia, and 100,000 deaths were averted because of outside assistance. Of those lives saved, 10,000 were saved after the U.S. Marines landed in December 1992.

The Americans stepped in on December 9, 1993, because UNOSOM—the UN Operation in Somalia—failed to hold onto a fragile peace among the Somalia's clan factions. UNOSOM (which is now known as UNOSOM I) with its military contingent of 500 Pakistani soldiers succeeded only briefly in intimidating the factions into any kind of compromise. Once the fighters adapted to their presence it was business as usual, looting, killing, and intimidation of aid workers. The Pakistanis were the butt of jokes among the Somali militias who realized very quickly that the force was utterly impotent. Mohamed Sahnoun had been saying all along that outside force was not the answer, and he embarked upon a grassroots diplomatic campaign.

In retrospect, many critics of the military intervention have said that Sahnoun's way would have brought peace to Somalia. That isn't at all certain. In all likelihood his tactic of conciliation and appeasement would have eventually left him and the UN where they ended up anyway—weak and ineffectual. What is certain is that UN headquarters in New York wanted something bigger and more sensational than one Algerian diplomat talking peace with Somalia's clan leaders. UN Secretary General Boutros Boutros-Ghali wanted his massive intervention. Sahnoun stood in the way. And Sahnoun's early successes in getting the factions to talk became a threat to the secretary general's plans. Sahnoun was ignored by New York and essentially given no option but to resign at the end of October 1993. The American-led, 30,000-strong Unified Task Force would take over from UNOSOM.

13

THE MOGADISHU LINE

A man who has warned you has not killed you, yet.

—Somali proverb

On Memorial Day of 1994, President Bill Clinton handed Congressional Medals of Honor to the widows of Master Sergeant Gary Gordon and Sergeant First Class Randall Shughart.* The two soldiers had been killed in combat in Mogadishu, October 3, 1993. "They were real American heroes," Clinton said. Indeed they were. Gordon and Shughart jumped from a helicopter into what they knew was near certain death to save the lives of their comrades. "They were part of a larger mission—a difficult one," Clinton said, a mission "that saved hundreds of thousands of innocent Somalis from starvation, and gave that nation a chance to build its own future."

This last part wasn't exactly true. Gordon and Shughart had arrived on a very specific mission with the Army Rangers and the secretive and specialized Delta Force in August of 1993, long after starvation was any kind of issue in Somalia. That very month, in fact, all feeding programs had been stopped. Theirs was a purely combat mission: to capture, or otherwise

---

*It was the first time the medals had been awarded since Vietnam.

punish, warlord Mohamed Farah Aydiid. On that October Sunday, eigh-teen Americans died, eighty-four were wounded, one was captured, and two had their lifeless corpses dragged through the dust by angry and victo-rious Somalis. And the Somali anger was understandable: perhaps 500 Somalis perished that bloody day, many of them civilians caught in the crossfire as the Americans invaded a densely populated neighborhood in what would be their final assault against Aydiid.

In his speech, Clinton was trying to put the best possible spin on what had become a tragic mess. He once again raised the humanitarian banner, reminding his audience of what had supposedly brought us to Somalia in the first place. It didn't work. In the previous four months, the images from Somalia had changed: One day we were looking at photos of beefy marines rescuing big-eyed starving babies. The next day it was equally compelling images of Cobra attack helicopters strafing Mogadishu streets. Suddenly the humanitarian intervention had become a military assault. The skinny Somalis who had so recently been seen as victims had become the enemy.

Congress and the press together wondered aloud: When did the mission change? How did the humanitarian relief effort, so simple, become a hunt for a warlord? When did we get involved in nation building? This is how journalists and politicians who supported the intervention in the begin-ning distanced themselves from the bloody finale ten months later. Writing in the November 1, 1993, issue of the *National Review*, Brit Hume echoed the sentiments of those who had woken up to the realities of Somalia: "Mr. Bush's humanitarian mission had been transformed, with little high-level discussion and almost no public debate." In Congress, Senator John Mc-Cain of Arizona, a supporter of Bush's intervention in Somalia, accused Clinton of changing the mission.

It was as if someone had thrown a switch while no one was looking, sending all of Somalia down a different track. In reality, however, Bush's "purely humanitarian" mission was a mirage. A realistic analysis of the sit-uation in Somalia would have shown that the policy path Bill Clinton wan-dered down during his first year in office was the logical extension of the direction in which the Bush initiative was heading. If the Somalia mission was to be more than a grandiose public relations stunt, the military would have to tackle real problems, the problems that were hidden behind the simplistic notion propagated by the media and the relief agencies: People are hungry; send soldiers to deliver food.

Somalia is not a story of how a humanitarian mission became a military adventure. It's about how the people running a humanitarian mission became so dedicated to their cause that they started to see strafing, bombing, and killing as humanitarian acts. And it's about how the institutions built to perform the mission became more important than the goals of that mission. President Bush never could have gotten public or Pentagon support if he'd asked for 28,000 marines to battle factional bandits in a distant African country. He had little trouble getting support to send 28,000 marines to feed people. But in reality it was the same thing, and Bush administration officials were aware of this.*

Starvation in Somalia was political. It was caused by the warlords. The solution was going to have to be political, and probably military. In the feel-good early days of the mission, no one wanted to hear that. They wanted to believe it was all about those kids in the CARE ads. They wanted to believe it was about delivering food and making them smile. But delivering food is easy. It took trucks, people to load them, and guns to get them past the bandits. That mission was accomplished quickly. Once again, withdrawing was going to be the problem.

The violent events that occurred in 1993 were not an aberration; they were, in fact, foreign aid carried out to its logical extreme. Foreign aid run amok. The desire to help had—as it almost always does—become the desire to control. In a routine foreign aid situation there is local government, even a corrupt local government, to check the tendency of aid organizations toward control. There is a point at which the interests of the aid organizations clash with the interests of the government. Aid organizations across the Third World have been lectured or deported in hundreds of instances where governments have perceived a challenge to their sovereignty.

Aid organizations regularly complain that local governments are the main obstacle to development. If only they were allowed total control, they might be able to really do development work. Somalia was the perfect chance to test this. There were no controls on aid agencies or what they could do. It was as if a tumor was set loose in a body without an immune system. The operation in Somalia became the primary focus of a number of aid organizations, including the International Committee of the Red Cross, which spent more than half its budget there in 1993.

Although the aid organizations had total freedom to do as they pleased, there was a catch: Without a local government, there were no police to

---

*According to a report in the Los Angeles Times just before the December 9, 1992, intervention, "Officials caution that once the food supplies are rolling again, the allies . . . would face an even more trying question: how to put together a viable government capable of running the country without increasing civil strife."

keep the peace. Somalia was dangerous. Organizations were subjected to extortion by warlords and petty bandits. Aid workers were being killed. They hired armed guards to protect them, but just as often ended up being robbed or held hostage by those very same guards. Since there was no government and no banking system, they had to deal in cash—boxes of cash. Planeloads of it were coming in every day, which only made them more tempting targets.

So they needed security. They needed to bring in an armed force from outside so they could continue to do relief and development work. Led by CARE and its president, Philip Johnston, they asked for military intervention, but they wanted it on their own terms. They wanted the military to act as facilitators for humanitarian organizations, serve their interests. But the military doesn't work that way. Aid organizations quickly realized that the military had its own agenda and its own way of doing business. It was like the early missionaries and traders in Africa who asked military backing so they could go about their business. One day you had a small British garrison protecting a trade route; a year later you had a colony and total political control. No sooner had the soldiers landed than the aid organizations began to complain about them: they did too much, they did too little; they failed to disarm the factions; they were violating human rights in their attempts to disarm the factions. Aid agencies were dismayed to find that the soldiers were acting like soldiers.

But the military intervention also opened the door to a flood of aid agencies. In the violent fall of 1992, there were only a handful operating in Somalia. On the heels of the military intervention, hundreds set up shop. The publicity generated by the military intervention meant that money was pouring into their coffers. Somalia was a business opportunity.

For the U.S. military and the UN, Somalia offered a different kind of opportunity. Their agenda was much more ambitious, their problem more daunting: The UN in Somalia was creating a model for post–Cold War intervention. The UN and Secretary General Boutros Boutros-Ghali wanted their own army. Somalia would set a precedent, a Chapter VII intervention—peace enforcement. Bush's New World Order was coming apart in Somalia and in Bosnia, but Bosnia seemed too dangerous. Ed Vulliamy, a reporter for *The Guardian*, got at least one State Department planner to openly admit, "There was no doubt that Somalia was instead of Bosnia, a way of staying out of Bosnia."* Bosnia was deemed too dangerous, the mis-

*The Guardian, May 20, 1996, p. 12.

sion filled with too many unknowns. Somalia would provide some answers. The idea was that an aggressive, muscular UN would emerge from Somalia ready to fight in Bosnia and probably in other sticky post–Cold War wars, wars where the United States did not have a defining national interest but where it nonetheless would want to intervene. Somalia would work the glitches out of the system. But there really hadn't yet been an opportunity to test out the military machine.

Aydiid and the other warlords had more or less cooperated with UNITAF. But Aydiid particularly had been a beneficiary of the Americans' control of UNITAF. For example, after negotiations with U.S. special envoy Robert Oakley, both Aydiid and his crosstown rival Ali Mahdi Mohamed had stored their heavy arms in Authorized Weapons Storage Sites (AWSS). However, whereas Ali Mahdi was told to move his weapons some 12 kilometers out of town, Aydiid's storage sites remained in town, accessible within minutes should a war flare up. During the UNITAF period, from December 1992 until May 1993, Oakley met regularly with Aydiid. The two men seemed to enjoy being seen together. General Joseph Hoar would later say, "We kept a level playing field between the clans by meeting with Aydiid every day."

Aydiid would not enjoy such favored treatment after Oakley and UNITAF departed.

On May 5, 1993, the United Nations Operation in Somalia (UNOSOM II) took over, eventually building to a 28,000-strong international military presence, including troops from Pakistan, Canada, India, Bangladesh, Zimbabwe, Botswana, United Arab Emirates, Italy, and a greatly reduced American contingent, the 1,300-man QRF, or Quick Reaction Force. The Americans were there only as backup in case of immediate threats or to support other UNOSOM troops if needed.*

The UNOSOM II mandate (UN Security Council Resolution 814) was much more aggressive and ambitious than what UNITAF had set out to accomplish. Where UNITAF was essentially a heavily armed food delivery service, UNOSOM was, in fact, a nation-building exercise. And it was im-

---

*Despite the partisan anti-UN hysteria that arose in the States after October 3, that was never the case. At no time was the QRF under UN command. They were commanded on the ground in Somalia by Lieutenant General Thomas Montgomery, who answered to CENTCOM in Florida, commanded by General Joseph Hoar. Hoar answered to General Colin Powell.

plemented under Chapter VII of the UN Charter, peace enforcement.* And aggressive military involvement. The Security Council resolution spoke of "the restoration of law and order throughout Somalia," the "re-establishment of local and regional administrative institutions, the reconstitution of the police," and it recognized the importance of disarmament to any progress.

American lawmakers would later belittle the UN, charging that these goals were unrealistic. The reality, however, was that Resolution 814 was not written by UN bureaucrats. It came almost intact from the office of General Colin Powell.

So a group of poorly equipped and disorganized Third World armies were set up to undertake a series of tasks that the U.S. Marines refused to even consider.

But this was precisely the idea. With all sorts of nastiness cropping up in places like Rwanda, Liberia, and Haiti, potentially in central Asia, and most immediately in the Balkans, the UN needed to build the capacity for dealing with these new things called failed states. The people behind Resolution 814 never actually believed it would succeed in Somalia. There were too many problems to begin with, starting with the fact that the country had never known anything like the democratic institutions 814 was purporting to set up. Or, as one high-ranking U.S. official put it, "You had to have a lot of imagination to think you could do anything with Somalia."

But to really test its wings, the UN needed an enemy; Aydiid was only too happy to oblige. In Aydiid, they had themselves a formidable foe, but one who could be beaten, or so the planners thought.

---

*The best explanation of the difference between Chapter VI, peacekeeping, and Chapter VII, peace enforcement, was articulated by British colonel Allan Mallinson, writing in *Jane's Defense Weekly*, October 28, 1995. Mallinson is responsible for the development of the British army's doctrine for operations other than war.

Peacekeeping is politically centered. The essence of peacekeeping operations is that UN troops operate in support of diplomacy, acting as a third party, transparently applying principles that sustain the belligerents' consent to international intervention. This facilitates dispersal and freedom of movement, essential for a peacekeeping force, and keeps force levels low, aiding operational endurance.

On the other hand, peace enforcement is ultimately about using force to compel compliance in the absence of consent: the probability is that one, or more, of the belligerents becomes the de facto enemy, and the intervention troops themselves become combatants. In these circumstances an approach akin to warfighting is required, with peacekeeping principles supplanted by the principles of war; notably surprise, concentration of force and offensive action.

• • •

In June of 1993, the UN went after Aydiid, invoking the full powers granted under Chapter VII of the UN Charter. A line had been crossed that would become known as the Mogadishu Line, the abandonment of a humanitarian neutrality, but the term would not be used until more than a year later, in a very different place. As Serb forces were shelling and capturing so-called UN safe areas, Lieutenant General Sir Michael Rose, the UN commander, spoke of his reluctance to call UN troops into action. He did not, he said, want to cross the Mogadishu Line.

In Somalia that line was crossed in a flash on June 6, 1993. In a special Sunday session, the UN Security Council declared war on Aydiid when it issued Resolution 834.*

On June 5, twenty-four Pakistani soldiers were killed and fifty-six were wounded in gun battles around Mogadishu. Without any investigation of what had happened, the UN charged Aydiid with a premeditated ambush and issued an instant indictment, launching a week-long series of attacks on Aydiid's various strongholds and Authorized Weapons Storage Sites (AWSS) around the city. When the bombardment ended, the Special Representative of the Secretary General (SRSG) in Mogadishu, American Admiral (retired) Jonathan Howe, issued a warrant for Aydiid's arrest and placed a $25,000 bounty on his head. Somalia became a war zone between the UN and Aydiid's militias.

Pursuant to Resolution 837, the UN hired Professor Tom Farer of American University to undertake a study, which was to become an indictment of Aydiid. Farer arrived in Mogadishu two weeks after the incident and just after the UN, employing the American QRF, ended its week of reprisals against Aydiid.

Aydiid himself had called for an independent investigation into the events of June 5, claiming that the UN was not a neutral party and had a

---

*Among other things, Resolution 834

> Strongly condemns the unprovoked armed attacks against the personnel of UNOSOM II on 5 June 1993, which appear to have been part of a calculated and premeditated series of cease-fire violations to prevent by intimidation UNOSOM II from carrying out its mandate as provided for in Resolution 814 (1993)....
>
> Reaffirms that the Secretary-General is authorized under Resolution 814 (1993) to take all necessary measures against all those responsible for the armed attacks referred to in paragraph 1 above, including against those responsible for publicly inciting such attacks, to establish the effective authority of UNOSOM II throughout Somalia, including to secure the investigation of their actions and their arrest and detention for prosecution, trial and punishment.

serious conflict of interest setting itself up as a fair and impartial jury in judging an assault on its own troops.* Admiral Howe's insistence that the UN could conduct an impartial investigation was early evidence that in the absence of any civil authority in Somalia, UNOSOM was taking for itself near dictatorial powers. The Farer report bears out Aydiid's suspicions. It is nothing if not a whitewash.

The report—never officially released by the UN—is absurd and arrogant. Although a scholar in international law who had written a book on the politics of the Horn of Africa,† Farer was by no means an expert on Somalia or Somalis. "The great bulk of our inquiry has consisted of lengthy interviews with military and civilian personnel associated with UNOSOM II." The report then goes on for two and a half pages about how difficult it was under the circumstances to interview Somalis.

Some facts are not in dispute. As part of the factions' agreements with the UN, heavy weapons had been placed in Authorized Weapons Storage Sites. UNOSOM officials decided to conduct a search of sites where weapons of Aydiid's faction—and only Aydiid's faction—were stored. The inspection would take place on Saturday, June 5. A memo went to Aydiid on Friday, June 4, the Muslim Sabbath and a day when Aydiid was not in his office.

The letter of intent to inspect the sites was therefore presented to Aydiid's lieutenant, Abdi Hassan Awale "Qeybdiid" (whom the Americans called "Mad Abdi"). According to an official memo, "Mr. Awaleh [sic] was

---

*In the early days of the military operation against Aydiid, most people seemed to accept the UN version of events without question. The following June 8, 1993, editorial from the *Buffalo News* is typical of the mainstream American reaction:

> The slap in the face a Somali warlord has given the United Nations is a direct challenge that cannot go unanswered if the international organization is to be viewed as anything more than a paper tiger, there or anywhere else . . .
>
> All evidence indicates the murders stemmed from a deliberate ambush set up by gunmen loyal to Somali strongman Mohammed Farah Aidid. The attack in the capital city of Mogadishu came as the UN troops, there to guard food distribution, went to check out weapons warehouses controlled by Aidid, who was told of the inspection ahead of time and did not object.
>
> Such a cowardly and brazen attack on U.N. peacekeepers cannot be merely condemned; it must be punished . . .
>
> Whether in Bosnia, Somalia or any of the trouble spots in which peons wreak carnage carrying out the orders of others, the United Nations must be able to go directly after those in control. That is the most effective way of stemming the violence that not only threatens U.N. peacekeepers, but that also keeps local inhabitants under the thumbs of unelected warlords.

†*War Clouds on the Horn of Africa: A Crisis for Détente.* Carnegie Endowment for International Peace, Washington, 1976.

somewhat shaken by the notification . . ." He then made several excuses about why he could not accept it. The memo, contained in Farer's report, continues: "After listening to all of Mr. Awaleh's comments, the representatives informed him of two facts. One, that he, Mr. Awaleh, is recognized as an appropriate high official of the SNA/USC. Two, the visit would be considered an official Notification."

So here were UNOSOM delegates informing a member of Aydiid's Somali National Alliance faction that his authority was based on UNOSOM's recognition. The memo concluded by saying that Awale was "upset over the matter." Understandably so. Abdi Hassan Awale "Qeybdiid" may have had an official position within the SNA, but the supreme commander was Aydiid. Qeybdiid was in no position to authorize anything. UNOSOM didn't care. From Aydiid's perspective, UNOSOM was telling him whom they would and would not recognize as authority within his faction. UNOSOM had crossed a line that was unacceptable to Aydiid.

The next morning inspectors and Pakistani troops arrived at AWSS 5, which was also Aydiid's radio station. A crowd gathered outside the radio station. It appeared to them that UNOSOM had seized their radio station, even though the troops were exiting.

Somalis love the radio. They thrive on news and information. It is as important to them as food and water. Every evening the entire country tunes in to the BBC Somali service. Activity in every town in the country slows to a crawl. Likewise, Aydiid's station was very dear to the people of Mogadishu, even those who didn't like him very much. The thought that UNOSOM might be shutting it down was incendiary in the extreme. The sight of troops near the station was enough to mobilize militias.

There's no doubt that Somali militias attacked the Pakistani soldiers at various points that morning. What is at issue is whether it was an ambush organized by Aydiid. That was UNOSOM's instant conclusion, and that is the conclusion of the Farer report, though he includes some evidence that would seem to cast doubt on that conclusion.*

Farer writes: "The elements of the ambush strongly evidence premeditation. Whether, in the absence of any disconfirming evidence, they establish pre-planning beyond a reasonable doubt is arguable, and of course is

---

*Was UNOSOM trying to close down the radio station or was it a legitimate inspection of arms storage sites? After the October 3 debacle, the UN did authorize an independent report on the violence in Mogadishu (S/1994/653). That report said: "Opinions differ, even among UNOSOM officials, on whether the weapons inspection of 5 June 1993 was genuine or was merely a cover-up for reconnaissance and subsequent seizure of Radio Mogadishu."

not essential for purposes of this inquiry which is concerned primarily with determining whether there exists evidence sufficient to support the indictment of General [Aydiid]. That evidence is built around a number of points about the way the Somali assault on the Peacekeepers was carried out: But they all revolved around the sophisticated and coordinated way the Somalis boxed in the Pakistanis, creating a "killing zone." Farer wrote that it evidenced "careful planning" and "sophisticated use of locations and camouflage."

Perhaps at this point Farer and others still thought the Somalis unsophisticated fighters. The truth is that Aydiid's militias had been battling in the streets of Mogadishu for four years. They knew every hiding place and every corner. A hundred times before, they had set up roadblocks and cordoned off "kill zones." They were conditioned to do it at the first sound of gunfire.

In the wake of the killings and the reprisals, I interviewed a number of Aydiid's fighters and got the story from their perspective. One of them, a quiet young man named Abdiwele Ali told me how his day went on June 5, 1993. Abdiwele had fought with Aydiid's militias when they had captured Mogadishu in January 1991. He hadn't participated in the clan war, but he had buried his rifle inside his family's compound.

"Radio Mogadishu had been giving out information every day about what the U.S. and UNOSOM troops were doing," he told me. "UNOSOM was not happy with this, and they accused the radio station of making propaganda against them. On June 5, a young boy knocked on my gate. He was out of breath and he said that Pakistani soldiers were sent to capture the radio station. With one of my neighbors I immediately ran towards the radio station. I saw people coming from the north and the west, and we joined at the main gate of the radio station. People started telling the Pakistanis to get out. 'This is our radio station. This is our country,' we were shouting.

"When the Pakistanis saw that some of the people were armed, they started firing in the air, but people would not stop coming. There were 2,000 people there now and they started collecting stones. Women and children began to throw stones and we were shouting, 'Go home UNOSOM. Go home.'

"Then the soldiers lowered the muzzles of their guns and shot straight at people. I saw a young child of four and a girl of about fifteen and a boy killed. I had not used my gun since the night at Villa Somalia [when Siyaad Barre was driven out of the city]. I did not fight in the civil war, but now I ran to dig it up from where it was hidden."

Abdiwele cleaned off his rifle and ran to his corner, a corner he had been assigned years before. All of Aydiid's fighters knew the drill. They didn't run into the gunfire. They moved to seal the city; they put up roadblocks. Abdiwele didn't see any more action that day. No troops moved through his checkpoint. Had they approached him, it might have seemed that Abdiwele was lying in a planned ambush. Over the following months I spoke with dozens of other fighters who told me similar stories.

In the reprisals that followed, UNOSOM did ultimately destroy the radio station. And they did complain that Aydiid's radio was broadcasting incendiary propaganda against UNOSOM even before the June 5 weapons inspection. Farer includes a few transcripts of radio broadcasts in his report. Here is one excerpt that Farer calls "exemplary."*

Does UNOSOM and the NGOs help the Somali people? UNOSOM and the NGOs came to Somalia to provide security and stability. The question is: are they helping the Somali people in the long run?

The Somali people are well aware of the Western ideology, which is divide and rule. The Western countries are creating more problems in order to get their own interest.

Let the Somali people know that there are political, religious and cultural manipulations. The foreign forces and the government are running our internal problems. They are intervening in any way possible. They are trying to create more problems in order to stay a long time.

It's no secret that Jonathan Howe was annoyed by the radio broadcasts. However, it's ironic that UNOSOM would try to bring democracy to a country by destroying free speech. The concerns expressed by this particular radio broadcast are legitimate, and the analysis, in my experience, fairly cogent. Howe's and UNOSOM's ire is also typical: People who claim to be helping tend to become extraordinarily irritated when their motives are questioned, or when they are accused of benefiting in some way from the misery of others. It must be noted again here that Somalis had a long and unpleasant experience with foreign aid. It was very natural for them to question the motives of those who had come to help.

There is also strong evidence that UNOSOM's annoyance with Aydiid arose because the warlord had successfully conducted a peace conference

---

*I've reviewed transcripts of more than forty broadcasts from the months prior to the incident at Radio Mogadishu and found a few instances where they were only slightly more provocative. On the whole, it was much less inflammatory than much of what passes for debate on American talk radio.

and concluded a peace agreement between his clan and a neighboring clan at the end of May. Aydiid had originally requested UN participation and, not incidentally, financial support for the conference, but then rejected UN requests that some additional subclan representatives be included in the talks. The dispute was over specific issues in a remote part of Somalia, far from Mogadishu, far from NGOs, and beyond the limited expertise of most UN advisors. The only person at the UN who understood what was going on was John Drysdale, the British longtime Somalia expert. Drysdale describes the reaction behind the walls of the UN compound: "There was general unhappiness among senior UNOSOM II political staff and the staff of the U.S. Liaison Office that Aydiid continued to upstage both UNO-SOM II and his political rivals." Drysdale explained, "As with all public confrontations with Somalis, the United Nations senior staff were excessively sensitive about a diminution of UN 'credibility'—the word they use, but in fact prestige would be more accurate."*

As it turns out, Aydiid's peace agreement has endured since it was signed in May 1993. None of the UN-brokered agreements lasted very long. Aydiid's radio broadcasts around the time of the "weapons inspection" were boasting of the success of the conference. Could the UN have been acting to preserve its own power and prestige? It's not unthinkable. Aydiid had become a threat to UNOSOM's growing authority—not necessarily a threat to peace. Aydiid's challenge was to the entire concept of a Chapter VII intervention, and that was intolerable to the UN's ambitious bureaucrats. Like most aid operations, UNOSOM II eventually became self-serving. Suddenly UNOSOM II became more about building UNOSOM II than about bringing peace to Somalia.

The man in charge, Admiral Howe, believed in his mission in Somalia, so much that he wouldn't tolerate dissent or even listen to the opinions of advisors like John Drysdale if they clashed with his view of the way things were. He tended to see things in black and white, good Somalis and bad Somalis. The good Somalis agreed with his policies and backed UNOSOM II; the bad Somalis didn't. It was okay to hunt down the bad Somalis.

Howe was no stranger to the process of hunting down fugitive bad guys. As assistant to Admiral William Crowe, then the chairman of the Joint Chiefs of Staff, he was directly involved in attempts to capture Panama's Manuel Noriega. Howe had a reputation as a savvy Washington insider, serving in a number of positions associated with national security policy, starting in 1969 as a military assistant on the National Security Council

---

*John Drysdale, *Whatever Happened to Somalia?* (London: Haan Publishers, 1994), p. 168.

staff. In 1991, President Bush appointed him as his deputy national security advisor, replacing Robert Gates, who became CIA director. Howe also served as a NATO commander. In positions at the Pentagon and State Department, he was involved at the highest levels of strategic arms negotiations and headed the delegation that implemented the U.S.-Israeli strategic cooperation pact during the Reagan administration. He was not Boutros Boutros-Ghali's first choice to represent the UN in Somalia. The secretary general would have preferred to give the impression that UNOSOM II was a true UN effort, not just a cover for American foreign policy. But the United States insisted, and, as usual, got its way.

Howe proved uniquely unsuited for the task. On several occasions, I met with the top Somali experts in his office, who were totally exasperated at their boss's refusal to deal with the complex realities of Somali politics. Howe just forged ahead doing things his way. He failed to see that offering a reward for Aydiid made the warlord all the more powerful and that much more difficult to catch, and that blanketing Mogadishu with Wild West wanted posters just made UNOSOM look stupid. (The posters became collectors items.) I asked him how he thought the situation should be resolved. "Ideally, what I would like to happen to Aydiid? The best idea would be that he would surrender himself. Maybe the next idea is that some Somali people would deliver him to us, and the next idea would be that we ourselves would capture him. But the main thing is that I would like to get him off the scene."

Capturing Aydiid would have provided Howe and the UN with both a problem and an opportunity. There was no court system in Somalia to try him, and questionable grounds to try him in an international court of law. A precedent needed to be set for future peace enforcement operations. "I think we all feel that sense that this is the first Chapter VII, and in a sense we are pioneering into new territory," Howe told me. "It's been our desire from the start to try to learn from this and set a model that will really benefit other people, to do it successfully, do it well, clearly document our lessons learned—there will be plenty of them and there have been—so that the next mission that comes along in another country will really benefit from our experience."

"It seems like a laboratory," I offered, "because you're obviously learning as you go."

"I think that's fair," the admiral replied.

Of all the violence that took place in Mogadishu, the most significant might have been on Monday morning, July 12. The U.S. military had completed its punishment of Aydiid on June 17. Heavily armed AC-130 gunships were withdrawn. The Pentagon said it was over.

However, the military was once again in the driver's seat in Mogadishu. There was a new, more aggressive military presence on the streets, like a city under occupation. And Aydiid's forces began to act like a resistance underground. Snipers started taking shots at soldiers. Six Somalis who worked for the UN were killed as a warning. On July 7, the Americans carried out some house-to-house weapons searches, and U.S. Army colonel Ed Ward, third-ranking commander of the UN force, boasted to the *Washington Post*, "We're going to retake the city in about five days." It was five days later that American Cobra helicopters took to the air and fired ten TOW missiles into a house where elders of Aydiid's clan were having a meeting. The house was owned by Abdi Qeybdiid and would hence be called Abdi House. Some fifty people were killed that day, many of them not necessarily allies of Aydiid and most of them respected members of the community. They were trying to discuss issues. Some were even there to urge Aydiid to step down. The military knew that Aydiid was not there that day.*

"It was a real destroy mission," an American officer told me. And, in effect, it was the first mission that really could have been a truly offensive initiative on the part of UNOSOM. It was also a mission that required the highest levels of approval. Major General Thomas Montgomery, who commanded the QRF in Mogadishu, did not have the authority to order his troops into an offensive posture; that command came directly from the White House.

It was designed to push the limits of Chapter VII. Presumably, all this was in the name of keeping the peace in Somalia and elsewhere. In effect, however, it was the beginning of the end of UNOSOM and of any chance for a UN settlement in Somalia. And it forced Aydiid to take the offensive. He had no choice if he was to retain his position as head of the USC/SNA. He could not stand by and let the foreigners kill the elders of his clan. What did Howe and UNOSOM expect?

The fighting escalated through August and September. When four American soldiers were killed by a land mine on August 8, Clinton sent in Task Force Ranger. That, in turn, culminated in the raid on October 3 that left so many dead.

---

*It was on this day that four journalists who went to view the destruction were killed by angry Somali mobs. Hansi Kraus of AP, and Dan Eldon, Hos Maina, and Anthony Macharia of Reuters were chased and beaten to death.

In the end, the Americans accomplished their mission on that day, capturing twenty militia leaders blamed for attacks on U.S. and UN troops. But the mission was never really worth accomplishing: None of the captured men was held very long. The only one who was really held, Mohamed Hassan Awale, had actually been helpful to the Americans in the past. As if to justify the raid and the deaths, he was sent to a place the Americans called Gilligan's Island, an island prison in southern Somalia, where Aydiid's then financier, Osman Ato, was also being held. A U.S. official later confessed that they learned nothing from any of the people they captured.

The reality is that there was nothing to learn, nothing to be gained. There were no plots; Aydiid had no plans. And the final horrible irony was that most of the men who were captured in that bloody battle probably would have shown up at the UN gates with flowers in their hands if they'd been invited for dinner.

The face of captured airman Michael Durant adorned the covers of every magazine and newspaper in America. The mission was over, ended by its own hubris and because it finally revealed itself for what it always was, an exercise in control. Mogadishu had been turned into a testing ground for various Western interests, and many Somalis recognized it as precisely that.

None of this exonerates Mohamed Farah Aydiid from any responsibility. The simple fact about Aydiid was that he was never willing to compromise. He would accept no agreement that didn't leave him in the position he believed he deserved, head of state of Somalia. He supported the UN and U.S. intervention when it seemed to suit his purposes and opposed it with single-minded intensity when it didn't. And he had no qualms about laying waste to Mogadishu and killing tens of thousands of his own countrymen to achieve that end.

After October 3, Robert Oakley came back to Mogadishu and met with Aydiid. He then announced that the hunt for Aydiid was over, and that Michael Durant would be released unconditionally. There would also be an independent investigation of June 5 and other incidents in Somalia. At Oakley's press conference, Keith Richburg of the *Washington Post* asked Oakley if that wasn't precisely what Aydiid had asked for in the beginning. Oakley avoided the question.

The Americans didn't learn anything on October 3 that they didn't know before. The difference on October 3 was that a photographer and a Somali cameraman with a Handicam were there to take pictures of the bodies of the Americans being dragged through the streets.

A week earlier, on September 25, three Americans were killed when their helicopter was shot out of the sky by Aydiid's militia. (A fourth was rescued by a Somali.) The bodies of the dead were torn to shreds. The head of one of the airmen was chopped off and put on display. The military knew it, yet General Colin Powell, in his final appearance as chairman of the JCS, told reporters that the UN mission in Somalia was going well.

"Let's not lose sight of the overall success of the mission," Powell said at the National Press Club. "We have had good days and bad." Powell went on to endorse the nation-building strategy. "The exit strategy for the UN is to stand up some sort of a political entity that can take responsibility for Somalia, led by Somalians [sic] with a Somalian police force to keep order."

The presence of nearly 30,000 heavily armed marines succeeded in calming the situation in Somalia—at least in the short term. As with the 500 Pakistanis, Somalia's fighters backed off and assessed the situation. As they grew used to the American presence, they became emboldened once again. Incidents of violence began to increase after January 1994. By the time the Americans departed in May, 1994, and were replaced with a much weaker and less well organized multinational UNOSOM II force, the militias were itching to get back into action.

In the weeks following the raids, I walked through the rubble. There were new designations in Mogadishu now—Crash Site 1, Crash Site 2—denoting where two U.S. helicopters had gone down on October 3. I went to the Olympic Hotel, where the raid had taken place, past the charred, hollow corpses of armored personnel carriers that had been sent on a failed mission to rescue the Americans. Children climbed on the remains of two American helicopters. As I passed deeper into this area of south central Mogadishu, near the Bukhara market, a man greeted me, saying his name was Artan, a teacher. Artan was tiny—about five feet four—with a beard and probably in his early forties. We talked and strolled past bullet-riddled walls.

As we walked through the rubble, a boy named Liban began to follow us. He told me he was sixteen. When I expressed some skepticism, he admitted to being fifteen. We stopped to rest a moment, and he squatted comfortably back on his heels, his feet pressed flat against the ground. He raised his AK-47 to his shoulder and lined his eyes up to the sight. His moves were rehearsed and fluid. The long barrel of the rifle extended far beyond his tiny compacted body. He yanked back the bolt and loaded a round into the chamber. Then he snapped off the safety and started imitating the sound of gunfire. American, American, American, he barked out, one for each shot. I used to play this game as a child, killing imaginary Germans. For a moment, he almost looked like a child, but the gun was loaded. The adults in the compound hardly noticed him.

"This was my sister's house," Artan informed me, pointing to a shredded pile of corrugated iron.

"Was anybody killed here?"

"Yes, my mother and one sister and two of my sister's children."

Artan's other sister, Haredo, arrived and began to tell me what had happened: When the fighting started on the street, she brought the children into the house. She was just beginning her afternoon prayer when bullets poured through the roof, turning the little house black with dust. Then, as the cloud settled, she found her two sons, mother, and sister cut to pieces on the floor. Haredo maintained a glassy stare. She was still in obvious shock. Her telling of the story was slow and dutiful. She didn't want to talk, but her brother had told her she must. She didn't want to talk because she was filled with guilt. "We told the children they would be safe," she kept repeating.

"Where is our happiness now? Our happiness has changed to fear," she said over and over. "When the Americans came, we greeted them with green leaves. Now our happiness has changed to fear."

Artan took me across the street to where they had buried the dead. There were graves, hundreds of graves. Some were mounds of dirt marked with rocks and branches. Some people with more money were able to buy a little cement and had built concrete cradles around their dead. Most were fresh.

"We call that area the American monument," Artan told me.

A donkey cart passed through the devastation with "Donated by the People of the United States of America" food bags on it.

After October 3, the battlefield switched from the streets to the pressroom at the UN compound. In mid-October, a thirty-six-member Pentagon Joint Information Bureau, or JIB, was dispatched to Mogadishu. It was headed by a crusty army colonel, Steven Rausch. The JIB would now handle all questions pertaining to U.S. involvement in Somalia. In most press conferences the "jiblets," as they were known, outnumbered reporters by as many as three to one. The what-the-hell-this-is-Africa atmosphere of the earlier UN press briefings—once held outdoors under the camouflage net—was replaced by a stiff Washington formality.

Rausch's JIB was the leading edge of a 12,750-member Joint Task Force composed of 4,150 troops on the ground and 8,600 afloat off the Somali coast. On November 1, the JTF was joined by heavy firepower: Some 400 vehicles, including Bradley assault vehicles and Abrams M1-A1 tanks, were paraded to the north of the city and parked on an empty stretch of desert they called, without irony, Victory Base.

The JIB assigned themselves parking spaces and launched an assault on the public perception that U.S. soldiers were under UN command. The image back home, the one that really got people worked up, was that of American soldiers ordered to their deaths by Pakistani or Egyptian officers. Rausch first refused to speak from behind the usual UN lectern in front of the backdrop of a UN flag. He stood, instead, off to the side behind a separate lectern, wrapped in green camouflage netting with a photocopied map of Africa pinned on the front. The message was clear: U.S. troops are *now* firmly under U.S. command.

In reality, of course, they always were. No American soldier ever took an order from a non-American officer, and decisions involving U.S. troop movements, especially the October 3 attack on Aydiid, were made entirely by the U.S. command, sometimes without consulting or even informing the UN.

The perception that the Americans were under UN control was the result of an earlier, more successful public relations effort, one that eventually backfired. When UNOSOM II officially took over from the United States in May, U.S. Army major David Stockwell became the chief military spokesman. He dutifully donned a blue UN beret and sewed a UN patch on his U.S. Army uniform. His press briefings always emphasized the multilateral nature of military activities in Mogadishu, even when they were carried out by U.S. troops under U.S. command. Then, because of concerns that Stockwell's increasingly frequent appearances on television made the whole thing look *too* American, he was replaced at the podium by a New Zealander, Captain Tim McDavitt. Stockwell, however, remained in charge, until the JIB showed up.

The new public relations effort got off to an awkward start. When there were no television cameras in the room, heads easily turned to Rausch when he addressed the press from his own lectern. When TV arrived, it became more complicated. Cameras and microphones had to be moved; sound technicians rushed to the front of the room as Rausch began to speak; chairs were kicked aside by cameramen looking for a better position. During one of these exercises, CNN let the cameras roll and aired the commotion. The U.S. lectern was immediately stashed in the JIB office.

Having gained control of the pressroom, the JIB set upon a second task, explaining what the additional U.S. troops and all that equipment were doing in Somalia. The primary reason, as stated, was to protect U.S. troops already there. But since the administration had called off the hunt for Aydiid, the troops already in Mogadishu didn't need any protection. The second stated goal was to "open lines of communication," that is, to clear roadblocks so humanitarian relief supplies could get through. This effort to re-spin the mission in humanitarian terms, so popular a year earlier, also ran into discrepancy problems with the facts on the ground. A few visits to relief agencies revealed that all the supplies they were sending were getting through anyway. And in the previous three weeks of driving around Mogadishu, I'd yet to encounter a roadblock on a major road. When I raised these facts with an American officer, he just grinned and said, "Exactly. The mission can't fail. We need to be able to claim one success before we leave on March 31."

Against the mounting evidence that thousands of U.S. soldiers were sent to Somalia on a purely face-saving mission, it was announced that the Americans would establish a "presence" on the streets. Exactly what that "presence" was to consist of or when it would begin was never made clear. When Ambassador Robert Oakley was in Somalia during the first days of November, he met with representatives of Aydiid's Somali National Alliance and informed them of U.S. intentions to venture outside their barracks. Oakley reported that an agreement had been reached and that Americans would be able to patrol the streets without fear of being shot by the militia. In fact, they never went back on the streets. They were kept safely away from danger. Their mission, to rescue the future of peace enforcement, didn't require that they actually use their weapons.

Then, just as all the new troops were finally settled in, it was time to go.

At the end of March 1994, on the final day of the U.S. presence in Somalia, I climbed up on a towering sand dune between the Mogadishu airport and the beach-front final command post of the American forces in Somalia. From the top of that dune, members of the Command Assault Vehicle Team had been watching the steady departure of their comrades. Off the south side of their dune, the white prefab, sandbag-covered bunkers of the officer corps were perched on modest cliffs above the Indian Ocean. Along the shore to the west, amphibious assault vehicles shuttled troops to the fleet offshore. To the immediate north was the airport runway with its steady flow of massive C-5 transport planes and Sea Knight twin-rotored helicopters carting away soldiers and equipment. Beyond the runway was Mogadishu, and Somalia. Staff Sergeants Olga Pohalski and Aaron S. Dudley and Sergeant John Hamen were spending their final days in Somalia avoiding the sun and sand and maintaining the mobile radio control center that was parked with them atop the dune.

"We're first in, last out," said Sergeant Pohalski.

"Last out?"

"Well, maybe not exactly last, but pretty close to last. When this truck goes, all communications will be shut down."

Locating the last soldier out, defining the precise moment the American adventure in Somalia would end, became an obsession for many of the reporters, who rushed back to Mogadishu to cover the American exit. Like the final episode of M*A*S*H, this would be the end of a TV event. Many of these reporters had stood on the beach at the beginning of Operation Restore Hope on December 9, 1992 as the marines stormed ashore and tens of thousands of Somalis lined the dunes, waving branches and wreathes to greet them. There was no question about the very moment the operation had begun. The departure would not be nearly so dramatic, that was certain, but the press needed at the very least to identify an event, a ceremony of some sort, a final gesture—a lowering of a flag, for example—to frame the adventure with the high and heady drama of that December morning. The military was determined that there would be no flag ceremony (although the cameras did catch some flags being packed away), no departing pomp that could be juxtaposed against any future violence in Somalia. The only Somalis who showed up to say good-bye were there to scavenge the crates of bottled water, MREs (meals ready to eat—military rations), and other items the military left behind.

For months, U.S. Marines had handled security at the airport, making sure that nothing interfered with the withdrawal. In the course of the morning, that duty was officially passed over to Egyptian soldiers, the transfer acknowledged with a quick handshake. And as journalists fanned out to watch the activity, the UN military spokesman, New Zealander Chris Budge commented, "Let us know where you're going so that there will be no problems with the efficient security elements that will be in place after the Americans depart." Budge couldn't hold back a smirk.

At 10:15 A.M., Major General Thomas Montgomery boarded a helicopter and left. At 11:30 A.M. a dozen massive helicopter transports arose from the beaches and took to the air in formation like a line of pigeons alighting from a telephone wire. They kicked up plumes of sand that could be seen all around the city. And then Lieutenant Dave Walcott, the last man boarding the last amphibious vehicle leaving the shore, said his final words to journalists: "We accomplished our mission: the safe withdrawal of our troops." Then, speaking to the assembled journalists, he said, "I suggest you get out of here while you can." It was not what the military PR brass wanted from their last soldier, but it was precisely what the press had come for.

The lieutenant was as unrealistic as he was quotable, emblematic of the Americans' total isolation from the country they had come to save. Since January, the Americans had sequestered themselves behind layers of security at the airport and along the beaches and had been quietly slipping away ever since. Many of the remaining soldiers were just there to cover the rear guard of the pullout. There wasn't much they could offer the press in terms of homespun American reflection on the events of the past sixteen months.

"How do you feel about leaving?"

"Can't wait to get out of this shithole."

"How long you been here?"

"Nearly two weeks now."

For most, their only contact with Somalis had been with laborers, employed to fill sandbags and with shopkeepers at a place called Walmart, an area at the end of the airport runway where Somalis had built souvenir stalls and cut holes in the fence through which they sold trinkets and bits of Africana, ebony statues of no particular ethnic origin. Carvings of Shaka Zulu with his spears and shield were big sellers, so the Somalis whipped up thousands of them, and neither buyer nor seller was the least bit concerned that Shaka had no connection at all to Somalia.

Pohalski and her colleagues on the sand dune were an exception. They'd been in Somalia since mid-October, arriving to shore up American troop strength in the wake of October 3. They'd been there long enough to know that there was more to Somalia than the people who dragged the dead bodies of their comrades through the streets. Curious about what lay outside their barracks, they were full of questions about Somalia.

But there was no way that they were ever going to see what was out on the streets. From the day they arrived, their main job had been not to embarrass the U.S. government, to serve as a symbol that America wasn't backing down. At the same time, they were to stay as far from potential harm as possible. On October 3, Operation Restore Hope had become Operation Don't Fuck Up Again.

On the streets of Mogadishu, the American withdrawal barely caused a ripple. Few Somalis turned their heads as the American choppers took to the sky. There was no reaction to Harrier jets booming overhead as a warning to potential last-minute troublemakers. Somalis know an empty gesture when they see one.

Likewise, there was little reaction on the streets to the "peace" accord signed the previous day with much UN-generated hoopla in Nairobi by Aydiid and rival Ali Mahdi. The ceremony in Nairobi seemed designed to mimic the signing of the Israeli–PLO accord on the White House lawn the previous fall. The former fugitive warlord and his murderous rivals had attained the status of statesmen in record time.

The accord repudiated "any form of violence as a means of resolving conflicts" and set up an April 15 meeting in Mogadishu to establish a national reconciliation conference to be held on May 15. The conference, predictably, was never held.

The only thing that was certain was that the United Nations got what it wanted; a semblance of an agreement to accompany the American departure. The UN was just happy to get the signatures, and the warlords had a nice time in Nairobi. They stayed in first-class hotels, were given phone and secretarial services by the UN (for a cost of $50,000 a day), and did a lot of shopping. Aydiid himself had been in Nairobi for months, staying at Nairobi's five-star Serena Hotel until he was asked to leave because he and his entourage were frightening the tourists. He moved to the Interconti- nental. Several Somalis commented that $50,000 a day was a bargain com- pared to the nearly $3 billion that was spent in Somalia, and it might be more economical just to keep them there.

When the Americans left, the press returned to the Sahafi Hotel and began packing up their gear. Satellite phones were folded up and video decks stowed away. Reporters filed their last stories and checked onto flights back to Nairobi. Most of what followed in Somalia did so without the world's attention. There were no Pakistani journalists in Somalia, no Egyptians, Indians, Zimbabweans, or Malaysians running around asking their troops what they thought of the situation here.

The press and the military together agreed to close a chapter on Soma- lia. Neat packages make for good newspaper copy and academic confer- ences. But in Somalia, today, there is nothing left. No electricity, no plumbing, no infrastructure, no wires on the poles. Except for some graffiti and prefab buildings, there is little evidence that more than 100,000 American soldiers marched through the country over sixteen months. Back in the States, plans were being made at academic institutions to pon- der the mechanics of peacekeeping. The "lessons learned" from Somalia are certain to be enumerated many times. Politicians will speak of "another Somalia," with the same intonation they once used for "another Vietnam."

Some of the people who were affected by the exercise had more basic questions. Families of the dead Somalis and peacekeepers can never be sure why their loved ones died. It's difficult to explain that policymakers were pushing for precedents, trying to establish the limits of Chapter VII power, seeking to define the Mogadishu Line between humanitarian intervention and political involvement.

"I'd really like to know what was going on out there," Sergeant Hamen said from atop his sand dune the day before he left Somalia. "I mean, what do we tell our kids? Was this a war, or what?"

14

THE SELF-LICKING ICE CREAM CONE

The statistics on sanitary improvements are not interpreted by the
native as progress in the fight against illness, in general, but as fresh
proof of the occupier's hold on the country.

—Frantz Fanon, *A Dying Colonialism*

The United Stated abandoned Operation Restore Hope in Somalia immediately after the fiasco of October 3, 1993. From that point on, nothing the Americans did was meant directly to affect the situation on the ground; everything was aimed at minimizing negative political fallout back home until they packed up and left five months later. With the Americans happily out of the picture and hostility raging in Mogadishu, the rest of the UN mission was doomed. It was only a matter of time before international will, and, most important, international funding, would dry up.

Any doubt about that was sealed two weeks after the American departure when a plane was shot down in Kigali, Rwanda, killing the presidents of Rwanda and Burundi and setting off what may be the worst concentrated massacre in human history. Journalists followed the events. Money followed the news. And NGOs followed the money. Somalia was forgotten, except by the UN, which continued operating in Mogadishu as if they were going to be there forever.

In May 1994, the Security Council voted to allow the mission to proceed for another three months.* The decision received little scrutiny from
the U.S. press, which, like the U.S. government, was busy with new crises
in Haiti and Rwanda.

With the press and the Americans occupied elsewhere, the UN civilian
bureaucracy in Somalia spread like a tropical fungus. Between March and
December 1994, Somalis saw the number of UN civilian employees double
to nearly 800, even as humanitarian activity ground to a halt. One worker
in the humanitarian office said she was "disgusted" with how little was
going on. Most of these foreign employees, she complained, were just doing
time there to help them climb the UN career ladder. "A Somalia combat
ribbon looks good on the résumé," she said.

A Somali employee in the same office was more bitter. Having worked
under five different foreigners at the humanitarian unit, he said he finally
had figured out that the expatriates were interested only in collecting their
daily subsistence allowance of $100 or more per day, beyond their salary
and perks. Somali employees were lucky to get $300 per month.

The UN spent $160 million renovating the former U.S. Embassy com-
pound (which was completed at a cost of almost $40 million by the U.S.
government just before Mogadishu descended into chaos). Even after it
became clear that the UN operation would be ending, the bureaucracy
continued to sink money into construction. A new airport terminal building was completed in August 1994. Then, in November, the UN installed
speed bumps inside the 80-acre compound; apparently, driving the same
two miles of road day after day had made people reckless. (Anyone could
walk across the compound in ten minutes.)

Despite continued UN attempts to "normalize" relations with Aydiid's
faction, the warlord did only what was in his own strategic best interests.
In July 1994, his soldiers attacked a Zimbabwean contingent in the town of
Beledweyne. One Zimbabwean was killed, and the rest were stripped to
their underwear. Automatic weapons, mortars, and armored personnel carriers valued at more than $2 million were confiscated. (After the American
withdrawal, the UN lacked the transport capability to reinforce any of its
troops in the field.) Aydiid apologized for killing the soldier, kept the
goods, and continued to meet cordially with new SRSG, Victor Gbeho—
who continued to express optimism that the UN could broker a peace

---

*UN Security Council Resolution 923 renewed the mandate until September 30, 1994, while
reaffirming the objective that UNOSOM II complete its mission by March 1995.

agreement.* Meanwhile, Aydiid had been complaining about the UN's failure to pay hotel bills that his delegation ran up during months of stalled negotiations in Nairobi and Addis Ababa.

Aydiid, preparing for the inevitable withdrawal, insisted that the UN leave behind all vehicles and other valuable equipment, arguing that any "aid" that came into Somalia belonged to the Somali people and, by extension, Aydiid himself. Though the request struck many at the UN as impertinent, Somalis considered this a perfectly reasonable request. From their perspective, the UN operation was inherently corrupt, and UN bureaucrats were in Somalia only to enrich themselves. They saw little evidence to dissuade them.

Since the beginning of the intervention, Somalis charged that the Egyptians and other Third World troops in Somalia were there only to "do business." It appeared they were right. Once the Western contingents had left, security collapsed. A few dollars passed to sentries bought anyone entrance inside the gates of the port or the airport to do business. In the five months following the American departure, fifty-seven brand-new four-wheel-drive vehicles were sold to Somalis by the security force for between $3,000 and $5,000 apiece. Some turned up on the streets of Nairobi—their UN markings faintly visible beneath fresh paint—where they fetched $50,000 to $60,000. In September 1994, four tankers filled with gasoline were simply driven out of the port, never to be seen again. Cash and goods alike fed the arms buildup.

The bill for the operation reached $4 million per day—one-third of it supplied by the United States. Most of that paid for foreign troops. Another large chunk went to foreign contractors such as Australia's Morris Catering and the Texas-based Brown & Root.† Somali businessmen who have tried to deal with the UN complained that procurement officers demanded kickbacks. Then there was the $3.9 million in cash that disappeared from the UN compound in April 1994. None of the money ever showed up—despite detective assistance from Scotland Yard—and it is generally considered to have been an inside job.

The expenditure might have been worth it if the UN had succeeded in brokering peace, but it never did. The two main factions drifted even fur-

---

*Victor Gbeho replaced Admiral Jonathan Howe, who left in February 1994.

†Brown & Root has collected around $250 million from the Pentagon for work in Somalia and Haiti and is now the primary U.S. contractor in Bosnia. The firm is owned by the Dallas-based Halliburton Company. The man who now runs Halliburton, Dick Cheney, was secretary of defense when Brown & Root won the Pentagon contracts.

ther apart and then splintered again as some of Aydiid's top lieutenants abandoned him.* As negotiations became more intricate, the UN personnel in the country had less and less experience. By the time the UN mandate was renewed, there was no one left with any institutional memory.

This led to a series of diplomatic blunders that only confused the situation in Somalia. Based on information that Gbeho's staff sent back to New York, the secretary general, on September 17, 1994, published a report that was packed with inaccuracies designed to justify the continued UN presence in Somalia.† For example, the report concluded that the UN had successfully brokered a settlement in the lower Juba area south of Mogadishu. Although signatures had been coaxed onto paper, fighting had actually intensified during the summer. NGOs such as the World Food Program, Oxfam, and the International Rescue Committee were forced out of the region due to threats from General Mohamed Said Hersi "Morgan," a participant in the "peace" process.

The report also listed a series of meetings and agreements among various Somali groups that it optimistically portrayed as steps to a wider peace. In reality, however, they were just more of the same hollow accords that the UN had been collecting signatures on for two years. No one who knew anything about recent history would have been at all cheered by the "agreements." What the UN failed to realize, or refused to acknowledge, was that, because of its reputation, its very participation in a peace process nullified agreements in the eyes of the participants. In contrast, agreements that the Somalis hammered out among themselves, usually after a dose of bloody confrontation, seemed to hold.

UNOSOM was viewed by the Somalis not as a credible mediator but as a resource to be exploited. Right up to the UN's departure in March 1995, many Somalis saw the mission as little more than a source of revenue. In part, this was the result of a series of UN threats to close up shop if the warlords refused to negotiate in good faith. But every time the warring factions refused to budge, the UN came up with a new excuse to stay.

---

*In the spring of 1994, Aydiid's financier and top advisor, Osman Ato, deserted him along with Mohamed Hassan Awale, the SNA's "foreign minister," and Abdi Hassan Awale Ato, who had been imprisoned by the Americans and had millions of dollars worth of equipment destroyed in American raids, thought that Aydiid was being too anti-American and too intransigent in negotiations.

†UN document S/1994/1068.

• • •

After the Americans and journalists departed, Matt Bryden and I took a trip through "the rest of Somalia," the areas where the UN and the NGOs weren't really working. We flew to Galkayo, in central Somalia, where a group of expatriates in a UNOSOM office quietly passed the time doing very little. They were in essence providing that all-important UN *presence* in Galkayo. The town was hot and peaceful. We dined with UNOSOM employees, who spoke openly about how UNOSOM was only making things worse.

On the streets of Galkayo we were approached by a man who asked, "Galkayo is so peaceful. Why are there no NGO's here working?" I suggested to him that maybe it was peaceful precisely because there were no NGOs there. He thought for a moment and then asked the question again.

We visited with the governor, Abdirahman Bixi, an acquaintance of Matt's. A member of the Omar Mahamoud subclan of the Majeerteen, Abdirahman Bixi became governor following the Galkayo accords engineered by Aydiid in Mogadishu in May 1993.

Matt described Abdirahman Bixi to me as warlord-mullah-businessman. When we arrived at his compound we found him sitting like Buddha— chubby, shirtless, and wearing a *macawis*—on the floor of his darkened bedroom. He greeted Matt with a roar and a huge hug, and then sent the children out to find some tea. So how were things in Galkayo? "Fantastic," he said. And what had happened to the technicals, we wanted to know. Galkayo had been filled with technicals from both the Majeerteen and Habar Gidir clans shooting the place up. Abdirahman Bixi waved his hand dismissively. "The boys are doing business," he said. They had removed the gun mounts from the sawed-off Land Cruisers and filled them with goods for the market. "Trucks come from Boosaaso bringing cheap goods. The drivers buy goats from the nomads. One sack of sugar equals 1.5 goats. They bring other goods from Berbera, goods at a cheap price."

We left Galkayo overland, heading north to Boosaaso in a pickup truck rented from the governor. It was a ten-hour drive along what was called the Chinese road to Hargeysa. Chinese aid had built it in the 1970s, and it was still in pretty good shape. This was the kind of foreign aid the Somalis liked. It was something useful that everyone could see. Chinese aid is a whole package deal. They bring everything, including the workers. They build it and then they leave. Osman Ato had once told me that the Americans were stupid with their aid. "You waste money on a lot of big projects," he had said. "The Chinese just build a stadium or a road and everyone loves them."

We drove for hours across the featureless desert, and Matt told me stories about his experiences in Somalia, each one reinforcing to me—and to him—what a disaster the vast majority of aid projects had been. The warm air ripped through the cab of the truck as we flew up the deserted road. I was riding in a car without guns for the first time in two years.

At a few points along the trip we saw roadblocks. In the area around Mogadishu this would be an indication that it's time to fear for your life. But the men at these roadblocks didn't even ask for money. They wanted a commodity more important: news. "What do you hear from Galkayo, from Beledweyne, from Mogadishu, from Kismaayo?" Like desert nomads, they passed information on and we resumed the journey.

After the town of Garowe, where Ethiopia juts into Somalia, the Chinese road heads west toward Hargeysa, and a new road continues a final 450 kilometers northward to Gardo, up over the hills of Al Maskab, and downward to the seaport of Boosaaso. The second road is often known as the Italian road, built with Italian aid under the Socialist government of Benito Craxi for a cost of $250 million.

In typical Italian colonial fashion, the Italian construction companies that got the contracts returned millions to Italian politicians in the form of kickbacks. Many of these arrangements were made through Siyaad Barre's "Chamber of Commerce" office in Milan. The Chamber had a commission deal on every "aid" project, allowing Barre to keep a chunk of the aid loot right there in Italy so he didn't have to bother stealing it from his own central bank. Some 114 aid projects were arranged this way during the 1980s, including factories that never opened and hospitals that were never used. This came to light in 1989 when another Somali official, a certain General Mohamed Farah Aydiid, sued Craxi, alleging that the Socialists had promised him half of the 10 percent commission on all arrangements made through the Somali Chamber of Commerce in Milan. A Milan court dismissed the case, not sure how to deal with allegations that kickbacks were not paid on illegal kickbacks.

Meanwhile, there was a beautiful, rarely used road in the middle of nowhere, and after seven hours of driving I was happy to feel it under the tires. Perhaps Osman Ato had a point. We traveled around the region, ending up in Hargeysa some days later. Hargeysa, the capital of the former British Somaliland protectorate, was now the capital of the de facto independent Republic of Somaliland. I made an appointment to see President Mohamed Ibrahim Egal and walked around the town a bit.

Hargeysa had been under almost constant assault since Siyaad Barre started bombing it in 1988. A further civil war among northerners had destroyed what was left. The independent Republic of Somaliland begged for foreign aid, but since no one recognized them, none came. What followed reminded me of a book I had read as a child: *Stone Soup.* In this children's story, some soldiers wander into a town somewhere in Europe and ask the villagers for food. The villagers lock their cupboards and plead poverty. In turn, the soldiers say that they don't need any food; in fact, they're going to cook a feast for the entire town: stone soup. They light a fire, fill a kettle with water, toss in some stones, and wait. The soup will be delicious, they say, but it would be so much better if they only had a carrot. So someone brings a carrot. And then it would be even better if they had some onions . . . and so forth, until the soup is full of vegetables and everyone marvels that soup made of stones could taste so good.

When it became apparent in Hargeysa that no outside money was coming in, a few local businessmen took it upon themselves to do a few repairs. Some houses were rebuilt. Money started to trickle in from relatives in Dubai and Toronto and London. Soon a mosque was repaired, a new hotel went up. Then someone built a power generating plant. And a satellite phone system was installed. It was a miracle, as if one of the most devastated cities in Africa had rebuilt itself.

It was evening, after 8:00 P.M., when I walked through the gates of the "presidential palace" in Hargeysa. Guards were lounging around, AK-47s lying carelessly on the ground. I strolled through the front door, past some guards sitting on the steps chewing qat. The stairs were frayed carpet on cracked marble. I wandered around the palace briefly until someone asked me what I was doing there. When I explained, he told me to wait in a room off to the right of the stairs. Inside, a little man with glassy eyes sat on a sheet spread on the floor. He had a bundle of qat on the sheet beside a belt-fed machine gun near the window. "Somali whiskey," he said, holding up a bundle. I stooped to examine the machine gun. It was old. The stock was wooden and worn smooth. I was then directed to a room across the courtyard, but it was too hot to stay inside, so I went and sat on the railing overlooking the rock garden below.

After a while, a small, round man with hennaed hair emerged from behind a door. He didn't say that he was Egal, and for a moment I wasn't sure. Then I remembered him from photographs I'd seen of the twenty-something prime minister meeting with LBJ at the White House, the young hope of independent Somalia, the Western-educated democrat. We went back into the hot room and started to talk. He was wet, having just washed and prayed, and he sat comfortably on the couch.

"What nobody else knows is that this is not a new entity," he said about his country. "We're not breaking away. We're withdrawing from a union we joined voluntarily in 1960. Our union was the first step to the idea of Greater Somalia, and we miscalculated. Greater Somalia is dead. We cannot fight with Kenya, Ethiopia, and Djibouti."

Egal was Somalia's prime minister in 1967, and he traveled the world, absorbing political realities that clashed with the Somali grand dream. He realized that Somalia could never be united without the help of the great powers. So he forged new relationships with Ethiopia and Kenya. He met with Charles DeGaulle in France and agreed not to pursue union with Somalis in Djibouti, at that time still a French colony.

"What I was doing was to the annoyance of the Soviet Union. It led to the coup d'état," Egal said. That was true, in part. The coup that started with the assassination of President Abdirashiid Ali Shermaarke was also initiated because Somalia's political system had fractured along clan lines—in 1969 there were some 60 political parties and more than 1,000 candidates vying for 122 seats—and his party used the national treasury as its personal campaign war chest.

Siyaad Barre emerged on top after the coup and sent Egal to jail for twelve years.

"The people of Somaliland have another chance now to determine their own futures. The Westerners think this is Biafra all over again. It's not. Somaliland is a state that was. We have our own traditions. We have eighty years of colonial experience to separate us from the south. British rule was indirect rule, different from the feudal rule of the south. No warlord could emerge from our people. That is a difference between us."

Egal is perpetually annoyed because he can't get recognition from any foreign country. He finds the West's attitude patronizing, especially since the breakaway republics of the Soviet Union and the former Yugoslavia received rapid recognition and aid from the West. "All of those European countries that had never been a state before are recognized already," he said. "Because of UNOSOM and the failure of the UN in Somalia, they aren't willing to acknowledge our successes here."

Egal has stayed away from the series of peace conferences staged by the UN in Djibouti, Nairobi, and Addis Ababa. "How can we go to Addis? I am a head of state. I cannot go as the equal of Aydiid. We are not a faction. We are a nation. We have no one to be reconciled with. There is nothing we can say to any of those factions. They have no mandate. UNOSOM wants us to come as one of the factions. Aydiid has issued an invitation to a defunct faction, the SNM. The SNM had a two-year mandate here and they couldn't succeed."

Egal was referring to a particularly dangerous UN blunder in Somaliland. Even though the Somali National Movement had won the independence of Somaliland and was in large part responsible for the defeat of Siyaad Barre, they had fallen from power. In 1993, in the town of Boroma in Somaliland, a meeting of elders "elected" Egal to lead. Yet when the UN was arranging a conference in 1994, they invited the SNM and its head, Abdirahman "Tuur," to participate. After Tuur had fallen from power, he had a change of heart and decided suddenly that Somaliland should not be independent and proceeded to cement an expedient alliance with Aydiid. The UN's "recognition" of Tuur and the SNM nearly threw Somaliland into a state of war.

"We don't want a federation with Somalia," Egal said. "Two governments can talk. For twelve hours I talked to Aydiid. 'You cannot talk to me about sovereignty. You are only a warlord,' I told him. What is inhibiting debate with our brothers in the south is an incongruity of status. I must have a counterpart to talk to. The warlords have no authority."

Then Egal explained something to me, something I'd heard before from Somalis on the streets. It was a crazy conspiracy theory in my mind, but here it was coming from the mouth of the "president" of Somaliland.

"UNOSOM and the secretary general have evolved a policy for Egypt to safeguard the Nile," he continued. "Sixty percent of the Nile water comes from Ethiopia, which is undergoing a population explosion. One of those countries, Egypt or Ethiopia, will be without water. Egypt wants to keep this part of the world unstable for a while. The best way to do that is to keep Somalia as a loose cannon. We are Boutros-Ghali's greatest enemy because we have removed the threat of Greater Somalia. UNOSOM's only work is to sabotage everything we are doing here."

My initial reaction was that Egal had just blown his argument. He was beginning to sound like a flake. But as I thought about it, his case began to make sense from his perspective. The entire colonial experience in East Africa was based on the strategic quest to locate and then protect the source of the Nile.

Outside intervention in Somalia has never really been about Somalia. The Italians held the Benadir coast because it provided them with seaports from which to mount their campaign against Ethiopia. The British held Somaliland in the north to secure a supply of fresh meat to their garrison stationed across the gulf in Aden. The Aden garrison, in turn, was there to protect the Suez Canal. The possession of Jubaland in the south was a result of their hold of the Kenya colony (which, in turn, was taken over to protect Uganda and the headwaters of the White Nile upon which their Egyptian venture depended). The Soviets and Americans during the Cold War both invested in Somalia because Ethiopia was on the other side. Ethiopia is the source of the Blue Nile, which provides most of the water that provides hydropower at the Aswan Dam and then fertilizes Egypt before seeping into the Mediterranean.

All Somalis know this. To them, Somalia has always been about the security of Egypt. So when the former Egyptian foreign minister turned secretary general of the United Nations, Boutros Boutros-Ghali, sent troops to Somalia, they were naturally suspicious. As foreign minister, Boutros-Ghali had been friendly with Siyaad Barre and had provided support for his repressive regime. It all seemed so very transparent.

Somalis tend to view politics somewhat differently from Westerners. To them it is personal. Acts are carried out by the man, not by the office he holds. Boutros-Ghali was the same man in New York as he was in Cairo. His aims were the same. Protect the Nile.

So when the Americans landed in Mogadishu in December 1992, most Somalis figured something was up. More was at stake here than Somalia. They knew that the foreigners would soon lose interest, and they planned to get as much as quickly as possible from them. Somalia is not about Somalia.

In the years since the Somalia intervention fell apart, most of the post-mortem has borne out Somali suspicions, with conferences and seminars dealing with such topics as "Somalia: What Went Wrong," and "Somalia: Lessons Learned." The real focus of the discussions was on how to improve the bureaucracy. Histories written about Somalia have concentrated on the actions of diplomats: characters who came and went but who ultimately were of little consequence to Somalis. To them, the UN was just another foreign entity on its shores, and one that would eventually go, leaving Somalis to sort out their problems as they always did. One year later the UN was packing its bags.

Sadness permeated the UN's departure from Somalia in March 1995, as if it were the premature closing of an underappreciated Broadway show. The giant operation collapsed into itself. UN personnel retreated from the 80-acre UN compound to the seaside port-airport complex, and finally to the port alone. Holes were dug in the sand and perfectly good vehicles were buried—just to keep them from looters. UN workers packed their bags and tore down the prefab houses they'd erected along the beach. Pakistani and Egyptian soldiers combed their hair and shaved and waited for the ships and planes that would take them away.

With every departing charter flight, the compound became a bit quieter and a lot emptier. The French-run PX, which formerly echoed with the happy sounds of UN employees buying party-size crates of beer, whiskey, and cigarettes, became a dormitory for the last UNICEF workers. Then buildings were abandoned, and the last foreigners moved into empty shipping containers. Somali staff lined up to collect their final paychecks and demand additional compensation for working overtime and holidays. The UN slowly backed away, covering their retreat with disbursements of more than $1 million a day to keep things quiet. Every night, fewer and fewer people were pressed into tighter and tighter quarters until the whole operation vanished into a dot on the horizon.

Above and beyond it all were the Americans, who had returned to cover the UN's retreat just a year after their own unceremonious withdrawal. This time the Americans were there to rescue and protect. They were the cavalry rushing in as saviors, their uniforms unsoiled by their own now-distant involvement in Somalia. This time the failure was all the UN's.

The Americans talked about how the UN mandate in Somalia had been overambitious, how a "purely" humanitarian intervention had somehow become "nation building," and how that was never the intention. Somehow the UN got out of control. It was that UN Security Council Resolution 814, which used terms like "political settlement" and "transitional government institutions," that had stretched this thing way beyond its original intent. Most of the UN officers were too diplomatic—or too tired—to point out that Resolution 814 was an American initiative rammed through the Security Council in March 1993 by the Americans, who then left Pakistani, Malaysian, Bangladeshi, Indian, Zimbabwean, and Nigerian troops to do what their own marines had decided was unfeasible.

It seemed that failure was written into the plan.

As the plug was being pulled, it was hard not to think of the way things had been: Not so long ago, the UN operated like a gigantic clock. The air was constantly filled with helicopters shuttling people around as if Mogadishu was some futuristic model city. Passengers and freight moved through an efficient transport web that covered the entire country. A satellite communications system made remote UN outposts easy-to-reach extensions of a New York City telephone exchange. Thirty thousand soldiers and several thousand civilians were supplied with food and water from abroad. Dignitaries came and went. Aid workers with radios attached to their belts attended security meetings every morning.

This was largely the accomplishment of Admiral Jonathan Howe: The man destined to be remembered for his ill-fated hunt for General Aydiid had wrested a vast functioning bureaucracy where once there was chaos and desert. And it all ran beautifully.

From the Somalis' perspective, however, the entire bureaucracy was an object of endless amusement. They saw foreigners, hundreds of them, darting about the streets of Mogadishu, risking their lives, occasionally getting killed or kidnapped, going from meeting to meeting, always busy, always going in and out of offices, always in a hurry, yet seemingly doing nothing. Nothing was ever built in Mogadishu that the Somalis didn't build for themselves. The only thing the foreigners left behind was military debris and trash—vast fields of empty plastic water bottles that poor Somalis first hoarded but soon had their fill of. The UN paid Somali contractors to cart off the refuse and sewage, but then showed little interest in what was actually done with the waste once it left the confines of their compounds. Other than this, the entire UN operation seemed totally isolated from Somalia, as if it were under a plastic dome.

For the last year and a half before the withdrawal, the UN troops were there only to protect UN troops. Most of the UN personnel were in positions that provided service only to UN personnel. The U.S. military ended up adopting the Somali view of the bureaucracy. American officers described the operation as a "self-licking ice cream cone."

George Bennett, the UN's spokesman—and one of a handful of people who had been with UNOSOM from the beginning—gamely continued in the last days to put a positive spin on the situation. But Bennett was tired, and his spinning lacked its usual energy and conviction. As with everyone else, his disappointment was tempered with relief: After many close calls and last-minute reprieves, the United Nations Operation in Somalia, UNOSOM II, was finally over. Bennett had represented three different UN special representatives in Somalia. One, Jonathan Howe, had tried to kill Aydiid, and the most recent, Victor Gbeho, had, in Bennett's words, been seduced by Aydiid. Bennett sat in his office, now stuck inside a hangar on the airfield, smoking cigarettes and trying to speak over the roar of jet engines and diesel trucks. I suggested to him that the entire operation might have been unnecessary or, at the very least, overambitious. Perhaps the UN could have saved the billions of dollars that it spent on building its own infrastructure and instead employed one person and a couple of assistants to sit in Mogadishu and offer to mediate whenever the warlords were in the mood to talk to each other.

Bennett sat silently for a moment and then responded with a Somali proverb: "If you sweep the earth with a broom, it is the broom that wears out."

The UN's peacemaking machine was cursed with a built-in flaw: It desperately needed to succeed. When the only way to bring peace to Somalia might have been to walk away, the bureaucracy was compelled to stay and find a peace for which it could take credit. The future of peacekeeping and peace enforcement around the world depended on it. Indeed, of all the conflicts in the world, Somalia was chosen because it was deemed, in the words of General Powell, "doable." The fight there was regarded as petty as compared to, say, the "ancient animosities" that were enflaming passions in Bosnia.

In fact, it was the petty nature of the Somalia dispute—small men lusting after power and loot—that made the conflict so intractable. There were no issues, no ideological differences, nothing to negotiate. As long as the UN remained in Somalia, it continued to supply the raw material of the conflict: loot. Each desperate move to get an agreement—any agreement—sapped the UN of credibility and respect. It paid massive hotel bills, flew warlords and their entourages to Addis Ababa, Nairobi, and Djibouti and literally begged them to put their signatures on documents. Ali Mahdi and Aydiid used these meetings not to make peace with each other but as political conventions where they lobbied and coerced other faction leaders, trying to convince them to sign on with a winning ticket. UN negotiators seemed to first favor Ali Mahdi, then Aydiid, then Ali Mahdi again. Neither Aydiid nor Ali Mahdi ended up with any respect at all for the institution.

Most Somalis couldn't understand what the UN was doing trying to scrape together a "democratic" government out of the remnants of the hated Siyaad Barre regime. Both camps were largely staffed by people who had worked for Barre's dictatorship—including Aydiid himself and Ali Mahdi's wife and closest advisors. In its eagerness to bring order to Somalia, the UN would have happily reinstated a dictatorship. Success for the UN would have been failure for Somalia.

But these details were of little interest to the UN's negotiators, who had no patience for the minutiae of Somali politics. For both the UN and the United States, Somalia had long ago stopped being about Somalia. It was about redeeming a faltering American foreign policy and about carving out a brave new world of peacekeeping. The more they strained to reach an agreement, the farther away it seemed to drift. The few people within the bureaucracies who were conversant with the important details of Somalia's clan system resigned, complaining that no one was listening.

Those details, of interest only to true Somaliphiles, were extremely important. For example, most people understood that Aydiid and Ali Mahdi were members of the same clan family, the Hawiye, but came from different subclans, the Habar Gidir and Abgaal. Fewer realized that both of these subclans were broken down into further subclans that didn't entirely support the faction leaders. Ali Mahdi's Abgaal-Harti were a minority and needed to keep the other subclans happy. And Aydiid's Habar Gidir-Sa'ad were dependent on the Habar Gidir-Ayr and Habar Gidir-Suleymaan for their infantry strength. And few were remotely aware that Aydiid's even more immediate clan, the Habar Gidir-Sa'ad-Jalaf, were involved in tense negotiations with the Habar Gidir-Sa'ad-Hilolwe, the group that supplied most of his money and top advisors.

Neither the Americans nor the UN ever seemed to get a firm grasp of the clan system. The walls of their offices were plastered with clan diagrams torn from academic books. Starting with Samal, the supposed founder of the Somali people, the charts broke down into clan families, subclans, sub-subclans. It was all very neat and very graphic. But the Westerners tended to see the family trees as if they were corporate organizational charts. They therefore concluded that power emanated from the top, and that everyone was really part of one big family. The fighting was internecine and therefore senseless.

What they never seemed to understand was that the Somalis themselves never thought in terms of organizational charts. Their perspective on their own lives was from the bottom up. Starting with the immediate family, and climbing up the family tree, the farther away you got, the more remote the connection. The loyalty of the foot soldiers to the chief at the top of the clan lasted only as long as the spoils of war came down through the ranks. Aydiid needed to deliver the goods. The resources dumped by the military, the UN, the NGOs, and the journalists ensured that Aydiid had enough to spread around.

The battles being fought in Mogadishu were for real resources, scarce resources, real wealth, and the stakes were high. It was a battle for survival, far from senseless. To the contrary, it made perfect sense. For the last ten years of the Barre government, relief food poured over the docks of Mogadishu. The government used that food to build its power base and control people in the hinterlands. Individuals used the food to get rich. It made perfect sense that the warlords would fight over relief food. Food was power and survival for the family.

By the time the U.S. Marines came ashore in December 1992, Aydiid and Ali Mahdi had fought each other to a bloody standstill. As early as March 1992, their factions had begun to turn inward, challenging their leadership. Photo ops with American diplomats were just what were needed to raise their profiles within their own clans. From that point onward, almost everything Aydiid did was an attempt to keep his own alliance intact. While the UN was exerting its energy to broker an agreement between the warlords, Aydiid and Ali Mahdi were worried about keeping their relatives happy. In other words, billions of dollars and several hundred thousand foreign nationals were involved in a global operation to settle what was, at its core, the politics of dysfunctional families.

The man who perhaps understood the least was the one who had taken on the largest burden: U.S. Ambassador Robert Oakley.

Oakley had grabbed for himself the reputation for being "the one American who really knew what was going on." He had the useful skill of projecting an enigmatic half smile whenever confronted with questions he didn't want to or, more likely, couldn't answer. Most of the assembled press corps interpreted this as a sign of higher knowledge. The few with more experience in Somalia figured he didn't know what he was talking about. One press conference stands out.

The day that Aydiid was taken off the UN's most-wanted list in November 1993, Oakley went to see him. As he drove back through the streets of Mogadishu with an Aydiid-supplied military escort, his little convoy found itself in the middle of a cheering throng of Aydiid supporters, who began chanting "Oakley, Oakley, Oakley." The ambassador wisely did not yield to the temptation to address the jubilant crowd. When I asked about it later, he pretended that it was all part of the plan.

"I've seen crowds here before. When they have on their smiling faces it's good," he said. "When they have on their nasty face it's bad, but I wasn't the least bit nervous." One of Oakley's assistants provided a bit more detail: "They led us on . . . we had no idea. We came down this street and there's this huge crowd . . . and I thought, Gee, this looks interesting." The truth was, as usual, that Oakley was being manipulated by Aydiid.

Several times during Operation Restore Hope, Aydiid's clan was close to running him out of town at the end of a technical. Each time he was rescued, inadvertently, by the Americans. Aydiid deftly learned that he could unite his forces only by focusing on a common enemy; a call to arms against infidels and imperialists still gets adrenaline pumping in that part of Africa. The best way to isolate Aydiid would have been to ignore him, not to put a $25,000 price on his head or send in Delta Force. Each bloody confrontation with peacekeepers raised his profile. Likewise, every time Aydiid was flown to a meeting or was visited by U.S. special envoy Robert Oakley, he walked away strengthened.

For that reason, the impending departure of UNOSOM was an immediate threat to Aydiid's power, and the announcement that the marines would return to assist in the withdrawal was a final opportunity for Aydiid to raise the banner of glorious combat.

In the months before the UNOSOM withdrawal, Aydiid's power had been seriously challenged from within his own clan and from his external allies. His closest advisor and primary financier, Osman Ato, and his most powerful military ally, Colonel Abdullahi Yusuf, had been talking with members of Ali Mahdi's faction and were united in their conviction that Aydiid had become power mad and was the main obstacle to peace in Somalia. Ato had gone to the Sa'ad clan elders and gotten their agreement on this notion.

Aydiid responded by playing his anti-American card once again. Through his radio station—the one he rebuilt after the Americans leveled the first one—he told Somalis that the Americans were coming to "recolonize" Somalia. Most Somalis saw it for what it was, a desperate gambit by a desperate man. But Aydiid's core supporters in his subclan rallied round. They attended twice-weekly demonstrations (as they had during the days of Aydiid's battle against the UN) and spread the word. In the coastal town of Merka a week before the Americans were to land, a group of elders asked me to explain why the Americans wanted to take over Somalia. I tried to assure them that the Americans would be there for only two days, three at the most. They remained skeptical.

Just before the Somalia landing, the Pentagon unveiled an array of high-tech nonlethal weapons that it had in its arsenal. These included Sticky-Goop, which would disable an onrushing crowd by engulfing people in a mountain of glue, binding them to themselves, other people, and the ground, and carpets that would release CS gas if trod upon. President Clinton had reportedly been upset by the numbers of civilian casualties involved in a series of U.S. operations in Somalia, starting with the deaths of at least 100 bystanders, many of them women and children, in a September 9, 1993, firefight. But his most immediate concern was with the Republicans, and avoiding anything that would serve as a vehicle for recalling the disastrous October 3 attempt to capture Aydiid. The plan was to keep it low-key and nonviolent. The announcement of these nonlethal capabilities was designed to let potential looters and troublemakers know that the United States was prepared to deal with them. The message to Somalis was, *Stay away.*

The Somalis didn't get it. For a week before the arrival of the marines, the streets of Mogadishu were abuzz with rumors about the fantastic comic-book science-fiction gadgets the Americans were bringing with them. People planned to go to the gates of the port and airport just to see the stuff. What the hell? It couldn't kill you.

So once again, the Americans had completely misread the situation on the ground in Mogadishu. Their humane gesture was interpreted as a sign of weakness and an invitation. Privately, U.S. commanders were concerned about just that. "Once the bad guys figure out we're not going to kill them, they become more dangerous and endanger the force on the ground," said one military planner.

But once again the Pentagon's eye wasn't exactly on the ball. They may have been back in Somalia again, but their concern was with future peace-keeping missions. If the United States ever hoped to employ Egyptian, Pakistani, or other forces in future multinational operations, it needed to demonstrate that Americans would put their lives on the line to protect them. And despite a real distaste for the peacekeeping business in Washington, Pentagon officials accept that the military had better be doing something if they're going to continue getting huge budget allocations. "It's becoming inevitable that we're getting these types of capabilities thrust upon us," said a Pentagon source. "The attitude is let's dance with it rather than wrestle against it."

The Pentagon is now dancing in the ruins of Yugoslavia, and Somalia has slipped back into its preintervention stateless state. There is almost no evidence that the United States and UN were ever there and little trace of the $4 billion that was spent. Mogadishu remains a collection of clan-based enclaves, each protected by its own militia. Somehow people eat and survive, children go to school, businessmen import and sell goods. Occasionally a battle erupts.

Somalis are now responsible for their own futures. There are no foreigners to blame for their failures. And sometimes a bright spot emerges. Elman Ali Ahmed, a Somali electrician, stayed through all the fighting and ran a technical school for Mogadishu's orphaned children and for former militia members. He was known in Mogadishu for his dreadlocks and his car, a beat-to-death Toyota with no roof. Journalists knew him because he would drop by to visit and help people repair computers and other electronic equipment. He spent all his days trying to convince Somalis to come to their senses and organize against the warlords for peace. On March 10, 1996, he was shot to death by gunmen who supported Aydiid.

He was unique in Mogadishu. He did what most people waited for foreigners to do. He never formed an NGO or asked for money from the UN. Elman always knew he was in danger. He understood that there was no such thing as a "pure" humanitarian intervention. Humanitarianism, like poverty and underdevelopment, is political. It takes commitment, and it comes with risks.

15

RUNNING TOWARD RWANDA

War is the beast which eats children. With food aid, we think we are feeding the children, but we may be feeding the beast.
—Lindsey Hilsum, British journalist

Buffalo Bill's is ripe with the stink of cooked meat, stale beer, and very cheap perfume. Rooted to the floor around a horseshoe-shaped bar, bare steel poles rise to menace customers who crowd around waiting for beer. Back when this was Nairobi's first American-style burger joint, the poles, topped with saddles, served as barstools. Parts of the western motif remain; Conestoga wagon tops arc above the booths nearest the bar. Early every evening young African women wander in and order soft drinks, which they share with each other while they wait for the men who will buy them alcohol, and maybe take them away.

Then the Land Cruisers start to arrive. Groups of white men enter the bar. They are as young as twenty and as old as sixty. They have a swagger about them; masters of this universe. At the very least, they own the night. Some of them are white Kenyans, known as Kenya cowboys. Others are foreign aid workers. Most of them make their money from the aid business. While some of them work directly for NGOs, many are part of a different class of aid workers. They are aid entrepreneurs—truckers, mechanics, consultants, engineers, pilots, and others who do the real work of aid, the moving and lifting. They execute the plans of the humanitarians and missionaries.

In the summer of 1994, they are having their best year ever. Just as the relief effort in Somalia was winding down, Rwanda exploded. For three months they waited on the sidelines while members of Rwanda's Hutu ethnic group took machetes, clubs, and knives to 800,000 Tutsi countrymen. Then, after the Tutsi-led Rwandan Patriotic Front captured the country and the Hutus fled across borders into Tanzania and Zaire, the good times returned. Two million people in refugee camps meant lots of work for everyone. And everyone at Buffalo Bill's is in high spirits.

Kevin, a middle-aged South African, runs a trucking company that is now covering the roads between Mombassa, Kenya, and Goma, Zaire, where a vast refugee camp has pitched itself on volcanic rock. The refugees need everything, and Kevin's trucks are there to deliver. Kevin talks loudly and throws back beers as a Kenyan woman rubs his neck and attempts to slide onto his lap. He passes her some money and says, "Fuck off and get some beers, will you darling."

The women at Buffalo Bill's, nearly all of them prostitutes, outnumber the potential customers by a factor of four. It's a buyer's market, but a few jobs a week can earn the women a lot more money than an African office worker with a good education and secretarial skills, and office jobs are impossible to find anyway. Many of the women are educated, and most of them have tried to find jobs in other fields.

In Nairobi and all over Africa, prostitution flourishes wherever it is not actively suppressed. From an economic point of view, going into prostitution is a rational decision for an African woman. It's one of the rare avenues open for her to make real money. The sex industry is one of the few points where the local economy and the expatriate economy intersect.

Like most African nations, Kenya runs on two parallel economies. The expatriate economy, which includes most high-level government officials and some powerful businessmen, is a First World economy. It is the world of Mercedes-Benz automobiles, palatial homes, servants, nightclubs, and expensive restaurants. Four-wheel-drive vehicles can cost $90,000. The average Kenyan earns less than $400 a year.

This really struck me one day when I arrived at a friend's home where I was staying in Nairobi with several bottles of whiskey I'd just picked up at a local liquor store. In my friend's absence, I was paying the salaries of his cook, gardener, and watchman. As I was handing them their cash, I saw price stickers, which were still on the bottles. I suddenly realized I'd just paid for a single bottle of a standard blended Scotch what amounted to the gardener's monthly salary—and he had a decent salary by Kenyan standards. In industrialized countries, even the lowest-paid worker can occasionally spring for a good bottle of whiskey or a decent pair of shoes. Rich and poor exist on opposite ends of a broad economic continuum. In Africa there are few places where the two economies meet.

Of the money that Western organizations, businesses, and charities spend in Africa, a small part goes into the African tier economy. This is the money paid to servants and workers, the pennies passed out to beggars and street children for watching their cars at night. The vast bulk of the money that Westerners spend is in the upper tier of the economy. Rents are paid at European rates, often in foreign exchange. Planes are chartered and trucking companies are engaged to move aid and relief supplies. The landlords and car dealers are the government officials who live in this upper tier with the expatriates, who show up at the restaurants and clubs. NGOs generally pay their local staff well, by local standards. But even the lowliest foreign-born volunteer aid worker exists in the expatriate economy; these unskilled Westerners earn multiples of what highly qualified nationals get paid.

The disaster in Somalia was a windfall for Kenya. The Kenyans charged landing fees for airplanes at Wilson Airport, where most charter and civilian planes are based. NGOs moved in thousands of personnel, and the United Nations operated most of their relief effort from Nairobi. In addition, hundreds of thousands of Somali refugees flocked into Kenya, where they were met by an army of aid workers to take care of their needs. Relief organizations purchased water, food, blankets, and other materials in Kenya. They rented houses. All of this was money going to Kenya's politician-businessman class. With Kenya's crucial tourism industry slipping, aid workers became a permanent tourist presence, filling hotels and restaurants as tourists once did. And just as the Somalia operation was ending, Rwanda arrived to fill the gap.

Most Kenyans stood helplessly by and watched the aid parade file through town. Only a few were in a position to benefit from it, and many of them hang out at Buffalo Bill's.

On this particular evening at Buffalo Bill's, I've come specifically to meet Kevin to ask about food diversions from the refugee camps in Zaire. A colleague of his told me with certainty that he would be here on any given night.

I find Kevin at a table with a group of others from the aid business. There is an American who works with CARE, and a Kenya cowboy in his late fifties who is head mechanic on Kevin's fleet. He has psoriasis on his wrists and a gaunt, infected-looking face. There is also a younger Englishman, tall, thin, blond-haired, drunk.

I tell Kevin I've heard that much of the refugee food is falling into the hands of the Hutu extremist hit men who engineered the massacre of the Tutsis in the first place and then frightened their own people out of the country and into the refugee camps. Yes, true, he tells me. His truckers deliver all the food. The food is checked in at the camps. But, he tells me, his trucks don't leave empty. They leave the camps with some of the food they came in with. "My drivers make what money they can on the return trip. They carry coffee or whatever they're paid to carry. So they truck food out of the refugee camps." On the return trip, the drivers are working for the Hutu leaders, who steal the food and use the money to purchase guns and ammunition to retake the country. Once again, it appears that an aid effort is financing a war. Once again, an investment in aid is ensuring that there will be another disaster in the future.

As I'm talking to Kevin, his attention is only half focused on me. I grab my answers as he alternately nuzzles and abuses the young Kenyan woman, who accepts the insults with professional good humor. "Didn't I tell you to piss off? I'm talking to a journalist here." His friends laugh and encourage him. Other women are gathering around and campaigning for their attention.

The tall blond Englishman says his name is John. When I'm introduced to him, he offers me his limp wrist to shake. He says that since I'm a journalist, I should buy a round. How long have you been in Kenya, he asks me, with undisguised hostility. This is a standard question, it is what determines the expatriate pecking order. When expats sit and talk about Africa, they display their combat ribbons. Length of stay is the most important. The ones who have been here the longest earn the right to say whatever they want. Their interpretations of African behavior and politics are given the most weight at gatherings like this. I've been here since 1977, I tell him, seventeen years. John is quiet for a moment.

"I was born here," he suddenly blurts from the silence. "Buy me a fucking beer."

His friends ignore him. They start talking about business and trucks and refugees. Kevin and his friends are the prime beneficiaries of the aid business, which is why they hold most NGOs in such contempt. They know they can overcharge, produce shoddy work, and still get paid. They joke about forming an NGO called Somalia Community Assistance Committee—SCAM. Everyone laughs. As in Evelyn Waugh's Scoop, where journalists invent a war to write home about, they've decided that they should invent a famine, to get the food and money and work. Who's going to know? Skinny Somalis always look like they're starving anyway. They live in hovels even when they're rich.

Kevin has been contracting for NGOs for fifteen years and doesn't see much difference between his business and theirs. To him it's all about contracts and getting paid on time. He turns back and tells me I should ride with his trucks for a week, see what happens to the food. John says nothing now but sporadically bangs loudly on the table. When people look at him, he affects an innocent look. Sorry. What did I do?

As the crowd gets drunker, the prostitutes move closer. They sit on laps. Fuck off, John says to one of them, getting into the spirit. But she doesn't fuck off. Later he corners me in the men's room. He looks to be about six feet four. He's blocking my exit, and asks to borrow money. No, I tell him. Then he demands money. I just met you, I say. Ask your friends. Then John begins to cry and starts telling me about the embarrassment and pain of not being able to buy a drink for his friends.

"No" I tell him again, and I push past him out the door.

"You're a bore," he shouts after me.

Rick, the CARE guy, tells me later that John wasn't born in Kenya. He came as a VSO volunteer, Britain's Peace Corps, about six years earlier. He fell into the Nairobi scene, the drugs and alcohol and prostitutes. He married a prostitute and now she works to support them both. Occasionally he finds good-paying work in the aid business, helping the poor African refugees.

The Rwandan Hutus who fled their country were frightened out of Rwanda by their own leaders, a situation similar to Siyaad's creation of a refugee crisis in Somalia after the Ogaden war. Refugees attract aid. Aid is a resource. As in Somalia, the Hutu militants wanted to use the camps to rest, regroup, and rearm for the second phase of the battle. The UN and the U.S. and the NGOs could provide day care for the women and children while the men prepared for war. They begged for mercy while making their own people prisoners of fear; they raised money on the shivering, emaciated bodies of their own children.

The Hutu exodus was a political success for the leaders for one reason: They knew that relief aid would be there when they crossed the border. They knew the West would respond. And when the West did respond, it was a signal to other refugees to desert Rwanda and head for the border. The word was out in Rwanda that food and medical care existed on the other side. Aid made the exodus possible. Aid made the exodus logical. Life was better on the outside, despite the scenic horror of the camps. The killers fled into the open arms of international charity.

Everyone involved knew that the Hutu leaders were preparing to reinvade Rwanda. A UN document states: "It now looks as if these elements are preparing an armed invasion of Rwanda and that they are both stockpiling and selling food aid distributed by caritative [sic] organizations in order to prepare for this invasion."*

The emergency nature of a refugee operation usually means that accountability is sacrificed. Losses and leakage of aid supplies are tolerated for the sake of expediency. In the short term, all hands are needed to dispense the aid, so there's no one around to really check what happens to it. And in the long term, no one cares. Few people will pay attention to an emergency after the dramatic crisis phase has passed. The consequences of misdirected aid are rarely brought to light. Who, after all, was going to blame charities if the Hutu invaded Rwanda? For the donating public, the aid workers are there to help. Whose fault is it if the damn Africans screwed up their own lives? The West is not at fault. The West is not accountable.

Hundreds of times I've heard aid workers heap blame for failure on the recipients of their generosity. I've often been reminded of these lines from Kipling's *The White Man's Burden:*

Take up the White Man's Burden—
   The savage wars of peace—
Fill Full the mouth of Famine
   And bid the sickness cease.
And when your goal is nearest
   The end for others sought,
Watch Sloth and heathen Folly
   Bring all your hope to nought.

In Nairobi I met with a Somali businessman friend who runs a trading company that had been bidding on relief projects. It's really the only business in town. The Red Cross and other international organizations pay promptly and in hard currency. My friend can import anything, and between the Somali refugees in Kenya and the Hutu refugees in Zaire and Tanzania he's been doing well in recent years.

He started complaining to me, however, about the Red Cross and a recent contract they just issued to supply blankets to Rwandan refugees in

---

*Africa News Report, November 28, 1994.

Goma. "They tendered to buy 100,000 blankets, specifying that they be 60 percent wool and 40 percent synthetic. Those blankets cost seven dollars apiece." He showed me a photocopy of the contract that went to another firm to buy the blankets: total cost, $700,000. The blankets were purchased from Raymond's Blankets, a huge Kenyan manufacturer in the Rift Valley.

My friend showed me another contract, this one from the blanket factory. According to the document, the Red Cross actually purchased blankets that were 20 percent wool and 80 percent synthetic. Those blankets were $4.50 each, total $450,000. Someone pocketed $250,000. My Somali friend figured it was a deal between someone at the Red Cross and the Kenyan contractor. At any rate, the money was gone, and no one is running around the refugee camps checking the fabric of the blankets that are covering cholera victims. "You want more stories? I've got more stories. Everyone is getting rich from Rwanda," he said.

The Hutu refugees attracted incredible media attention. Refugees make better pictures than the slow slaughter of 800,000 people. They're in a neat package in concentrated areas. They look like victims, long lines of people trudging toward somewhere or other. It raises sympathy like nothing else. Across the industrialized world, NGOs raised hundreds of millions for Rwanda.* Rwanda came with its own slogan: Worse than Somalia. More dead, more refugees in a smaller place, more bang for the buck. A new benchmark in horror had been reached.

"This was no Somali refugee camp with total and permanent confusion," Gérard Prunier wrote in his remarkable book about Rwanda. "Here food could be distributed in an orderly fashion. There were authorities and even a form of order. But this order was the order of death which had prevailed in April–July."†

The authorities in the camps were the same people who had organized the amazingly efficient slaughter of Tutsis in Rwanda. They knew how to keep things under control. It was this "order of death" that made things so convenient for the NGOs.

NGOs had built their strength and numbers during the 1980s over a series of disasters, Ethiopia, Somalia, and Bosnia being the best known. Mozambique was another NGO growth opportunity that received far less

---

*InterAction, a coalition of some 150 American nonprofit organizations, reported that nearly $100 million in cash and goods was given to their members alone.

†Gérard Prunier, The Rwanda Crisis: History of a Genocide (New York: Columbia University Press, 1995).

publicity, but plenty of money. By the time Rwanda rolled around, an unprecedented number of organizations were funded and ready to roll. No one actually knows how many organizations are doing this kind of work. They're not required to register or to check in with any central authority. But in the United States alone, the increase in numbers over the last decade has been substantial. In 1982, there were 144 NGOs registered with USAID; by 1992, there were 384; and by 1994 that number had increased to 419.* And these are just the ones that registered to get federal grants. Most had no knowledge of Rwanda or Rwandans, and some had never worked in Africa before. A lot of mistakes were made.

One of the legendary blunders of the Rwanda refugee campaign came from CARE Germany, which sent 267 German doctors and nurses to Goma, Zaire after a nationwide appeal for recruits. CARE, however, didn't check with anyone else in Goma and, as it turned out, the doctors weren't really needed. In addition, many of the doctors had no experience in places like Goma and were immediately beset with a kind of post-traumatic stress that incapacitated them.

Red Cross officials turned away CARE volunteers, citing lack of qualifications. One Red Cross official, John Parker, told the press, "I need someone here who has been selected for his attitude and his behavior. I do not need a bunch of do-gooders around." In addition, the do-gooder doctors were only scheduled to stay for a few weeks, not enough time to acclimate to working conditions, let alone actually do any good.

The episode reflected a prevalent Western attitude that anything we send, anything we can do, is needed and useful. It is the same attitude that hammers home the message that for the price of a cup of coffee, we can alter the lives of poor children in the Third World. It is bargain-basement charity.

The charity AmeriCares, for example, sent 10,000 cases of Gatorade to Goma intended for cholera patients. "It is the same ingredients you would get in an I.V.," the AmeriCares president, Stephen Johnson, said.† Well, no, it's not. AmeriCares is one of those charities whose prime purpose seems to be to provide an outlet for corporations looking for tax-write-offs.

Pamela Winnick, an attorney who has worked for both CARE and Save the Children, now spends much of her time investigating charities. She re-

---

*These figures come from a General Accounting Office report, *Foreign Assistance: Private Voluntary Organizations' Contributions and Limitations* (GAO/NSIAD-96-34), December 1995.

†Raymond Bonner published this in an excellent *New York Times* article, "Post-Mortem for Charities; Compassion Wasn't Enough in Rwanda," December 18, 1994.

ported that AmeriCares sent two million Mars chocolate bars to St. Petersburg, Russia; seventeen tons of Pop Tarts to Bosnia; and 12,000 Maidenform bras to victims of the 1990 earthquake in Japan.* Winnick journeyed to Bosnia, where she found stocks of Prozac in a medical center that was desperately short of vaccines and other emergency drugs. It was, predictably, supplied by AmeriCares. Winnick quoted from a leaked document from UNHCR in which one official advises another: "I would strongly advise that you treat . . . AmeriCares with extreme caution. UNHCR's experience with [AmeriCares] in the former Yugoslavia, former Soviet Union and Burundi/Rwanda emergency have shown it to be an irresponsible, publicity hungry organization capable of making grandiose generalized offers of assistance and providing planeloads of highly questionable 'relief supplies.'"

Defending itself in a letter to the *Wall Street Journal*, AmeriCares was unusually candid: "By donating . . . products to AmeriCares, our companies save massive destruction costs, warehousing expenses and headaches . . . while they gain tax benefits, good public relations and brand-name recognition in emerging markets."

Chris McGreal of *The Guardian* reported on some of the other less-professional aid organizations working in Goma in the December 17, 1994, issue. One of them was Operation Blessing, operated by American evangelist Pat Robertson.†

Operation Blessing's head in Goma, David Rosin, says his organization dispatched "medical missionaries" at the height of the crisis after Mr Robertson launched a nationwide television appeal likely to have raised large donations.

At present, the organization has more evangelists than medical staff working from its small clinic. Luxury accommodation for Mr Rosin and one other worker costs £4,000 a month.

---

*AmeriCares was founded by Bob Macauley, a kindergarten and Yale classmate of George Bush. Barbara Bush and two Bush sons have been on the board of advisors.

†Pat Robertson owns a company based in Zaire called the African Development Co., which has invested in diamond mines, lumber, agriculture, and other large-scale industries in Zaire. He has a close personal relationship with Zaire's dictator, Mobutu Sese Seko, the man who has outdone all others in his abuse of foreign aid, pocketing an estimated $5 billion from his nation's treasury. In the process, he has turned what could be Africa's wealthiest country into an anarchic mess. Through sanctions and aid restrictions, the United States has been trying, unsuccessfully, to coax Mobutu back to sanity. Pat Robertson has opposed these measures. He told the *Washington Post*, "The attitude of the State Department toward Zaire is outrageous, and has been for years." In Zaire in 1995, he met with Mobutu and promised to use his friends in the Senate like Senator Jesse Helms of North Carolina to change U.S. policy.

Although Operation Blessing says those it helps are not forced to take a dose of religion, the United Nations medical coordinator in Goma, Dr Claire Bourgeois, thinks otherwise. "Operation Blessing is no longer under UN co-ordination . . . personally I don't think they should use health care to reach people to teach them religion," she said.

Operation Blessing is one of those organizations that invests a lot in the show, the spectacle of compassion that makes such great TV. Pat Robertson's organization spent more on flying volunteers and television crews to Zaire than it did on anything else—$356,000 for transportation alone.*

Only the host country can apply its laws, and in the case of Zaire, they weren't about to insult Pat Robertson—or any NGO for that matter. Zairean officials have made a handsome profit from the NGOs and journalists, who pay landing fees, bribes, and other levies as part of the cost of doing business.†

As in Kenya and Somalia, ordinary Zaireans haven't benefited much from the presence of so many foreigners and so much aid money. To the contrary, local farmers have been forced out of business by tons of free food. Few NGOs have hired Zairean engineers, doctors, or other professionals, preferring to bring people in from abroad. And while the UN has doled out millions in contracts to foreign NGOs, local NGOs have had to make do with nothing. Zaireans, some of the poorest people in the world, struggling to survive in a country where absolutely nothing works, have stood by while the international community has focused on the plight of the refugees.

On the Rwandan side of the border, the new government, with all its concerns, tried to exercise some control over the situation. At the end of 1995, more than twenty NGOs were booted out of the country. Again, McGreal reported:

> Christine Nyinawumwami, a senior Rwandan rehabilitation ministry official, has threatened to expel organizations considered abusive, including those which sweep children into their orphanages because they offer better fund-raising prospects.
>
> "Some agencies are taking children from the villages and putting them in centres, taking their pictures and using them to raise money," she said.
>
> "They should be helping the community to look after the children. These agencies are going to leave and there will be no one to look after the children."

---

*Bonner, "Post-Mortem for Charities."

†A UN investigation also concluded it was "highly probable" that Zaire had been supplying weapons to Hutu exiles so that they could mount a coup against the new Rwandan government.

Emma Visman, of Save the Children [UK], found a similar problem around the camps in Bukavu, Zaire. "Everybody wants to start children-only centres. They're very vulnerable to being used to get more funds."

The Catholic agency, Caritas, has been criticized for giving children for adoption into Zairean families without keeping tabs on their fate. A UN source reported Zaireans trafficking in Rwandan children through Burundi.

But the organization which most outraged aid workers was Americans for African Adoptions International which arrived in the chaos of post-war Kigali intent on scooping up orphaned, abandoned and other children in distress for transport abroad, against Rwandan law.

"Those people came through here looking to find African babies to ship to the US and UK. I couldn't believe it. It was disgusting. We wouldn't have anything to do with them and made it clear how we felt about what they were doing. They never came around again so we don't know how many children they took away," one UN official said.

I had seen the exact same thing in Somalia fifteen years earlier. There is perhaps nothing more wretched than the exploitation of children for fundraising, yet nothing more common. NGOs that focus on children had always fallen back on this "mission" whenever outsiders questioned their motives or practices. "We may have made some mistakes, but if you write anything that reduces our donations, you'll only be hurting the children," is a refrain I've heard often over the years. And for the most part, journalists kept their suspicions to themselves.

But that has slowly begun to change. Many of the journalists who went to Rwanda and Goma had also been in Somalia. Never before had the press and the public been exposed to so much horror and charity in such a short time. Slowly, the message had begun to sink in. At Goma, the NGOs all had their banners and bumper stickers and T-shirts. Logos were everywhere, like the Nike "swoosh" or Coca-Cola. It was like being at a grand trade show of charity. Too much of this, mixed with shameless and aggressive self-promotion, and the gloss starts to wear off. What once looked so pure and selfless starts to smell.

Lindsey Hilsum, who writes for *The Guardian* and reports for the BBC, was one of those journalists who finally saw enough. Hilsum, whose coverage of Rwanda was second to none, had seen a lot. On December 31, 1995, she wrote in *The Guardian*:

In the past decade, I have watched the emergency aid business from the famines in Ethiopia and Mozambique in the mid-Eighties to genocide and the refugee exodus from Rwanda last year grow from a small element in the larger package of "development" into a giant, global, unregulated industry worth £2,500 million a year. Most of that money is provided by governments, the European Union and the United Nations. Increasingly, they, like the general public, channel funds through non governmental organizations (NGOs), which descend like migrating geese on every civil war and refugee crisis. . . .

But the bland assurances of the advertisements "we are making things better, you can help" mask serious doubts about emergency aid. What would be called profits in any other sector have enabled NGOs to grow and proliferate. When a million refugees swarmed across the border between Rwanda and Zaire last year, more than 100 NGOs turned up. . . .

The needs of lost, weeping children sitting next to their parents' corpses were undeniable, but some refugees abandoned their children believing the aid workers would do a better job of looking after them. They were wrong. Malnutrition and death rates in some children's centres were higher than in the camps in general.

Hilsum and I were at a conference in Geneva in December of 1995 where someone remarked, "You need a license to drive a taxi in New York City, but anyone can form a charity and start working overseas." The United States government has passed laws that govern the behavior of U.S. businesses abroad, but there are no such rules for charities. There is no accountability. The UN can attempt to run a refugee camp but has no authority to tell an organization they can't pitch a tent and start working. There's nothing to prevent a group of Westerners with money from setting up shop and performing surgery on refugees. No one is going to ask for their medical diplomas or evidence of liability insurance. When I was a Peace Corps volunteer in Kenya, I remember meeting a doctor working in a bush hospital who elatedly told me, "I'd have to wait another five years before they'd let me do the things I'm doing here at home."

On top of this, much of what these organizations do, they do with public money. In 1993, American NGOs received more than $1.7 billion from USAID, including $414 million in food commodities and freight. Other federal agencies, such as the Department of State and the Department of Agriculture, handed over an additional $439 million. A decade earlier, NGOs received just over $1 billion from the federal government. More than 60 percent of American NGOs receive some kind of federal funding. And this doesn't include taxpayer monies channeled through UN agencies.

Organizations like the National Charities Information Bureau do a de-

cent job monitoring expenditures and the proportion of funds NGOs de-
vote to overhead and fund-raising, yet they're in no position to make any
judgments about the work these groups do. By NCIB's standards, Ameri-
Cares is among the best charities. Because most of what they get are contributions in kind, 100 percent of which they are able to pass along to
recipients; AmeriCares is able to make the amazing claim that 99.1 percent of donations go to the needy. No one asks if the needy want those donations or need those donations. Most organizations follow suit and do
their best, as Save the Children does, to make that pie chart look good because that's the only thing critics and watchdogs tend to look at.

Journalists are currently in the best position to judge NGOs, but those
who are too critical of the organizations aren't allowed access to their projects, and NGOs are under no obligation to open their books or reveal
their activities to the press. At any rate, few journalists are equipped to do
a detailed and accurate analysis of development activities. It takes more
time than journalists generally have. You can walk into a village, see happy
children and a Save the Children logo on the local school, and judge that
everything is fine. Recipients of aid aren't stupid enough to complain to
journalists about projects, especially if someone from the NGO is within
earshot.

In a place like Somalia or Rwanda, it was particularly difficult to criticize
NGOs. They had all the money and all the airplanes. The only rides to
Goma, for journalists who weren't backed by big news organizations with
money to charter planes, was with aid organizations. They were more than
happy to help. The return on investment makes it all worthwhile because
NGOs need nothing more than publicity. Their prime interest is in reaching their customers, the donating public. These are the people who must
be convinced that the organizations are doing what they say they're doing,
and NGOs look after their customers at all times.

What is really required is a truly independent agency—not one like InterAction, which is composed of NGOs—to look after the interests of the
targets of development and relief, a.k.a., the needy. The organization
should be staffed by professionals who have the time and resources to produce detailed analyses of what these organizations are doing for the poor of
the Third World. Those that do effective aid work should be singled out so
"customers" know where to spend their money. In the short run, that will
stop the wildfire proliferation of NGOs, and eventually reduce them to a
manageable number so that relief circuses like Rwanda don't ever happen
again.

16

MERCHANTS OF PEACE

You daren't handle high explosives; but you're all ready to handle
honesty and truth and justice and the whole duty of man, and kill
one another at that game. What a country! What a world!

—George Bernard Shaw, *Major Barbara*

"Peacekeeping '94 is dedicated to the memory of all those military and
humanitarian aid personnel who lost their lives in the service of
peace—lest we forget."

The words were printed on a placard hanging along one side of the entrance to the exhibition hall. On the other side hung a life-size image of a
soldier—a peacekeeper—silhouetted against a bright red sky, as if he were
standing guard over some sacred ground. But the solemn sentiment lin-
gered for as long as it took to pass through the gate and ride the escalator
to the showroom below. There, any sense of reverence dissolved in a haze
of fluorescent lighting and the steady low-level chatter of salesmen. In a
room the size of a large gymnasium, in the basement of the Washington
Sheraton Hotel, dealers in arms and other military hardware stood by sales
samples and stacks of pamphlets scanning patiently for customers. Trade

show veterans, most could spot a hot prospect in a sea of suits and then lure him in with a nod and a smile.

Many of the buyers who strolled through wore military uniforms. Most were attachés from various Third World embassies in Washington. They admired the new M998A1 Series High Mobility Multi-Purpose Wheeled Vehicle (better known as a Humvee) and checked out the interior of an armored personnel carrier from General Motors that had been dubbed "The Peacekeeper." They took practice shots with an M-16 assault rifle modified to fire a laser beam at computer images of enemy soldiers. They browsed over a display of handcuffs and other restraining devices and fondled the kind of paramilitary paraphernalia usually advertised in *Soldier of Fortune* magazine.

But they walked right by booths set up by the American Red Cross and Interchurch Medical Assistance. Few seemed interested in stopping at a display from InterAction, a consortium of 160 NGOs such as CARE and Save the Children. Megan Meier, who sat at the InterAction booth, said she wasn't exactly sure what she was doing there. She shrugged and smiled. Then she remembered the script and explained that InterAction wanted to promote cooperation between NGOs and the military.

Peacekeeping '94 was a product of Baxter Publishing, a Canadian firm that used to sponsor an arms bazaar called ARMX. That show was designed to promote the sale of Canadian weapons and was met annually by demonstrations from peace activists. Then, in the glow of good feelings generated by the not-yet-failed Somalia intervention, they changed the name of the enterprise to Peacekeeping '93 and went global. Their first exhibition in Canada was held at the Ottawa Congress Centre, a city-owned building that is specifically prohibited from holding arms shows. Protesters showed up crying foul and called the show a clever cover for the same old merchants of death.

Baxter, which now owns the "Peacekeeping" trademark, has now made the show a profitable, regular international event. The company's marketing manager, Alan Crockford, said that he expects to attract more exhibitors from the arms industry as well as a lot more NGOs for a regular schedule of shows. The evangelical relief group World Vision was supposed to exhibit in Washington but didn't show up, but Crockford said they'll definitely be on board in the future. He also pointed to a representative from CARE who was checking things out. "They'll be here, too," he said.

For future "Peacekeeping" shows to maintain their credibility and for the credibility of the nascent peacekeeping industry it is essential that the humanitarian agencies get in line with the hardware producers. "It's a humongous growth project," Crockford said. "Very exciting."

The arms industry and the NGOs—the merchants of death and the purveyors of mercy—are still in the process of working out their relationship to their mutual benefit. At first, the relationship in Somalia was strained. Organizations such as the Red Cross refused military protection but then made sure to tag along behind military convoys when they needed to go to dangerous places. The organization insisted they were not using military escorts, but the distinction was a puzzling bit of semantics.

As the NGO–military relationship developed in Somalia and then in Rwanda, Haiti, and Bosnia, NGOs discovered a gold mine: The soldiers attracted more press than they could. The grandeur of military movements—massive C-5 transport planes depositing thousands of soldiers and tons of supplies—and the high-level government involvement ensured that the relief operations would dominate the media. The publicity, in turn, attracted huge donations. In places like Goma, Zaire, the military did jobs the NGOs couldn't. Military equipment was used to dig graves in the rocky ground. Military engineers installed filters and purified millions of gallons of water, ending a cholera epidemic that was beyond the capabilities of the charities. Hundreds of NGOs invaded Somalia, Rwanda, and Haiti on the heels of the military and on funds generated by the publicity. The partnership was solid. Now Red Cross representatives are standing beside salesmen from Barrett Firearms Manufacturing, makers of shoulder-fireable, heavy recoiling weapons, in one big marketplace of goods and services.

Although the presentation is new, the reality of the NGO-military relationship has long been developing. Most American NGOs, just like the army and the marines, had been instruments of U.S. foreign policy all along. They had been government contractors, taking a large part of their working capital from USAID, going where USAID wanted them to go, and helping the people and the countries the U.S. government wanted helped. Whether the government gives CARE a grant to do a water project or sends in the Army Corps of Engineers makes little difference in the end.

From the military's perspective, the NGO relationship gives them credibility as humanitarians and opens up new vistas of intervention. Despite complaints from Jesse Helms, Newt Gingrich, and the right that all this humanitarianism is turning the military into a bunch of pansies, and beyond the protests of conservative commentators like Rush Limbaugh, who called humanitarian intervention "a counterculture use of the military," it was the Pentagon that pushed hardest for the Somalia operation. The generals and military bureaucrats at least seem aware that the future of war lies in keeping peace in places where America doesn't have an obvious strategic interest. The people who were at Peacekeeping '94 accepted this as an act of faith and seemed utterly unconcerned that the new Republican majority would spoil the party.

Separated from the trade show by the escalator and 200 yards of Washington Sheraton lobby was the seminar room, where Peacekeeping '94 took on the air of an academic conference. This part of the show was sponsored by the Canadian Institute of Strategic Studies, a private policy think tank, but essentially a government contractor. One of the first speakers, Canadian Major General Romeo Dallaire, former commander of the UN forces in Rwanda, spoke passionately of how the world had ignored the mounting catastrophe in the months before the massacres began. The whole tragedy was, he said, preventable. A million lives and immeasurable human misery could have been avoided had the world chosen to act—or even if someone had donated working vehicles so he could transport his troops.

Dallaire proposed that the UN be given a kind of standing army that could be called into emergency situations on short notice. He wanted the UN to have its own intelligence agency since, logically, if you're going to be doing things like chasing warlords, it helps to have some idea what's going on out there. He envisioned a world where the UN acted as the police force, with the big powers available to be the cavalry if things got really out of hand.

Dallaire's plan also had the UN coordinating all humanitarian activity in every crisis. He criticized some of the more than 200 NGOs that showed up around Rwanda with the military. The small NGOs, he said, were "mom-and-pop organizations with heart and no capabilities," while the large NGOs "have capabilities but no heart." The small ones were in the way most of the time and the big ones didn't do much good. Dallaire's obvious sincerity for a moment overshadowed the reality of the goods being sold in the basement and the fact that most of the people in the room were there because they had hardware to sell in a shrinking market.

The next generation of automatic assault rifles may be sold with the slogan, "Never Again," but for now, many of the salesmen in the basement seemed unable to grasp the peacekeeping spirit. A representative from Firearms Training Systems was visibly annoyed when his assistant allowed journalists and other noncustomers to play with his rifles. "It's not a game," he said, after it was suggested that the system might turn a profit in a shopping mall. "I've got to see one more customer and then we can pack this thing up and go home," he said on the first day of the show. The salesman was awaiting some Arab buyers—from countries more likely to create a need for a peacekeeping operation than to actually participate in one.

A representative from Hiatt Thompson handed out free samples of plastic handcuffs. They're cheap, they're secure, they're disposable. And they once appeared on the wrists of Bosnian Muslims photographed lying face down in the mud beneath the boots of some victorious Serbs.

The seminar speakers weren't selling arms directly. Most had something bigger to sell. Once war making and peacekeeping are removed from the realm of immediate national security, they become a very competitive business. With billions of dollars being poured into peacekeeping operations around the world, there are lots of armies willing to hire themselves out, and there are plenty of alternatives to calling in the UN. That was the case being made by Robin Beard, NATO's assistant secretary general for defense support. Boasting that NATO was "the most successful alliance in the history of the world," Beard went on the offensive: The UN didn't win the peace. NATO won the peace and now NATO will keep the peace. "Are we going to become a subcontractor of the UN?" he asked the crowd without waiting for an answer. Unlike the rag-tag bunch of armies the UN puts together, NATO already had experience, standardized equipment, and leadership superior to that of the UN. "I don't personally feel comfortable with that relationship between the United Nations and NATO," he concluded.

Other contenders for peacekeeping are regional organizations such as ECOMOG, a force of West African countries that had enjoyed limited success in Liberia until the whole thing came apart in 1996.* Dennis Beissel, the UN's acting director for field operations, was speaking when a Ghanaian representative in the audience raised the issue of ECOMOG. Since Beissel handles multibillion-dollar logistical matters for the UN, he wasn't in the mood to have his operation compared to some rinky-dink African project. Beissel quickly dismissed the Africans, stating that the force was incapable of handling a real peacekeeping operation: "There's a lot to know about. There's food, there's uniforms, there's enormous complexity

---

*ECOMOG soldiers were reported to have participated in some of the looting when fighting flared up there. And some of the troops profited from arranging charter ships for desperate Liberian refugees to flee the country.

in medical issues." He was annoyed that anyone would ask such a question. The real reason for his annoyance was, as he himself had said earlier, "Our new growth will be in Africa."

Beissel was more comfortable taking questions from military contractors in the room who were drooling over the money that was under his control. "In 1993 the UN system procured goods and services worth over $3.5 billion, making it one of the largest purchasing entities in the world," said a pamphlet available at the show. According to the literature, $1.5 billion of that was used for peacekeeping.

This pamphlet was advertising a book entitled "How to Do Business with the United Nations." The guide, which sells for $295, tells you how to get a piece of that action and helps you navigate the Byzantine UN bureaucracy and obstacle course of multiple procurement divisions. Sitting next to it was another pamphlet that sheds light on how some businesses sneak through the maze. It was for corporate membership in the United Nations Association of the United States of America—a kind of boot camp for executives looking for those multimillion-dollar contracts. Memberships range from $1,500 to $25,000 a year, and benefits accrue proportionately. Members get field trips to peacekeeping operations ("Business leaders who participate in these trips gain valuable knowledge about product requirements for peacekeeping") and lunches with ambassadors, which are described as "an exclusive series of private conversations with leading public figures from around the world, senior United Nations officials, and other international decision-makers."

Beissel was acting like one of those international decision makers, a man with $3.5 billion in his pocket. As questions were fired at him about future UN operations, he started answering them in the first person, talking about the money "I" am going to spend, how "I" will deal with procurement, and other decisions "I" will be making.

"There are no protesters here," said Brigadier General Al Geddry, relieved and relaxing after the "gala" banquet on the first night of the show. Geddry, a retired Canadian military man turned New Brunswick rancher, sat down with me as the crowd filed out and the hotel staff stripped the banquet tables down to their raw plywood surfaces. Geddry now does public relations for Baxter and wanted to know what I'd thought so far. I agreed that they were doing a fairly good job reinventing the arms show: The dinner featured lots of ceremony, a bagpiper playing "Amazing Grace," and a speech by Elliot Richardson, still floating on the moral capital he earned by standing up to Nixon back in 1973. (He was introduced as "one of the most honorable men ever to have served his country in the cabinet of the United States of America.") Richardson is now the head of the United Nations Association of the United States of America.

He spoke about "the king's peace" imposed by William the Conqueror and the subsequent Norman and Plantagenet kings on the unruly Celtic and Saxon barons (warlords?) in Britain. That was the role he saw for the UN in the New World Order. With the end of the Cold War, apparently, the big strategic issues have been settled and now the nations of the world can work to put an end to the "small wars," the unimportant, senseless wars that others fight. I thought that Richardson missed the point that "the king's peace" had already been attempted in Africa. It was called colonialism and it wasn't so different from the feudalism the Normans used to pacify their British subjects.

The rest of the dinner went according to the organizers' schedule. It read:

- Piper will play twice during dinner, one tune being a lament.
- After coffee is served, piper will play around the room and will cease playing when he arrives at Mr. Richardson's seat. He will then be thanked (quietly) by Mr. Richardson and others at the Head Table. Following this sociable moment and a drink he will play out of the room taking the long route.
- Mr. Richardson will call on Mr. Blais [Jean-Jacques Blais, Chairman of the Board of Directors of the Canadian Institute of Strategic Studies] to propose a toast.
- . . . Mr. Blais will propose a toast to all men and women, military and civilian, who have paid the supreme sacrifice in the service of peace and to all who are serving today. Piper will play a short lament . . . Mr. Blais will then raise his glass and say: "To All Peacekeepers."
- Mr. Blais introduces Maj.-Gen. Cordy-Simpson.

The keynote speaker, Major General Roderick Cordy-Simpson, former chief of staff for the UN operation in Bosnia, spoke in a tight-jawed, upper-crusty Prince Charles sort of manner that seemed to suck all the air out of the room and make everyone sit up straight and take their elbows off the table. He described the Balkans conflict as "a thoroughly evil three-sided civil war," and painted a nightmare scenario about what would happen if the world failed to keep the peace: "Kosovo will be next, and if Kosovo is next then Albania will be called in, and if Albania comes in Macedonia will, and if Macedonia comes in Greece will, and if Greece comes in Turkey will, and if Turkey comes in Bulgaria will. Oh no, it won't happen, we all know it won't happen. Of course it won't. Our grandfathers said it wouldn't happen. And then . . ." He went on to describe the start of the First World War. All of this was, of course, the domino theory again. The enemy this time wasn't communism, it was chaos. But the call to arms was just as clear.

A representative from the Canadian Institute of Strategic Studies stood to sum up the show. He spoke of the "inspiring and educational displays" that were in the exhibition hall. Then he presented Eskimo carvings to the general and to Elliot Richardson.

"It's really nice. A seal on the ice." Richardson said when he accepted it. Then it was as if at the last minute he remembered that he must address the commercial aspects of Peacekeeping '94. He tossed in a little plug for the $295 book on UN procurement his organization had published, "which means, of course, procurement of the kinds of things that Peacekeeping '94 expo is all about." Richardson went on: "People my age grew up with the familiarity with the phrase, 'merchants of death.' Merchants of death were, of course, the manufacturers and traffickers in weapons. You represent—this expo represents—a new and far more open generation of the merchants of peace."

One of the waiters working tables was Mohamed Aweis, a refugee from Mogadishu who had been in the United States for about two years. He paid little attention to the conference, didn't really care what it was about, and just wanted everyone to leave the room so he could clean up and get home to his family. His constant presence around the table reminded me that Somalia had hardly been mentioned.

Perhaps this was because Canada is now going through convulsions similar to what the United States went through after the My Lai massacre. In the town of Beledweyne in March 1993, several Canadian soldiers from their elite airborne unit found a Somali boy sneaking onto their compound. One of the soldiers beat the boy, Shidane Abukar Arone, to death while others watched and took pictures. It was later revealed that the soldiers were members of the neo-nazi Heritage Front. Some of those pictures were published in the *Washington Post* the day before Peacekeeping '94 began.

Although one incident shouldn't cripple an entire peacekeeping industry, it nonetheless should have raised questions about the assumed moral superiority with which the powerful nations now address the small wars of the world. No one asked where that moral superiority came from. There was no banner honoring Shidane or the uncounted hundreds of Somalis who died at the hands of UN troops. No one raised a glass in their honor. Then again, the purpose of all of this was to sell hardware.

The marketplace of ideas is as important to this new industry as the market for hardware. For the NGOs, these ideas are reduced to buzzwords and clichés. The military, the NGOs, and quite a few journalists have now invested heavily in the idea that the world after the Cold War will be one of chaos and violence. In their forecasts, it is possible to sense a degree of excitement.

While the problems that NGOs once sought to address are arguably worse, they are seeking ever new tasks to tackle. Where they once spoke of basic human needs, women in development, and sustainable development, they are now addressing the issues of land mines, conflict avoidance, and, the latest and trendiest cause, "civil society." The same aid workers and volunteers who once tried (and largely failed) to teach farmers to grow things are now fanning out and sowing the seeds of "civil society" across the world.

Generally speaking, a civil society is one that is held together by rule of law, not one of loyalties to clan. It is the essence of the cultural struggles taking place in Somalia, Bosnia, and even New York City. In many ways it is a constant struggle, and one that seems bizarrely juxtaposed with the traditional notion and capacities of an NGO. Yet it is a growth opportunity. Along with land-mine clearance and conflict avoidance/resolution, it's where the money is. Few NGOs have ever seen a contract they didn't like, or a problem they didn't believe they could solve.

The first priority of an NGO, like any bureaucracy, is its own survival. Nowhere is this more clear than with NATO, the ultimate relic of the Cold War. Yet with the new mood of doom and gloom in vogue, NATO has been able to advertise itself as more necessary than before. During the Cold War it seemed we rarely heard about NATO. Then, with the Cold War over, the organization seemed threatened by internal squabbles and a lack of focus. The decision in the summer of 1995 to ignore the United Nations and bomb the Bosnian Serbs into submission, and the apparent success of NATO's peace implementation force (IFOR), has led to the rebirth of the organization. Now, with their reason for existence gone, the headquarters in Brussels is busier than ever. Perhaps the organization was just ahead of its time.

In June of 1996, sixteen NATO member states announced a new strategy of "combined joint task forces" to be their instrument of intervention outside NATO territory. This, they said, would give them the flexibility to deal with everything from peacekeeping to insurrection to wars. The new JTFs are modeled on the mission to Bosnia. Presumably if Somalia had been a "success," the UN's model would be ascendant.

Apparently some see NATO as the instrument for bringing civil society to Eastern Europe. Clinton administration security adviser Anthony Lake sees it this way: "We are . . . deepening security cooperation with all who share our values and our vision of peace. A key part of this process is NATO's enlargement. NATO can do for Europe's east what it did 50 years ago for Europe's west: prevent a return to local rivalries; strengthen democracy against future threats; and provide the conditions for fragile market economies to flourish."*

If governments start putting their faith in and channeling their money through NATO, it is almost certain that NGOs will follow. Everyone involved in the global fixit industry is fond of raising the specter of the "new world disorder," much the same way they once might have announced death rates they could not substantiate. For NGOs, it has been a rallying cry for more money and resources, whatever is really happening out there.

Most of the disorder seems to reside in the minds of policymakers and analysts, who have lost the lens through which they once viewed the world. The world may not have changed as much as they would have us think. The Cold War, with its clear and present threat to Western interests, only *seemed* simpler. With the Soviet Union gone, we have lost focus. The proliferation of media, particularly television, has also served to add to the sensory confusion. Chaos in Africa seems more threatening because we can see the refugee camps in Goma or the violence in Monrovia. But is this any more threatening than Biafra, the brutal war in Angola, or earlier massacres in Rwanda and Burundi? It is the intense media attention that makes it seem more dangerous and confusing. It is the perceived immediacy of the crisis that makes everyone cry out, "Do something."

In April of 1981, I was living in Beledweyne, Somalia. Rains in Ethiopia forced the Shebelle River over its banks and into the streets of the town. As the river continued to rise, the townspeople and the refugees from the surrounding camps evacuated to higher ground. The UN dropped in some large, white military-style tents for the expatriates, and we set up a camp on the highest point we could find. The Somalis set up a vast makeshift encampment across the plains below us.

---

*Address to Chicago Council on Foreign Relations, May 24, 1996.

One evening I was drinking Scotch with some of the expatriates—demographers, disaster relief experts of all sorts, and scores of doctors: an American from the Centers for Disease Control in Atlanta, a French doctor from MSF (Doctors Without Borders), and several others. We were talking about the flooding, the evacuation, the suffering. We talked in numbers: 20,000 people here and 50,000 there. We came up with solutions to everything. We computed how many tons of food and how much medicine it would take to relieve this disaster upon a disaster.

It was a calm night with a cool breeze. Below us we could see the fires from the vast encampment. Then out of the darkness, a young couple approached us. The man held a bundle in his arms. As he offered it forward, the woman carefully unwrapped the package; it was a sleeping baby. As they moved toward the lights of our tent, we could see that the baby had been burned over its entire body. The man explained that a pot of scalding hot water had tipped and covered the child. If we'd been in America, if the couple had had insurance, if the child had survived, he would have spent years in a sterile burn unit and received hundreds of skin grafts to save his life. It would have cost fortunes. The parents knew how serious the child's injuries were, but they also believed they were fortunate this night. We could see that they had full confidence that these foreign doctors would give the baby some injections and some balms, and the child would be fine. The doctors knew the child would die, painfully, over days. One of the doctors went and brought some pain killers for when the baby awoke. There was nothing else to do.

We went back to drinking our Scotch, in silence.

SOMALIA TIMELINE

1960

July 1
British and Italian Somali territories join to form an independent Somalia.

1969

October 15
President Abdirashiid Ali Shermaarke is assassinated.

October 21
Siyaad Barre seizes power in military coup.

1970

October 21
Siyaad commits Somalia to "scientific socialism," and officially aligns Somalia with the Soviet Union. The Soviets begin a massive arms buildup designed to shore up Somalia against the U.S. ally, Ethiopia.

1974

September 12
Ethiopian Emperor and U.S. ally Haile Selassie overthrown in military coup. U.S. continues to supply arms and aid to new regime in order to counter Marxist elements in the junta.

1977

February 3
Mengistu Haile Mariam takes control in Ethiopia and moves toward a radical Marxist agenda. Citing human rights abuses, the U.S. ends military and economic aid several months later.

September
The Western Somalia Liberation front launches a massive attack on Ethiopia and advances through most of the Ogaden region.

1978

April
Ethiopia retakes the Ogaden with the aid of Cuba and the USSR. Refugees flee into Somalia.

1980

August
The U.S. and Somalia sign an agreement exchanging U.S. arms for access to the abandoned Soviet military base at Berbera.

1981

January
The Somali National Movement (SNM) is founded to oppose the Barre regime.

June
CARE joins with the National Refugee Commission and forms CARE/ELU to deliver food to refugees in Somalia.

1988

April
Somalia and Ethiopia sign peace agreement forcing Ethiopia-based rebel SNM to return to Somalia. They occupy Hargeysa and the government re-

sponds by bombing the city, killing tens of thousands and creating new refugee problems.

1989

January
The opposition United Somali Congress (USC) is founded by members of the Hawiye clan.

1990

December
USC forces approach the city of Mogadishu. Most aid workers leave the country.

1991

January 26
Siyaad Barre is finally driven from Mogadishu by the USC.

January 29
Ali Mahdi Mohamed is declared interim president by the USC. Part of the USC, led by General Mohamed Farah Aydiid, opposes the appointment.

May 18
At a conference in the town of Burao, the SNM declares the independence of the Republic of Somaliland.

July 5
Aydiid's faction of the USC, now called the Somali National Alliance (SNA), declares him as their leader.

September
Siyaad Barre's forces stage a comeback bid. He seizes Baidoa. His troops loot grain storage bins and destroy farms. Counterattacks against Barre by Aydiid's militia lead to further destruction of agriculture. Both armies pursue a scorched-earth policy in Somalia's agricultural region leading to the famine.

November 17
The beginning of four months of fighting in Mogadishu between the factions led by Aydiid and Ali Mahdi. The city is leveled.

1992

January 1
Boutros Boutros-Ghali becomes Secretary General of the United Nations.

March 3
After a conference at UN headquarters in New York, Aydiid and Ali Mahdi sign a peace agreement. Other factions continue to battle in the south.

April 24
UN Security Council Resolution 751 establishes UNOSOM. Mohamed Sahnoun is soon appointed Special Representative.

April 25
Aydiid drives Siyaad Barre's forces out of Somalia and across the border to Kenya. Famine conditions become serious in the south.

August 12
Aydiid and Ali Mahdi agree to the deployment of a 500-man peacekeeping force to protect humanitarian operations.

August
A unilateral American operation, Provide Relief, airlifts tons of needed food into famine regions.

September 14
The 500 Pakistani peacekeepers arrive. Famine conditions begin to subside.

October 13
The UN approves the 100-day emergency Program for Somalia. Philip Johnston of CARE heads the program. For the first time the UN begins talking about 300,000 deaths in Somalia.

October
Aydiid decides he doesn't want UNOSOM in Mogadishu and moves his troops into the city from Bardera. Siyaad Barre's forces return from Kenya and capture Bardera leading to a spike in famine deaths. Speculation that the U.S. will send the Marines fuels press coverage of the violence and starvation.

November
WFP ships are attacked attempting to deliver food to Mogadishu. Both factions in the city engage UN troops.

November 25
U.S. President George Bush officially offers to intervene militarily in Somalia.

December 9
UNITAF forces land on the beaches of Mogadishu in full combat gear and are greeted by hundreds of journalists and cheering Somalis. The UN asks that UNITAF disarm the Somali factions.

1993

January 4–15
A meeting of 15 Somali factions in Addis Ababa agrees to cooperate with UNITAF and store heavy weapons at authorized inspection sites.

March 9
Admiral Jonathan Howe becomes UN Special Representative in Somalia in preparation for the U.S.'s handing the operation back to UNOSOM.

Late March
The forces of warlord Mohamed Hersi Morgan (loyal to Siyaad Barre) sneak weapons and soldiers past UNITAF troops into the port city of Kismaayo and defeat the forces of warlord Omar Jess, who is allied with Aydiid. Aydiid supporters feel betrayed by UNITAF.

March 26
Under Chapter VII of the UN Charter, the Security Council adopts Resolution 814 establishing UNOSOM II. The ambitious mandate talks of reestablishing political structures, a.k.a. nation building.

May 4
UNOSOM II officially takes over from UNITAF. The U.S. leaves behind a Quick Reaction Force to protect the UN from any attacks or to respond to emergencies.

June 5
24 Pakistani UNOSOM soldiers die in Mogadishu in clashes with forces loyal to Aydiid.

June 6
In a Sunday emergency session the Security Council adopts Resolution 837 authorizing UNOSOM II to take "all necessary measures" against those responsible for the attack.

June 12–17
UNOSOM forces, predominantly the American Quick Reaction Force, go on the offensive against Aydiid, destroying his radio station and other strategic locations.

June 17
Admiral Howe issues the arrest warrant against Aydiid and puts a $25,000 bounty on his head.

July 12
U.S. Cobra helicopters firing TOW missiles attack "Abdi House" where a group of Somali elders from Aydiid's clan are holding a regular meeting. Around 50 are killed. Four foreign journalists are killed by angry mobs.

August 8
Four American soldiers in a Humvee are killed by a command-detonated mine in Mogadishu

August 26
Task Force Ranger arrives in Mogadishu to capture Aydiid.

September 25
Three U.S. soldiers are killed when their helicopter is shot down by Aydiid's militia using a rocket-propelled grenade. Their bodies are desecrated, but the military keeps the information under wraps.

October 3
The debacle: 18 Americans and perhaps 700 Somalis die in a failed attempt to snatch Aydiid. Again the bodies of the dead are desecrated but this time a cameraman from Reuters is on hand to record the event. An American flier is kidnapped and photos of his battered body are broadcast and published around the world.

October 7
President Bill Clinton announces that the U.S. will beef up forces and also leave Somalia within six months.

October 9
Ambassador Robert Oakley returns to Somalia. The hunt for Aydiid is called off.

November 16
The Security Council agrees to an independent investigation of the events of the summer.

1994

March 26
The last U.S. forces pull out of Somalia.

1995

January 2
Siyaad Barre dies in exile in Nigeria.

March 2
The last UN forces pull out of Somalia.

April 6
The Security Council declares that "the people of Somalia bear the ultimate responsibility for achieving national reconciliation and restoring peace to Somalia."

1996

August 2
SNA leader and self-styled "president" of Somalia Mohamed Farah Aydiid dies from bullet wounds sustained several days earlier. Within days, his son Hussein Mohamed Farah "Aydiid," a former U.S. Marine, is named to take his place.

INDEX